GRACEFUL
RESISTANCE

INTERPRETATIONS OF CULTURE IN THE NEW MILLENNIUM

Norman E. Whitten Jr., General Editor

A list of books in the series appears at the end of the book.

GRACEFUL RESISTANCE

How Capoeiristas
Use Their **Art**
for **Activism** and
Community Engagement

LAUREN MILLER GRIFFITH

**UNIVERSITY OF
ILLINOIS PRESS**
Urbana, Chicago, and Springfield

Publication of this book was supported in part by the University
of Illinois Press Fund for Anthropology.

Library of Congress Cataloging-in-Publication Data
Names: Griffith, Lauren Miller, author.
Title: Graceful resistance : how Capoeiristas use their art for
    activism and community engagement / Lauren Miller Griffith.
Description: Urbana, Illinois : University of Illinois Press, [2023]
    | Series: Interpretations of culture in the new millennium |
    Includes bibliographical references and index.
Identifiers: LCCN 2022049618 (print) | LCCN 2022049619
    (ebook) | ISBN 9780252045066 (cloth) | ISBN 9780252087196
    (paperback) | ISBN 9780252054389 (ebook)
Subjects: LCSH: Capoeira (Dance)—Political aspects—United
    States. | Capoeira (Dance)—Social aspects—United States.
    | Political activists—United States. | Social justice—United
    States. | African Americans—Social conditions.
Classification: LCC GV1796.C145 G74 2023 (print) | LCC GV1796.
    C145 (ebook) | DDC 793.3/1981—dc23/eng/20221215
LC record available at https://lccn.loc.gov/2022049618
LC ebook record available at https://lccn.loc.gov/2022049619

For my sons, Harper and Roland

CONTENTS

ACKNOWLEDGMENTS

This is a project that has been working on my mind for at least half a decade. Given the tumult of the past few years, there were times when writing felt like an impossible prospect, but listening to my interlocutors' voices and thinking about the passion they bring to their work with capoeira and social justice compelled me to continue working even when it seemed like the world as we knew it was crumbling. It was a reminder that I was writing not despite the chaos around me, but because of it. There are so many individual capoeiristas that I would like to thank. I am refraining from naming them out of an abundance of caution for anonymity, but I hope you know who you are and how much I value your input. It has been an honor to count DaleChé among my friends, and his feedback is something I value greatly. Deacon warmly and enthusiastically welcomed me into his group and has consistently buoyed my faith in this project. Riser has been so generous with his time, and I sincerely hope our paths continue to cross. Bruno's input at the very early stages of this project charted the path I would follow throughout. Rene's words anchored me whenever my writing veered off track, and listening (and relistening) to Bram's interview never failed to bring a smile to my face. To my own mestre, *obrigada* for priming me to see the connection between capoeira and social justice, even if it took a few years for your lessons to sink in. Though I have opted not to thank individuals by their real names, I am happy to share a list of charitable organizations that they support in the hopes of raising these organizations' visibility: Community Ready Corps (http://www.crc4sd.org), United Way, and Drums Not Guns.

None of my work would have been possible without the mentorship I have received from Tom Green. Not only did he introduce me to capoeira, but he believed I was worth investing in even as a naive undergraduate making her first forays into ethnographic fieldwork. I will never be able to repay my debt to Anya Royce, who encouraged me to keep working on capoeira throughout graduate school and who models both creativity and consistency in everything she does. There are simply no words for the gratitude I feel toward Helena Wulff, who has been a steadfast supporter of my writing and professional pursuits. Her belief in me inspires me to work harder and be better. Norm Whitten has believed in this project from the very beginning, and his support has been crucial not only to the publication of this book but in my professional development and success. It has been a pleasure to work with the editorial team at the University of Illinois Press, and I am so grateful for the care they have taken with this project.

Paul Bowman at Cardiff University has had a tremendous influence on my involvement with the *Martial Arts Studies* community and I am so fortunate to count him as a colleague and friend. Working with Paul, Benjamin Judkins, and Wayne Wong as part of the *Martial Arts Studies* editorial team is not only a high point of my career, but just plain fun. I am grateful to colleagues in anthropology like Noah Johnson and Frank Ramos who find martial arts to be a fruitful area of research. I would also like to thank Ashley Kerr, who generously gave of her time to read and comment on a draft of chapter 1, as well as the reviewers who provided such careful and thought-provoking feedback. I hope you will see a reflection of your intellectual labor here and know that I will carry your feedback with me as I continue working on related projects.

At Texas Tech University, I have to thank Evangeline Jimenez, who spent a semester reading and discussing the literature on performance and resistance with me in preparation for her qualifying exams. Not only were these conversations intellectually productive, but they sustained me through an otherwise bleak semester of pandemic isolation. I consider myself fortunate to learn alongside our bright graduate students like Anna Margrét Sverrisdottir, Lauren Swanson, and everyone who took Alternative Ethnographic Representations with me in spring 2022. You kept me on my toes, made me laugh, and brought joy to our intellectual pursuits. I am also appreciative of Texas Tech University's Women Faculty Writing Program. The existence of this program was a contributing factor to my joining the faculty at Tech, and every semester I find a new reason to be grateful for the safe spaces my colleagues create.

I would also like to express my deepest gratitude to the Humanities Center at Texas Tech University for providing me with a fellowship during spring 2021. Dedicated time for writing is a great gift no matter the season, but without this support during the COVID-19 pandemic, I simply would not have been able to bring this project to completion.

I am grateful to my family for tirelessly supporting my academic pursuits. As I was working on this book, we mourned the loss of my grandmother, Deloris Stiers, who modeled open-minded curiosity and who always made us "look it up" when we had questions about the world. I am grateful to my wonderful parents, who have encouraged me and my work through every stage, and to Cameron, who has always cheered on my accomplishments. Finally, to Harper and Rollie: thank you for bringing so much sunshine into our lives. I care about social justice because I want you to live in a better, more compassionate world.

GRACEFUL
RESISTANCE

INTRODUCTION

There was a sniper posted on top of the YMCA building, just in case. Today the potential for violence at any public gathering, particularly one with a revolutionary message like racial justice, cannot be ignored. But on the ground, the carnivalesque atmosphere was akin to that of a county fair: the park was full of booths selling artery-clogging fried foods, mobile vendors sold tacos and popcorn, a radio station handed out free T-shirts, and various organizations passed out literature about their services. Conservative estimates put the crowd at one hundred thousand attendees, many—if not most—of whom were people of color and members of other marginalized communities. Some carried signs with slogans like "Respect for All, from Ferguson to Palestine." A few Black fraternities and sororities were marching together, Greek letters emblazoned on their jackets. Many wore T-shirts proclaiming that "Black Lives Matter" or "Love Is Love." Others wore items of clothing that were less overtly political but still displayed the wearers' identification with the African diaspora via their affinity for reggae or hip-hop music. Still others—like myself—carried nothing, and wore nothing that could be construed as political, but nonetheless sent a message just by being in that space.

This celebration, held in a public park in one of the poorer parts of the community (a midsize, southern US city), was the culmination of a three-mile march in remembrance of Dr. Martin Luther King Jr. I was there with several members of a capoeira group I have dubbed Grupo de São Miguel.[1] Importantly, the members of Grupo de São Miguel that marched on this day were a collective of individuals who just happened to train capoeira together; they were not formally participating in the march as an organization. This was not an official group *evento* (event),[2] but an extension of individual commitments to social justice that most members of the group tend to share. It was not a political event per se, even though the politicians who were on hand used the event as an opportunity to highlight their community-mindedness. But—as a white man who has not only trained in capoeira for years but is deeply involved in the African drumming community reminded me just a day or two before—"the personal *is* political." And that is what this book is about.

Grupo de São Miguel is an international capoeira contemporânea group,[3] whose founder was among the first wave of capoeiristas to move to the United States. Though some contemporânea groups privilege Brazil's role in the development of capoeira, this organization explicitly pays homage to its African roots. My interaction with this organization has been limited to the one locale (the city where the Martin Luther King Jr. festivities were held), although it has branches stretching from coast to coast in the United States as well as in South America, Europe, and Asia. I use the term *franchise* to refer to an organizational structure in which local teachers have been given permission by a presiding *mestre* (master) to offer classes under his—or, less often, her—name. There may be financial ties between the local teacher and the presiding mestre, but their relationship certainly goes beyond the commercial. It takes years to move up within the ranks of a capoeira group and be given authority to teach, and these teachers, who often carry the rank of *treinel* (coach) or *contra-mestre* (assistant master), tend to develop a close, almost filial relationship with their mestre.

Dense strands connect the local chapters of these groups. Graduation ceremonies, called *batizados* (baptisms), bring members of the capoeira community together. It is an honor for the franchise's mestre to attend these eventos. The mestre may also visit the local groups at other, less predictable times. These points of contact ensure some continuity across the franchise, but the character of each local group is shaped by its members and, perhaps most importantly, the temperament and inclinations of its local leader(s).

This particular chapter of Grupo de São Miguel feels like a family. Its training space, which sits well across town from the popular tourist district, has something a bit raw about it, with a roll-up garage door that makes it look like a storage unit from the outside. The burned-out house across the street and railroad tracks just beside the building make the neighborhood feel run down, even if gentrification is pushing the cost of its little bungalows into the US$200,000 range. But inside the building, the walls have been painted a vibrant orange, and it is clear that all the group members take pride in having secured a space of their own (it is far more common for a capoeira group to hop from place to place until a business or organization can be found that will let it use the space for free or for reduced rent, an arrangement that is often temporary). Even with the improvements the group members have made, however, their space is a far cry from the gleaming floors and glass windows of the shiny, strip-mall studio next to a Starbucks housing one of the other groups in town. And they like it that way. An activist who trains with Grupo de São Miguel said she chose this group *because* it didn't feel gentrified.

This is the kind of group where people come early and stay late because they want to be together. Music class may end only to have people take up the instruments again and start a jam session just for fun. After physical training ends, they may lie on the floor utterly exhausted and start talking about whatever is going on in the world or in their lives. Or they may end practice only to relocate to a cafe or someone's house to hang out and play board games. Attendance, too, is not rigidly enforced. Members might conclude that so-and-so is missing practice today because it's someone's quinceañera, and if someone has other engagements on a Saturday, they may just drop by in street clothes to say hi while everyone else trains. Not only does it feel like a family, there are some actual families in the group. When I have been there, it seemed perfectly normal for a couple to bring their child and take turns watching him while the other parent trained. Every individual in the group contributes to this *axé* (energy or "vibe"), but the leader sets the tone.

Deacon, the leader of this particular group, is the kind of person who, while certainly achieving great things and pushing himself to high standards, sacrifices for the sake of others. Having started his postsecondary education at an Ivy League school, he completed it at a small liberal arts college back home because of his family's finances. He shoulders the responsibility of caring for his elderly father while working full-time and teaching capoeira classes on the side, both at his own academy and at a community center in an economically depressed area of town that is populated mostly by people of color. Even a brief chat about national politics makes clear which way he leans, but he is strongly committed to the idea that capoeira should be inclusive. People of all faiths and political persuasions are welcome in the group. He believes that it isn't necessarily the most naturally gifted who become the best capoeiristas; rather, the hunger they have for the art determines what they can achieve. The kindness and generosity of spirit that he has unfailingly demonstrated to me no doubt play a part in creating the family feel of this organization.

At the group's Saturday afternoon training session ahead of the Monday morning march, Deacon announced that he and a few others from the group would be gathering at his father's house and walking the Martin Luther King Jr. parade route together. This announcement was not unexpected: the group had participated before, and I had made the trip specifically to march with it. Even so, no one was required to participate, and no one wore shirts that linked them to the group (though two marchers wore items of clothing that said "capoeira" on them). The city has one of the largest and longest-running memorial marches in the country. I was told by many people that this march would have around three hundred thousand participants, even if the official reporting was lower. Actual numbers aside, I got the sense from everyone I talked to during that January weekend that this is an important event for the city, one that represents its commitment to unity. It is not surprising that many capoeiristas in this city participated. I open with this story because it highlights the complementarity of the practice of capoeira (an Afro-Brazilian martial art that was introduced to the United States in the 1970s) and local forms of civic engagement, community outreach, and social justice. What exactly I mean by social justice—and how it aligns with the orientations of various mestres and rank-and-file capoeiristas—is something I address more fully in chapter 2. Here, suffice it to say that I use the phrase to refer to caring and compassionate efforts that seek to disrupt and subvert social structures perpetuating inequality, as well as acts that seek to achieve a more equitable distribution of wealth, opportunities, and well-being across all segments of society. I am talking about purposeful action, not indiscriminate violence or retaliative venting of frustrations (e.g., looting, setting fires, destroying property). In short, I mean working to undo the ways society has both intentionally and unintentionally marginalized certain groups of people.

A celebration of Martin Luther King Jr.'s birthday should, at least theoretically, cut across political differences, reflecting as it does the now-widespread view of him as a national hero (and obscuring just how polarizing his speeches and actions were during his lifetime, polarizing enough that he was assassinated). A scan of the day's crowd, the signs and flags they carried, and the clothing they wore, however, made it pretty apparent that most marchers were progressive if not explicitly left leaning. Perhaps because of this, a small group of protesters gathered at the interstate underpass, standing on the hillside with antiabortion banners and heteronormative commentary about the nature of family. There wasn't any logical connection between their platform and the purpose of the march; we just provided a large audience for their message. When we got there, my friends averted their gaze, not dignifying the protesters (who take up the same position year after year) with their visual attention. I stole a peek out of the corner of my eye. One sign said something about kids needing a mom and a dad. This was a new sign, apparently. The old one said that marriage was between a man and a woman, but when people from the march started taking pictures of themselves posing in front of the sign—cleverly covering the *w* and *o* in woman—the family values protesters realized they had lost control of their own rhetoric.

Another banner proclaimed that abortion was Black genocide. This, of course, is a powerful statement that the protesters surely hoped would find resonance among the marchers, who were there to support a Black leader. This slogan, which is often backed up by statistics about the number of Black women who have abortions relative to their white peers, is designed to get an emotional reaction. It completely disregards the sociological explanations for differential abortion rates. I nudged the capoeira leader and referenced the sign. He acknowledged it, and the way the protesters were playing on their perception of the crowd's feelings about the importance of Black lives to make their own ideological point, but also told me to "look who is holding the sign." Indeed, the protestor could have been cast as a small-town sheriff in a 1950s sitcom: a white guy with white hair, potbelly, and cowboy hat.

No one seemed to pay much attention to these protesters. There was no point in trying to engage with them, particularly in that setting. Angry confrontations do not change hearts and minds. And, for the most part, neither does logic. What changes a person's mind, Deacon told me, is getting to know someone from another identity group. That humanizes the issue, he argued, and combats the Othering—the exaggeration of differences—that so often happens between people on different sides of a conflict.

This serious moment aside, the atmosphere of the march remained light for most of our three-mile trek through the city. Deacon had grown up in this neighborhood, and as we walked, he pointed out the various schools he attended and even the daycare he went to as a child. We couldn't go more than a few blocks without someone waving to him or calling us over to the curb. At one point, a white boy carrying a red "Republicans for MLK" sign that was nearly twice as tall as he was rushed into the crowd to hug his capoeira teacher. It seemed everyone knew this teacher and respected him, regardless of their individual positionalities or political stances. We were having fun, chatting about all sorts of things from our families to the latest candidates to enter the 2020 presidential primaries. We danced along to the music that blared from car stereos and portable sound systems along the street and gratefully accepted water bottles handed out by people reminding us to stay hydrated. But a few blocks from the park, I got a chill that was hard to shake.

We passed a small home with a marquee out front listing the names Trayvon Martin, Cameron Redus, and Michael Brown. Suddenly, I felt the gravity of the day return. I asked the capoeirista beside me whether that sign had been put up especially for today. No, she said, they used to add to it every time another Black man was killed, but they stopped a while ago because they ran out of room. This list also contained the names of police officers who were killed, presumably, out of retaliative anger over Eric Garner's death. Garner died in 2014 while police had him in a choke hold. It wasn't really a Black Lives Matter sign, but it also wasn't a Blue Lives Matter sign. It was an outcry of frustration over the senselessness of so many lives lost, deaths that would not have happened if we truly lived in the kind of society that Dr. King imagined for us. That is what I carried with me for the last several blocks of the march.

I knew there was to be a speaker at the end of the memorial march, but it wasn't until we were gathered at the starting point that I found out it would be Shaun King. Before moving to Brooklyn for his career in journalism, King was a student leader at the historically Black Morehouse College and established a church in Atlanta. He has been an advocate and fundraiser for families whose loved ones have been victims of deadly police violence. I first became aware of his work in 2016, shortly after the presidential election, when he publicized the many cases of identity-based violence, discrimination, and intimidation that came across his desk. Controversies surrounding him aside, it was the weight of his list, more than anything, that brought home to me just how much trouble we could be in if Americans ignored the hate fomenting around us.

In his speech, Shaun King quoted Dr. King's 1963 "I Have a Dream" speech. One can hardly appear at an official Martin Luther King Jr. Day event without doing so. But he did not stop with the trite reiteration of Dr. King's line wishing for a future in which his children—and all people—could "live in a nation where they will not be judged by the color of their skin but by the content of their character" (King 1968, 17). This line has been reduced to a sound bite, a feel-good sentiment that it would be almost un-American to dispute. But Dr. King's address on the National Mall was not a feel-good speech. His rhetoric was beautiful, but as students of the martial arts know, oftentimes beauty can disguise deadly power. Dr. King was calling out the US government for writing a bad check, failing to deliver on a promise of equality for all American people. And if we look at his "Letter from Birmingham

Jail," drafted in April 1963, four months before his speech, the message is even clearer. Dr. King (1964, 91) wrote that "freedom is never voluntarily given by the oppressor; it must be demanded by the oppressed." Those in power rarely if ever hand over that power, particularly to the very people they have been exploiting and repressing. In his letter, he states that "over the past few years I have been gravely disappointed with the white moderate. I have almost reached the regrettable conclusion that the Negro's great stumbling block in his stride toward freedom is not the White Citizen's Counciler or the Ku Klux Klanner, but the white moderate, who is more devoted to 'order' than to justice; who prefers a negative peace which is the absence of tension to a positive peace which is the presence of justice" (96). Regrettably, I think that this observation still holds true. This is the danger in the heroes-and-holidays model of diversity education. We as a society tell ourselves we have done due diligence when our children spend one month learning about Black leaders, inventors, and athletes, but slavery is glossed over as an economic model or an example of states' rights, rather than being interrogated as a systematic form of violence and disenfranchisement that elevated one group over another. Certain states' legislators have even taken steps to prevent educators from presenting history through this lens to their students, for example by banning critical race theory.

Some capoeira groups do take a heroes-and-holidays approach to the history of their art. Those are not the groups I focus on in this book. They may mention slavery as a facet of capoeira's history, but they do not focus on capoeira as a tool of liberation for enslaved Africans and their descendants. These groups drop the Afro- from Afro-Brazilian when they talk about capoeira's origins. To use the language of one man I interviewed for this book, this is "gentrified capoeira," an admittedly inflammatory phrase that suggests that the history of capoeira is being whitewashed to make room for those who can afford the high rent. My goal is not to disparage these groups for taking a different approach to capoeira, one that may focus on fitness or the joy of creative movement or even national pride. After all, given the very real health problems associated with our sedentary lifestyles, most US residents do need to be moving more, and given the beauty of capoeira as an art form, I absolutely understand why Brazilians would honor it as a national treasure. Furthermore, it could be argued that just keeping a tradition like this alive is an act of resistance. For capoeira to be commonplace enough now that a white kid in the rural Midwest can find classes in their town is a success story that flies in the face of the Brazilians who outlawed it in the late 1800s. There are also very real risks that come with promoting one's art as a tool of liberation, and not everyone is willing or able to take those risks. But the individuals and groups I profile here have found resonance in the idea of capoeira as a model for civic engagement, and I am privileged enough to write about it as such without fear of serious backlash.

So far I have not said much directly about capoeira, an Afro-Brazilian martial art that blends sparring with song, dance, acrobatics, and theatrical improvisation. Chapter 1 addresses the history and form of the art, with an eye toward the elements that make it ripe for use as a tool of community engagement and activism, connections that are fleshed out in chapter 2. I begin with the vignette about capoeiristas' attendance at an Martin Luther King Jr. Day event, however, because it raises questions about why people engage in the particular civic behaviors that they do and what relationships might exist between different facets of an individual's identity. Is there any connection at all between being a capoeirista and attending an event in honor of Dr. Martin Luther King Jr.? A person who only knows that capoeira is a martial art that came from Brazil in the 1970s probably wouldn't see the connection. And someone whose interest in capoeira is restricted to the physical aspects of its practice—training one's reflexes and developing a lithe body—probably wouldn't see the connection either. But if we take into consideration that capoeira was, according to legend, developed by enslaved Africans in Brazil and disguised as dance so they could continue training without interference from the enslavers, then we start to see an underlying logic that links these seemingly disparate worlds. When one understands that many capoeiristas value this tradition because it represents both physical and psychological survival in the face of unimaginable oppression, it becomes easier to understand how their involvement in capoeira might lead to their involvement in other forms of civic engagement that support marginalized people living in the present. This book's biggest contribution is in showing how involvement in a leisure community, something often written off as spurious, can fundamentally alter one's way of being in the world. It is by changing individuals that we can change society.

When we talk about the artistic creations of marginalized peoples that have become popular, the issue of appropriation almost inevitably comes up. For a white American, the issue of appropriation in capoeira is twofold. It is both a foreign art and a Black art. What gives me, or anyone not from these demographic groups, the right to claim it as my own? This is a hotly debated issue within the capoeira community, and not one that can be resolved here or in any single publication. The popular and scholarly preoccupation with misappropriation has, I believe, prevented us from considering other ways of analyzing capoeira's global spread. A second significant contribution of this book is its claim that the right to belong to the capoeira community has less to do with one's ascribed identities (e.g., race and nationality), and more to do with one's attitude. I made a similar claim in an earlier book on capoeira (see Griffith 2016), but in that text I discussed one's humility, dedication to the group, and commitment to one's own training as the keys to acceptance within the community of practice. Here, I go a step further, arguing that engaging with capoeira as a means of respecting and supporting the African diaspora is an *appropriate* appropriation, by which I mean that one is taking capoeira as their own but doing so in a manner that is consistent with its underlying ethos.

Oftentimes, the engagement I discuss is directed toward activism on behalf of the African diaspora (e.g., attending Black Lives Matter protests). Indeed, some capoeira groups use an individual's commitment to serving and uplifting the African diaspora as something of a litmus test to decide whether and how to accept a white student's involvement in the group. Regardless of their own ethnicity, the individuals who use capoeira as a tool of civic engagement in the United States emphasize African contributions to capoeira, naturalizing its use as a tool for racial justice. This applies to capoeiristas performing all three major styles: angola, regional, and contemporânea.

An oversimplified dichotomy has presented capoeira regional (and the derived form, contemporânea) as the "whitened" form of capoeira, owing to Mestre Bimba's requirement that students in his school either be gainfully employed or be enrolled in school (see Reis 2004), and capoeira angola as the more African form, given Mestre Pastinha's involvement with members of the Afrocentric intelligentsia (see D'Aquino 1983). I will return to these issues later, but the overall implication is that regional has been modernized while angola remains traditional. Regional is more martial, angola more cultural. These binaries have been repeated by practitioners and scholars (myself included) so much that they have almost taken on a life of their own. But—as with most binaries—they do not capture the nuanced reality of capoeira as lived experience. Given my prior training as an *angoleiro* (practitioner of capoeira angola) and my background knowledge of the literature on capoeira, I expected to find that angola groups in the United States would be far more engaged in activism than would regional and contemporânea groups.[4] I was wrong: as I found, the use of capoeira as a platform or springboard for social justice work crosscuts these stylistic differences. It is my hope that US practitioners reading this book will set aside their preconceived notions of the various styles and see the common project in which many of them are engaged.

I was also wrong in assuming that racial justice would be the only form of social justice work in which capoeiristas engage. For reasons that become obvious when we look at the origins of capoeira, racial justice is a pronounced theme in the work of socially engaged groups. But many groups are also involved in environmental justice, challenging their members to make small changes in their daily habits that add up to something bigger. Some groups focus on helping job seekers develop the skills they need to secure a solid economic future for themselves. These are the more visible projects, actions with tangible outcomes that can be photographed and shared or talked about on social media, which I discuss in chapters 5 and 6. There are also more private, amorphous, or even ambiguous aspects of social justice work that affect individuals on a personal level, like changing one's attitude toward the hegemony of capitalism (see chapters 3, 4, and 7).

CAPOEIRA AS SERIOUS LEISURE

For too long, those things coded as leisure have been given short shrift in academia and in society at large. Leisure is often defined by what it is not: it is not work, not family time, and not domestic labor (Pickard 2017). This understanding alone, before we even begin to account for the Protestant work ethic, casts leisure in a liminal role. Even after anthropologist Clifford Geertz (1972) pointed out that a game may have far more serious ramifications than a surface-level analysis might imply, topics like play and sport have remained understudied and undertheorized, particularly the play done by adults in Western societies. Since one idea I propose here is that under the right conditions, groups centered on the promotion of particular body cultures have the potential to fundamentally alter an individual's sense of social responsibility, I find great utility in the perspective of "serious leisure" (Stebbins 1982), which helps explain the value of elective pastimes in individuals' lives.

Because leisure studies is an interdisciplinary field, it has few theoretical constructs that are truly its own, with the exception of the serious leisure perspective, a concept that has remained useful even forty years after its initial articulation (Gallant, Arai, and Smale 2013a). In his early formulation of serious leisure, Robert A. Stebbins (1982, 256–58) distinguished it from unserious leisure by arguing that (1) serious leisure demands perseverance in the face of adversity or struggle; (2) participants have "careers" in serious leisure, with involvement that can be traced over a significant span of time with its own ups and downs rather than being episodic or fleeting; (3) serious leisure demands individual effort based on knowledge, training, and skills that are specific to that community of practice; (4) serious leisure yields a number of benefits (e.g., self-actualization, belongingness, enhanced self-image) that are not characteristic of casual leisure; (5) each form of serious leisure has a "unique ethos" into which the participant is socialized; and (6) participants come to identify with the form of serious leisure in which they have chosen to participate.

Stebbins (1982, 253) predicted that people would eventually shift their primary identification away from their work and toward forms of leisure that they find personally fulfilling. He contrasted serious leisure—which can be subdivided into the categories of amateurism, hobbyist pursuits, and career volunteering—with "a bewildering array of unserious forms, such as sitting at a football game, riding a roller coaster, [and] taking an afternoon nap." Stebbins believed that the postindustrial condition would lead many people, presumably in Western societies, to increasingly seek opportunities for fulfillment and identity in the realm of leisure, rather than in their work. Given the culture of busyness that seems to have taken hold in US society, one might question his assumption that people would soon have an abundance of leisure time available to them. What is worth focusing on, however, is his prediction that "a steady diet of casual, unserious leisure [in one's free time] ultimately tends to cause spiritual dyspepsia" (267). Serious leisure pursuits, on the other hand, contribute to an individual's personal growth, sense of belonging, and overall sense of self.

The pursuits that have been studied as forms of serious leisure are staggering in their variety, including everything from beer brewing to sadomasochism. Studies often focus on the satisfaction one derives from such practices, a sense of accomplishment in exercising field-specific skills and expertise that is different from the pure hedonism that accompanies more casual forms of leisure (see Stebbins 1997). This framework has been particularly helpful for those of us studying activity-based forms of leisure, like sport, dance, and martial arts. Individuals who participate in serious leisure come to self-identify with the activity, often defining themselves in terms of their participation in that community of practice (see Ribeiro 2017 on boxing as a form of serious leisure). These spaces become important loci of socialization and belonging for members.

The setting where leisure takes place becomes a "third place"—neither work nor home—where an individual experiences a respite from normal duties and responsibilities (Ribeiro 2017). However, this is not to say that participation in such a community is free from obligation. Indeed, as the serious leisure pursuit becomes an integral part of the individual's sense of self, significant duties may fall on their shoulders. While an individual may feel less obligation to a leisure pursuit than to a job, the serious leisure participant will have more obligations and duties than a more casual participant (Stebbins 1982). Theoretically, they could walk away from these obligations at any time since there is no remuneration obliging individuals to fulfill certain duties and expectations; however, one's commitment to that leisure pursuit or the community in which that form of leisure is practiced is often great enough to compel them to show up and do whatever is expected. As a form of serious leisure, capoeira is still play, but it requires commitment on the part of practitioners. This commitment can sometimes feel onerous, and I have seen many students say it has become "too much" and walk away. But those who stay are rewarded by becoming more and more centrally situated within this community of practice (see Lave and Wenger 1991).

Numerous studies have found an association between serious leisure and positive outcomes like joy, happiness, expanded social networks, stronger social relationships, self-actualization, and self-esteem. In a quantitative study of tae kwon do practitioners, Junhyoung Kim and colleagues (2015, 154) argue that "personal growth and happiness are additional indicators of serious leisure outcomes." Though they do caution that "the magnitude and direction of the relationship in the model may differ if the study was conducted using participants in different activities" (156), there does not seem to be anything intrinsic to tae kwon do that leads to these outcomes. Rather, it is the nature of serious leisure that yields these results. Similar trends could most likely be seen in studies of running, cycling, or volunteering as forms of serious leisure. In other words, many studies present the particular community of practice almost as if incidental to the attainment of these outcomes, attributing them to the intention and intensity of the individual's engagement with the activity. In contrast, and while caution should be exercised in generalizing my findings to other communities of practice, I am convinced based on my in-depth case study of capoeira that some outcomes are specific to the form of leisure, even if others (e.g., happiness, personal growth) likely *do* result from nearly any form of serious leisure.

Scholarship on serious leisure to date has paid woefully little attention to demographic factors like socioeconomic status, gender, and ethnicity (Pickard 2017), to political participation as a form of serious leisure, or to the community-level (rather than individual-level) dimensions of this phenomenon. One notable recent exception, however, is Lise Kjølsrød (2013), who asks whether there might be democratic relevance in forms of serious leisure that take up significant amounts of time and constitute social worlds unto themselves. Scholars have been split on the matter, with some seeing these communities of practice as tenuous stand-ins for real forms of connection and others sensing something concrete and meaningful at the heart of serious leisure. To support her position, Kjølsrød presents several examples in which serious leisure communities—rock climbers, boat collectors, and live action role-players—either become involved in broader political discourses or express political ideologies through their play. She notes that "the chosen commitment is not patently obvious but still has a close resonance with the core activity, thus, the actors are already primed by emotional and intellectual affinity to the concern" (1213). Indeed, one need not be a conservationist in order to be a rock climber, but it is not difficult to imagine why one who is committed to a nature-based activity of this sort would be invested in preserving the natural environment. She also points out that these members' activism is not rhetorical so much as it is practical or applied; serious leisure provides the opportunity for members to enact their political philosophies. Kjølsrød then asks the next logical question—one I too am asking—which is about the circumstances that lead to politicization. Her answer is that "what is latent can become manifest under variable conditions—as long as the individual actors do not have to sacrifice their gratification" (1213). I do not disagree, but I think this important question remains largely unresolved. Bearing in mind that capoeira is but one case study of serious leisure leading to politicization and local activism, I nonetheless think there are some specific trends and mechanisms worth examining more closely.

Based on a feminist communitarian framework, Karen Gallant, Susan Arai, and Bryan Smale (2013a, 104) revised Stebbins's definition of serious leisure, describing it as "the committed pursuit of a core leisure experience that is substantial, interesting, and fulfilling, and where engagement is characterized by unique identities and leads to a variety of outcomes for the person, social world, and communities within which the person is immersed." This revised definition improves on the original by highlighting the benefits of serious leisure to the broader communities in which the individuals pursuing leisure are embedded. Through a quantitative analysis of three hundred volunteers in Canada, Gallant, Arai, and Smale (2013b, 333) confirmed that "social experiences facilitated through serious leisure strengthen community." By augmenting their use of the serious leisure perspective with the framework of communitarianism, these authors were able to better understand the relationship between individuals and their communities. This shift away from liberalism (which focuses on the individual) and toward communitarianism balances a concern for individual interests and responsibilities with a commitment to the common good and welfare of the community.

What Gallant, Arai, and Smale (2013a, 94) did is provide a critical corrective to the serious leisure framework, opening the possibility that future scholars might shift their attention to serious leisure's "potential to engage the social contexts in which it occurs, and hence, to address broader issues of community and social justice." My work responds to this call by focusing on how the individual, affected by their involvement in capoeira as a serious leisure pursuit, becomes involved in social justice issues that affect their community. This, in a broad sense, may be considered a form of political action. Here it is important to remember that political action is not restricted to a particular set of settings and institutions (e.g., Congress, town hall meetings, elections). Rather, people develop political orientations, express their positions, and influence one another in a range of social contexts in both planned and unplanned ways (see Kjølsrød 2013). And while some scholars have begun asking whether political participation might be considered a form of serious leisure (see Pickard 2017)—primarily because one's participation may become part of their identity and provide significant rewards in terms of belonging, self-actualization, and so forth—this question does not address what I have seen in capoeira. My engagement with the capoeira community for nearly twenty years suggests that participation in capoeira as a form of serious leisure develops a unique ethos that happens to be political. More specifically, it inculcates a left-leaning political orientation that is highly attuned to instances of social injustice and inequality. Although there are similarities between capoeira as it is practiced in the United States and as it is practiced in Brazil (and in other countries too, for that matter), I have limited my exploration to the United States because the "experiences of serious leisure influence and are influenced by the socio-political context in which they occur" (Gallant, Arai, and Smale 2013a, 96). Even if the United States and Brazil have both recently witnessed a rise in open hostility toward the rights and interests of marginalized groups, the contexts are not the same, and many issues capoeira groups in the United States are responding to are decidedly local concerns. Yet while my work draws primarily from the US context, the injustices faced by capoeiristas here have parallels in other parts of the world, particularly as populist governments continue to grow in power, and as world events push vulnerable peoples into positions of even greater precarity.

GLOBALIZED RESISTANCE ARTS

Some outcomes I discuss in this book might be "generic" in the sense that they could be produced by almost any form of serious leisure. In long-distance trail running, for instance, unexpected and sometimes unlikely friendships emerge as fellow athletes encourage one another to fight past exhaustion, pain, and their own limits. In these moments, it does not matter what someone else's race, ethnicity, age, gender, religion, or political affiliation may be. Commitment to the activity allows us to transcend those divisions. And yet—as significant as these meetings and relationships are—these personally transformative engagements tend to be situational, short lived, and modest in terms of impact beyond the individuals involved. What I am interested in here is how participation in certain arts—specifically capoeira, though this model will ideally be applied to other forms as well—can catalyze action beyond the level of the individual and actually transform communities.

With this in mind, I am introducing a new term, *globalized resistance arts*, to refer to art forms with a real or imagined connection to resistance that have entered the global milieu but have retained a discourse of subversion in their global circulation.[5] Capoeira is an exemplar of this category. It is difficult to talk about the origins of capoeira without mentioning slavery. Even the one capoeira teacher I interviewed for this project who was adamant that capoeira is first and foremost a martial art (and that teaching culture is not particularly of interest to him) insists that his students write essays on things like capoeira's history, which includes discussions of slavery, before they can progress to the next belt level. This history is just something one is expected to know in order to advance within the community at large. Even if there are multiple theories on the exact process by which capoeira came to Brazil and developed into its current forms (see chapter 1), the dominant discourse includes references to enslaved Africans who disguised their fighting as dance so that they could train without interference from white enslavers, who were both fearful of the enslaved population developing proficiency in defense and concerned about potential damage to their "property." If this narrative is what motivates capoeiristas' actions, then the veracity of the story itself, at least in this particular context, is irrelevant (see Green 2003).

The more channels an art has for conveying information about oppression and resistance—think folklore, song, ritual, and the movements themselves—the more likely it is for students to absorb these messages. This is one reason capoeira has become such a powerful tool of socialization. Capoeira uses a call-and-response format of singing, a common practice in arts of the African diaspora. Greg Downey (2005) has discussed the ways in which this practice calls the past into the present. The call-and-response format actually compels students to subjectively identify with enslaved Africans. We sing lyrics such as "no meu tempo de cativeiro, quando o senhor me batia" (during my time of captivity, when the master would beat me). What does it mean for me, a white woman, to sing this song? I was never a slave; my ancestors were never enslaved. So why do I sing that song? Quite simply, because my mestre tells me to. I'm compelled to do it by the hierarchical structure of the community I've chosen to join. Some people won't give this much thought; those who don't know Portuguese might not even know the meaning of the words they sing. But others will stop to critically consider the implications of a song like this, and the appropriateness of their voicing it in the first person. These are the moments that make all the difference in terms of changing one's consciousness.

With regard to the movements, there is a greater degree of variability in terms of how much information a teacher passes on about resistance during class. I was always taught that the straight kick to the stomach was named *benção* (or blessing) in an ironic jab at the enslavers who mandated that their enslaved workers be baptized and who often "blessed" them during Mass but continued to exploit their labor in a decidedly unchristian manner. I've also been taught that the *chamada* (a ritualized break in the flow of the game) is actually a parody of how white enslavers danced, similar to the cakewalk in the United States (Shrumm 2016). Again, I cannot necessarily verify these stories or point to the historical moment when they took root, but the important thing for my purposes is that they provide another channel of information about how capoeira has been used as a form of resistance. When students are exposed to this discourse repeatedly, and in different situations, it begins to take hold.

South African gumboot dance is another form I classify as a globalized resistance art. South Africa's history is tainted by apartheid, in which Black, white, and mixed-race residents were kept segregated and heavily punished for transgressing these boundaries. Miscegenation was a crime. Black people were moved to townships lacking basic infrastructure, without regard for the hours it sometimes took them to commute into the city for domestic-service jobs. The appropriation of Black-controlled land pushed hundreds of thousands of men into laboring in gold mines, where their lives were constantly endangered for the benefit and enrichment of the white people who controlled the mines.

Gumboot dance—in which dancers stomp and slap the sides of their rubber boots as well as parts of their bodies—developed as a form of communication between apartheid-era mine workers, who were forbidden from speaking to one another (Mills 2016). Though the dance was also used for entertainment, certain sequences could be used inside the mine to send particular messages, like alerting fellow miners to the presence of police. Mine workers adapted traditional dance forms to their new physical and material conditions and sometimes added songs that dealt with both domestic and sociopolitical themes. Dana Mills (2016, 68) considers gumboot dance "a political language." Despite the white mine bosses attempting to take control over the performances of this dance form—by organizing competition teams and staging displays for tourists—it nonetheless retained its subversive power. It was "a shared symbolic system between those who were not allowed to speak" (Mills 2016, 70).

During my brief involvement with a gumboot dance troupe in graduate school, I saw some of the same trends that I did with my capoeira group. The first priority was learning the movements. Unlike with capoeira, however, we had to work together as a group to perfect our timing so the dance would look and sound right during performance. In the course of teaching the movements and practicing the routines, our teacher—a Black man from South Africa—would tell us a bit about the horrifying history of apartheid or explain the meaning behind a song we were using. "The Lion Sleeps Tonight," for example, he said was about a man comforting his lover and telling her the train that would take Black men away from the village to work in the mines was not running that night. We affixed bottle caps to our boots to amplify the sounds we made with each movement, but we were also told that doing this represented the chains that would have encircled the legs of the mine workers (though no historical sources were ever offered to validate this statement). Explanations such as these had the effect of raising our awareness of the social conditions experienced by Black South Africans under apartheid.

When these globalized resistance arts become valorized in new locations, instructors from the places where the art originated also attain a new level of prestige. Elsewhere (Griffith and Marion 2018), I have written about the importance of traveling experts in establishing translocal communities of practice. What I want to emphasize here is that when there is demand for instruction in a globalized resistance art, people who have been on the receiving end of discrimination and oppression now have a new avenue for communicating their experiences and having those experiences validated by a sympathetic audience of receptive students. Individuals who may not have seen themselves as agitators or cultural ambassadors may suddenly find themselves in this role.

There are without a doubt other art forms that would fit this idea of a globalized resistance art and other dimensions of their global spread that should be examined (e.g., how these arts change in their new context, who is attracted to them, and to what ends they are used). These arts exist because a marginalized people asserted their agency within the set of constrained circumstances they found themselves in vis-à-vis a politically and militarily dominant Other. I have focused here on capoeira and, to a lesser extent, gumboot dance because they are cases I know well. It is my hope that other scholars will find this concept useful for describing other arts and their potential for becoming socially and politically transformative in the new places they take root, a point to which I return at the end of the book.

Will everyone who practices a globalized resistance art like capoeira achieve new levels of social awareness? No, of course not. What one considers the role of a capoeirista to be in modern life will depend in large part on the attitudes and commitments held by the leader of the individual training group. The stances of other group members matter too. Capoeira is many things to many different people. To some, it is a potentially deadly fighting art that must be hidden in order to retain its power. For others, it is a cultural art that just happens to combine martial skills with artistic elements like song, dance, acrobatics, and theater. Most people consider it to fall somewhere between these rather extreme poles. But for the individuals I am profiling here, it is without question an art of performative resistance.

I define *performative resistance* as a process through which the performance of certain arts leads to the embodiment of social justice ideals and activism. By singing in the first person and performing movements that have been passed down to us from the Afro-Brazilians who kept capoeira alive despite persecution by enslavers and the state, capoeiristas from all demographic groups—at least temporarily—embody diasporic knowledge. These performances have the potential to open an individual up to a deeper understanding of things like power, injustice, and systemic oppression, which may result in that individual engaging in civic action. As Judith Butler (2016) argues, performativity is a dialectical process. We are acted on by discourse before we ever take action ourselves. Through capoeira, individuals are socialized into a discourse of resisting oppression while also working to bring about a more just state of being for their communities.

PLAN OF THE BOOK

For readers who have limited familiarity with capoeira, chapter 1 provides an introduction to the history of the art as well as its defining formal features. It is my hope, however, that even experienced capoeiristas will find something new, or at least a new take on an old tale, in this chapter. This version of capoeira's history is written with an eye toward social justice. This is not a rewriting of history per se, but a shift in emphasis and a questioning of some of the foundational myths that have become ossified, particularly in the context of US capoeira groups. I also address some key moments in the globalization of capoeira as a way of explaining why so many groups in the United States have taken a turn toward social justice within their practice. Chapter 2 builds on the foundation laid in the previous chapter by highlighting some of the stories that have informed capoeiristas' interpretation of their art as a tool of resistance. This chapter also defines social justice.

This introductory chapter has argued that we must take seriously various forms of leisure that become central facets of individuals' identities, but that certain arts are particularly likely to become loci of socialization for participants and are thus worthy of even more critical attention. Through the act of performing these arts, performers actually bring that resistance into existence. This element of performativity has the potential to lead to change in one's own life and in one's community. In chapter 2, I present a model to explain how performative resistance works, framing it within the context of capoeira's role as a catalyst for social justice. These are primarily stories of individual change, often told from the perspective of the individuals whose lives have been changed by capoeira. Many individuals I profile in chapter 3 were simply unaware of the social injustice around them when they started playing capoeira. This is not to say they were spewing hate on white nationalist websites or calling liberals "snowflakes"; rather, they had not yet had any experiences that caused them to confront the realities faced by people unlike them. Chapter 3 is also where I introduce the concept of *affective habitus*, an emotional orientation toward the world that one acquires as a result of engagement with a particular social field.

Chapter 4 addresses the quotidian aspects of training that shape the capoeirista's affective habitus. These are things like afterclass discussions that facilitate connections between the history of capoeira and current, local events. Many pedagogical choices made by justice-minded teachers contribute to the overall tenor of the group, but the chapter also addresses ways in which individuals acquire this habitus without explicit guidance from their teacher. Even if a capoeirista pursues a self-guided course of study, these acts are still social insofar as they rely on materials that have been produced by the larger capoeira community (e.g., online repositories of song lyrics) and are done in real or imagined dialog with other members of the capoeira community, who may be geographically dispersed around the world.

Chapter 5 deals with the nature of the capoeira community and its pre-figurative politics. One interlocutor told me that capoeira "naturally by force" exerts an emotional pull on the people who find a home in it. This is an apt description of how structural diversity can lead to meaningful changes in how people relate to one another. This chapter also explores an anticapitalist thread within the capoeira community that is related to a larger project of justice and equity.

In chapter 6, I highlight some public expressions of capoeira groups' commitment to social justice. This includes things like teachers' taking their students to a Black Lives Matter protest. These individuals are willing to put themselves at risk, either physically or reputationally, because of their beliefs about justice and the ends to which capoeira should be used.

Not all social justice work, however, is as overt as my earlier chapters might suggest. Plenty of capoeiristas prefer to do "quiet" social justice work. In chapter 7, I pay special attention to what that looks like: less marching, more private but purposeful forms of justice work. In some instances, participating in overt forms of activism is a form of privilege. This is not to suggest that only privileged people protest, but to say that oftentimes the most vulnerable individuals in our society do not find explicit activism worth the risk. There is a reason the original capoeiristas kept their fighting prowess hidden, whether that was by disguising their fight as a dance or by trickily downplaying their skills until they were needed, and more privileged people should respect the reasons why those who have been marginalized may not feel comfortable engaging in the same channels of resistance as they do. In this chapter I also push back a bit against the claim of some interlocutors that they aren't involved in justice work. Even when they do not classify what they are doing as activism in a strict sense, simply following the example that has been set by one's own teachers frequently if unconsciously instills in individuals an impulse to use capoeira to better their community.

Thus far, I've painted a positive portrait of capoeira, particularly in the United States, but this is not to say that the community is without issues of its own. There is a vein of hypocrisy in certain groups that would be wrong to ignore. Chapter 8 addresses some of these shortcomings. These issues are becoming well known within the community but are unpleasant to talk about and often glossed over in favor of preserving harmony. In particular, there are the problems of sexism and sexual predation in capoeira that some groups are working to rectify. These are particularly important to discuss in light of larger trends in both Brazilian and US society (e.g., the Me Too movement, #MeuPrimeiroAssedio [#MyFirstHarassment]), where fallout from major scandals like the Harvey Weinstein case has led to widespread awareness of how common sexual assault is. Sadly, these acts of injustice are sometimes perpetuated by the very same people who claim to be using capoeira as an art of resistance. This chapter also discusses the more apolitical tendencies of certain capoeira groups, in order to present a more holistic and realistic portrait of the diversity of this community.

Chapter 9 summarizes the main arguments I have made in this book, but also asks whether capoeira is unique in terms of its potential to raise individuals' awareness of injustice. Why, for instance, do we see this happening in capoeira and not in Brazilian jiu-jitsu, which has become even more prevalent on the global stage than capoeira has? Are there other martial arts or dance forms that might follow the same path as capoeira in the future? Serious leisure in general and martial arts in particular serve a myriad of functions for the individuals who pursue such activities. Activism is merely one possible outcome of participation, but an important one to understand in light of our current sociopolitical moment.

1

THE MAKING OF A POLITICIZED ART

We are standing in a circle, excited to begin our weekly *roda* (improvisational game) but reverent as our mestre walks around the inside of our circle, waving an incense burner over each of our shoulders. Some stand still; others use their hands to waft the incense over their heads and down the length of their bodies. We've never received explicit instructions about what we're doing or why—or maybe I missed that day of class—but we implicitly understand that our mestre is doing this to purify the room and prepare us for the ritual that is about to begin. No longer are we *just* hanging out in a somewhat dusty music room at the "hippie" charter school in town. We are ready to summon the ancestors and play capoeira.

After the room is purified, we sit cross-legged in our circle. The mestre is at the front of the room, balancing on the last joint of his little finger a long musical bow with a hollowed-out gourd that serves as a resonating chamber. This is the *berimbau*, arguably the most important instrument in modern-day capoeira. With the index finger and thumb of that same hand, he presses a coin into the wire that stretches across the length of the bow. He lightly holds a stick in his other hand, which also has a woven basket rattle looped over his ring and middle fingers, rattling every time he strikes the wire. Dreadlocks tumbling over his shoulders, he calls out "iê!" and our focus intensifies. He begins singing a *ladainha*, a solo that praises the ancestors or references famous places in Brazil. When he transitions into a call-and-response song, the other instruments in the orchestra join in. There are two other berimbaus that complement his rhythm, two *pandeiros* (tambourines), a scraping instrument, a double-sided cowbell, and an *atabaque* (drum). The mestre tips his berimbau toward the ground, striking the wire several times, and thereby lets the two players crouched at his feet know that it is time to begin.

The two players are mirror images of each other as they strike a pose called *queda-de-rin* (kidney stand). Each has an ear and cheek touching the ground, with one hand positioned on either side of their head. The elbow of one arm is tucked into the body, its knobby joint pressing against the kidney. Their legs are pulled into their chest and then slowly raised straight up into the air, the full weight of each player's body being supported by the side of their head and their two hands, so that each body looks like the letter *L*. A smile curves the lips of one player as she realizes her opponent can no longer hold this position, and at last they enter the circle and begin to play.

This is capoeira angola, where practitioners spend much of their time in crouched movements, upside down as they cartwheel over each other, sliding under the other's legs and sending circular kicks skimming inches above their opponent's body. Other styles feature fast spinning kicks, flips, and other flourishes, but this style focuses on cunning and strategy. From time to time the opponents come upright, swaying back and forth in front of each other, their feet tracing a large triangle on the floor, tempting the other to attack only to launch a counterattack of their own. This movement, the *ginga*, is one of the main ways through which individuals signal their own unique style. It constitutes a form of embodied knowledge; it is a way of "perceiving others in relation to oneself; and of constructing one's own processes of self-making in front of a participant audience" (Rosa 2012, 163). These lessons have clear applications outside of the roda, and attention to these kinesthetic properties can help us understand how Afro-Brazilians have used their cultural art to enact resistance in the larger sociopolitical sphere.

The roda is sacred and must be treated as such. Capoeira rodas are supposed to summon the ancestors.[1] We do this through our songs, praising the mestres of the past and referring to their struggles, and through the use of sacred instruments like the berimbau and the atabaque. We also call the ancestors through our movements, giving new life to the corpus of bodily techniques that they developed for use in the roda and applying the lessons learned from those physical tricks to the tricky worlds we navigate on a daily basis. This book is my own attempt to summon the ancestors. I reference historical capoeiristas like Zumbi and Mestre Bimba, who took stands against injustice during their own lifetimes; I also call on ancestors that might be more familiar to US audiences like Martin Luther King Jr. and Maya Angelou.

Though on the surface there may seem to be little connection between non-Brazilian historical figures like King and Angelou and the Afro-Brazilian martial art of capoeira, they have been incorporated into the praxis of contemporary capoeiristas in the United States. In this chapter, I offer a brief overview of the form of capoeira (see also Griffith 2016; Rosa 2012) to provide context for the rest of the book. I also summarize the historical development of capoeira with an eye toward how these events have laid the foundation for capoeira to be used as a tool of social justice, a concept that I explore in more depth in chapter 2.

BASICS OF THE GAME

I start with a description of the form of capoeira, though potentially redundant for practitioners, to establish common ground for the diverse readers who might find this book of interest. A basic understanding of what capoeira demands physically from its practitioners is important for at least two reasons. First, although capoeiristas are discouraged from engaging in fights if there is any alternative, capoeira is a martial art, and several individuals I interviewed for this book reminded me that if they found themselves in a confrontation (e.g., at a protest) and could not run away, they were capable of and prepared to defend themselves physically. Second, the focus on flexibility, fluidity, and finesse that is built into the form of capoeira underscores how the people in this book use capoeira as a metaphor for navigating society in general. Engaging with capoeira as a metaphor is, in fact, one essential way in which it serves as a tool of social justice, making it possible for a mestre to compare something like unintentionally injuring a fellow player in the roda to committing a microaggression by, say, misgendering someone. Both result in harm; both necessitate redress.

Capoeira has been called a "dynamic pugilistic game" (Desch Obi 2012, 211), though this description does not capture the range of what makes it so entrancing. It has been described as a dance, a fight, and a game. It combines the seriousness of sparring with the explosive energy of gymnastics and the graceful artistry of dance, all done to the rhythm of an orchestra and call-and-response singing. Yet we never use the term *sparring* to describe what we do. One thing that is often missed in official histories of capoeira is the element of *brincando* (but see Willson 2001). While it is well documented that capoeiristas use the verb *play* rather than *spar* when describing the improvisational contests between two capoeiristas, the only Portuguese

The game of capoeira and the circle in which it is played are both referred to as a roda, seen here with the typical accompaniment of the orchestra. Photo by the author.

word often offered for this is *jogar*. *Jogar* and *brincar* both mean "to play," and it is true that the former term is much more commonly used than the latter. However, there is an important distinction between the two words that to me at least, captures one of the most beautiful elements of capoeira. Whereas *jogar* connotes the kind of play that one does in sports (e.g., playing soccer) or games (e.g., playing chess), *brincar* means to play in a carefree manner like children. It is a joyous kind of play that doesn't necessitate an objective. It is more akin to "messing around" than to competing. The most pleasurable games of capoeira I have experienced or witnessed would all be described as brincando. When this concept is applied to one's everyday life, it is a reminder to not take oneself too seriously and to maintain a sense of humor. Even when that play turns serious, maintaining good humor means one can avoid showing their hand, holding on to the possibility of catching their opponent at a future date.

In addition to physical play, song has an important role in capoeira, which I explore in more detail later in the book. What bears mentioning here is that capoeira song helps bring the past into the present (see Downey 2005).

Capoeira songs often reference historical events, but the details communicated through the songs themselves are sparse, requiring that a student learn the full tale by conversing with a mestre or someone more knowledgeable in the art (Assunção 2007). The songs can also comment on some aspect of the game in progress. If a player is using their hands to grab an opponent—something that breaks the unwritten rules of etiquette—the leader of the roda might start singing a song about a grasping woman who tried to hang on to her man too tightly. Players in the know will understand that this song is being sung to chastise the player for trying to grapple.

One's knowledge of capoeira is eternally incomplete. A player is always in the process of becoming, responding to the environment and social context in which they are situated (Habjan 2015). The skills of *malícia* and *malandragem* offer excellent examples of this. The word *malíca* does not translate perfectly into English. Though some translate it as "malice," the connotations of this word in English are inappropriate. Malícia can be better thought of as being sneaky or using deceit to trick one's opponent. Malandragem is a related concept and can be thought of as being roguish. As one capoeira mestre in Rio told Katya Wesolowski (2012, 86), "malandragem is the provenance of the malandro, the con artist. But malandragem is survival, it is surviving the fight that is everyday life." These strategies are applied both within capoeira and outside of it and are particularly useful for individuals existing at the bottom rungs of a grossly unequal society, in which getting ahead through purely aboveboard means is unlikely. It is widely believed that these qualities cannot be taught—indeed my own teachers have said this during class—but they most certainly can be learned. One develops these skills as a result of playing in the roda, falling victim to an opponent's tricks, and learning through trial and error the best ways to circumvent a sticky situation. It is a way of being in the world that readily translates outside of the roda.

This uncanny ability to deceive others through trickery is a source of great power (González Varela 2013, 2017). The public at large may consider deception to be a negative thing, but for the capoeirista, who becomes intimate with the practice of embodied deception, it is a morally neutral resource for navigating an often unfair and politically fraught world. Capoeiristas feign a kick that sends their opponent dodging downward only to pull back at the last second and attack from the other direction. As important as it is to learn how to be tricky, it is equally important to learn how to discern the attack in a partner's graceful movements. Being suspicious of one's opponent is something that comes with time, generally after a capoeirista has a bruised backside from falling victim to some sneaky attack in the roda. This is also an important skill in the real world. In capoeira, it is widely accepted that learning to disguise one's attacks in the roda translates into a tricky way of being in the world, one that serves the underdog well in all aspects of life. What is less often recognized, however, is that the capoeirista also transfers this skill of skepticism and reading between the lines of an adversary's actions. Rather than taking everything at face value, capoeiristas become adept at protecting themselves from exploitation.

Unlike in martial arts that carefully match opponents based on factors like size, weight, and sex, capoeiristas can play against anyone, which quite possibly reflects an understanding that there is no such thing as an even match in any context (MacLennan 2011). It is actually useful to play against a larger, stronger opponent because it encourages the player to outsmart that person, which is another useful life skill. Using malícia to subdue a physically more formidable opponent not only reverses the expected power dynamics of a physical contest, but (ideally) leaves the outwitted person laughing at their own folly for falling into the trap rather than angry and ready to seek revenge (Fuggle 2008). Should the defeated player not demonstrate good humor, they reveal themselves as someone who does not understand the ethos of capoeira.

Today, capoeiristas generally recognize three styles of the art: angola, regional, and contemporânea. Some might go so far as to claim that angola and regional are two different arts (Rosenthal 2009), though I find that position too extreme. Capoeira angola is the style depicted in the vignette that opened this chapter. It is the style I know best because I spent more than six years training in that style. Capoeira regional is the lineage associated with Mestre Bimba, which includes a comprehensive pedagogical system and is characterized by faster rhythms and hence faster movements in the roda. It includes more acrobatic flourishes than what is typically seen in angola, and angoleiros would rarely if ever perform the aerial movements or throws sometimes seen in regional. The regional tradition has been kept alive by Bimba's son Mestre Nenel and is taught by several teachers around the world; however, in popular discourse it is often conflated with the style known as capoeira contemporânea. Contemporânea was derived from regional, but its practitioners claim to revere both regional *and* angola, and they move from the slower rhythms of angola to the faster rhythms of regional in the course of a single roda, adapting their pace and style of play to match the music. Some observers consider this third style to be an amalgamation of the two older styles (Mwewa, Oliveira, and Vaz 2010). Contemporânea has the most practitioners both in Brazil and abroad, which means that when most people see capoeira for the first time, this is the version they are witnessing.

Key moments in the historical trajectories of each style are briefly discussed below, though I avoid going too far into distinguishing these styles from one another both because this divide has already been exaggerated in the existing academic literature and because my concern is with how capoeiristas in the United States from all stylistic backgrounds use their art as a springboard for local activism and community engagement. That said, there are two caveats that I must address here. First, Inkeri Aula (2017) argues that the political distinctions between capoeira styles are not as important abroad as they might be in Brazil, where regional has enjoyed much more endorsement as a national art than has angola. I am hesitant to agree that this holds true in the United States, at least in larger cities, where students can choose between the different styles. In our national context, I have yet to encounter an angola group that is completely unconcerned with issues of racial justice or with support for the African diaspora in some way. Contemporânea groups, on the other hand, may or may not explicitly voice their affinity for the African diaspora, depending on the inclinations of the leader and their core students. Second, Joshua M. Rosenthal (2009, 155) argues that "to say capoeira was Brazilian in the United States, where many see all Brazilians as people of color, is an implicit recognition that Africans had played a part in its creation." I disagree. For one thing, many people do not have a solid-enough grasp of Latin American history to understand the sheer magnitude of slavery in Brazil or the percentage of Brazilians with African ancestry. After all, I still run into people who think Brazilians speak Spanish. While some might hold the assumptions Rosenthal is describing, I do not think this is a majority opinion. Dropping the Afro- from the Afro-Brazilian descriptor of the art (as some capoeira contemporânea schools do) is a form of symbolic violence that implicitly denies Black authorship of this art. As I argue throughout the book, this issue of Black authorship and ownership is a core issue informing capoeira activism.

ORIGIN STORIES

The exact process through which capoeira came to be is the subject of much contention. Most capoeiristas—regardless of the style they play or where they learned the art—have been taught that capoeira developed when enslaved Africans had to disguise their fighting prowess as an innocuous dance in order to escape punishment. However, there is reason to be suspicious of certain aspects of this origin story. As is common in many forms of martial arts, which aspects of the narrative an individual emphasizes may tell us more about that person's ideological commitments than about the art itself (see Bowman 2016). Capoeira practitioners (Assunção 2007) and scholars alike

(Dettmann 2013) are influenced by their ideological positions. My telling of the tale begins with the transatlantic slave trade and focuses on capoeira as a creolized art—that is, one that developed here in the Americas as a result of the interactions between peoples and cultures. I maintain that capoeira is an African diasporic art whose most important contributors were from Africa, but the origin story with the strongest intellectual underpinnings, to me, centralizes developments that occurred in the New World.

Of all the countries in the New World, Brazil imported the largest number of enslaved Africans. Salvador in the state of Bahia was a major port of entry for the four million Africans who were taken to Brazil. Unlike Britain's northeastern colonies (e.g., New England), which were settled for religious purposes, Brazil was always considered, at least as far as the Portuguese crown was concerned, to have an economic function (Costa 1985). Life on Brazilian plantations was exceedingly hard, with the death rate so high and the birth rate so low that the colonists had to continually replace their workforce by importing more Africans. The implication of this for the study of capoeira and other Afro-Brazilian practices is that enslaved peoples in Brazil had repeated opportunities to learn from and exchange ideas with Africans who had newly arrived from the continent.

Brazil was the last country in the New World to abolish slavery. In 1871, the Free Womb Law granted freedom to children born to enslaved mothers, though their freedom was not official until they reached adulthood. Slavery was finally abolished in 1888, when Princess Isabel signed imperial law number 3,353. Unsurprisingly, the official end of slavery did not end prejudice toward Afro-Brazilians, and the nation aggressively pursued a strategy of *branqueamento* (whitening), encouraging the immigration of Europeans and hoping that miscegenation would eventually "breed out" any trace of Blackness in the population. This policy is consistent with an overall pattern of absorbing what was valued about Black culture without properly valuing Black people themselves.

Other books have dealt with the history of capoeira more completely than I aim to do here (Talmon-Chvaicer 2008; Assunção 2004; Taylor 2005–7, vol. 1; Lewis 1992), but unfortunately, any attempt at telling the history of capoeira will inevitably fall short, as no one has (yet) been able to definitively identify its origins. Not only do official histories often lack information about Indigenous and Black cultures, but the official records pertaining to slavery in Brazil were burned by governmental decree in 1890 (Fontoura and Guimarães 2002). Some of the most useful material from this era actually comes from nineteenth-century artists like the German painter Johann Moritz Rugendas

(1802–58), whose now-famous works include a painting of two Black men squaring off in some sort of physical contest, which is labeled *jogo de capoeira* (Rosenthal 2009; see also Rosa 2012). However, this painting does not contain all the elements that a modern-day capoeirista would expect to find in a roda such as the berimbau. Were berimbaus not used in conjunction with capoeira at this time, was their use haphazard and thus not captured by the painter, or was there another reason it was left out? Our inability to answer such questions leaves a gap that when filled by conjecture, drives a wedge in the field.

Scholarly writings about capoeira can largely be divided into two diametrically opposed positions. There are multiple ways of describing these different camps: Africanists versus Brazilianists (Griffith 2016), Afrocentrists versus creolizationists (see Dettmann 2013), and traditionalists versus modernists (Willson 2001). Africanists tend to disregard the role of Brazilians in developing capoeira, preferring to see it as an already-formed art that enslaved Africans brought with them to the New World (even if it had to be modified somewhat due to the conditions of oppression they encountered in Brazil). The Brazilianists, on the other hand, support a view of capoeira as a creolized art that owes a significant debt to the Africans who provided its source material but that would not have its present form if not for the specific mix of cultures that thrived in Brazil (i.e., African, Indigenous, and European).

The stylistic elements of capoeira—such as its use of polyrhythms, the call-and-response format of the songs, and its multidirectionality—are consistent with the "African ethos" (Dossar 1992, 7–8). This might be enough to convince some that capoeira is, at its core, an African art, but those I have labeled Africanists typically look to a dance called the *n'golo* or *engolo* (both terms appear in the literature) as the original form of capoeira. This dance from Angola was part of a puberty rite in which male dancers imitated the movements of zebras and aimed to kick their opponents in the face. Whoever gave the most virtuosic performance would be able to choose his bride from the eligible women without having to pay a bride price. The similarities between this game and capoeira were noted by Angolan painter Albano Neves e Sousa (1921–95). Unfortunately, because of political instability in Angola, these claims could not be adequately investigated at the time of Neves e Sousa's observation (Dettmann 2013).

In the Brazilianist/creolization camp are scholars like Adriana Raquel Ritter Fontoura and Adriana Coutinho de Azevedo Guimarães (2002), who point out that elements of capoeira doubtless came from Africa but that it developed into its present form in Brazil under a certain set of social and material conditions. One benefit of the creolization thesis is that it accounts for the addition of elements that have thus far not been accounted for in the earliest recorded depictions of capoeira. For example, despite the popular story about the martial efficacy of capoeira's being disguised as a dance, there is no concrete evidence of the berimbau being used in capoeira contests prior to the late 1800s (Mason 2013). Whether or not one believes the berimbau to be a defining feature of capoeira, however, is an entirely different question (see chapter 2). Assuming for the moment that the berimbau *is* a key feature of the art we know as capoeira, we can see evidence of it being played in Brazil during the early 1800s, such as in the paintings of *escravos de ganho* (enslaved wage earners) by Jean-Baptiste Debret (1768–1848). There is also evidence of physical contests that look like capoeira, such as in the Rugendas paintings. However, the absence of images including *both* the berimbau and capoeira suggests that the fusing of these practices occurred in Brazil rather than in Africa (Brito 2012). In addition, Paul H. Mason (2013) suggests that the *rabo-de-arraia* (stingray tail), one of the most iconic kicks in capoeira, may actually have been borrowed from savate (French boxing), as there are paintings demonstrating a similar movement being done aboard French ships and these sailors were known to participate in capoeira rodas while in Brazil.

In line with the creolization thesis, dance scholar Barbara Browning (1995, 91) acknowledges that the individual movements used in capoeira may very well have come from Africa, but states that "the strategic blending of fight and dance occurred in Brazil, under specific pressures." I concur with J. Lowell Lewis (1992) that capoeira likely took on its present form in the late eighteenth century. The holistic "metagenre" (MacAloon 1984) that we know as capoeira would likely not exist had it not been for the colonial conditions that forced people from disparate communities together and disincentivized the open practice of their martial skills. Regardless of how literally we take this part of the capoeira narrative, African-descended peoples throughout the New World have had to conceal the nature of their fighting systems to avoid persecution from white enslavers (see Green 2003). With Brazilian enslavers being on alert due to the success of slave revolts throughout the Caribbean (Taylor 2005–7, vol. 1), drumming was seen not as a pastime or religious activity but as a potentially subversive means of sending messages between communities. Enslaved and free Black and mixed-race people greatly outnumbered white people in colonial Brazil (Marquese 2006); their coordinated action could have been devastating for the white population, increasing its anxiety about maintaining control. These conditions could not help but change the form of capoeira.

Based on the available evidence, I find the creolization thesis most compelling. That said, caution must be exercised here; proponents of the Africanist position argue that the creolization thesis risks denying the creativity of Africans, an allegation that has been true of many academic debates over the genesis of various Black Atlantic cultural forms (Rosenthal 2009). T. J. Desch Obi (2012) takes issue with the ways in which the term *creole* is selectively applied to African-derived cultural traditions in the New World, while the arts, sports, and other practices developed by white people in the New World are seen as novel innovations. This double standard is evidence of some scholars' subconscious bias toward Africa and the diaspora. Desch Obi rightly argues that "it is only logical that for the label 'creole' (indigenized or hybrid) to be intellectually meaningful, there must also be 'non-creole' (nonindigenized or 'pure') cultural forms. But since few if any cultural practices are 'pure,' and all cultural forms carried into new places and eras became indigenized to the new environment, then all are 'creole' and the label is epistemologically and ontologically useless" (224). If everything is really creole, then one must ask why this label is typically only applied to the arts and practices created by people of color. While I strongly agree with Desch Obi on this point, I align myself with Wesolowski (2012)—and the creolization camp more broadly—who argues that capoeira most likely originated as an amalgamation of fighting styles from western and central Africa but came together on Brazilian plantations, where enslaved Africans from different cultural traditions encountered one another, and thus has always been a global art form. Global forms do change as they spread around the world. Acknowledging these changes need not mean undercutting the creative genius of those who originally developed the art, provided that we do not obscure their contributions through racist scholarly constructs.

MODERNIZATION

Ironically, it wasn't until after the abolition of slavery that practicing capoeira became punishable by law. During the slavery era, one could be given four hundred lashes if caught playing capoeira, but it was not technically illegal (Willson 2001). Following the abolition of slavery in 1888, unemployment, prejudice, and police harassment were significant problems for newly freed Black people. It was within this context that many capoeiristas joined gangs like the infamous rivals Guaimuns and Nagoas in Rio de Janeiro (Fontoura and Guimarães 2002). As Brazil sought to establish itself as a legitimate democracy following the 1889 coup d'état that established the First Brazilian Republic, capoeiristas in Rio were often implicated in political intrigue.

They not only served as bodyguards for politicians but were also accused of intimidating voters and "render[ing] elections farcical" (Assunção 2004, 93). For this reason, the Criminal Code of 1890 (articles 402–4) threatened capoeiristas with a two- to six-month jail sentence for practicing their art. Despite the risks, capoeira continued to be practiced clandestinely. Some even proposed that capoeira be used as a form of physical training for the military (see Downey 2002), but this movement was ultimately defeated because Parliament preferred European traditions to Brazilian ones (Talmon-Chvaicer 2008).

The dawn of the New Republic also marks one point at which the capoeira traditions of Rio de Janeiro and Bahia diverge. Because Rio was the political center of the nation during the early part of the twentieth century, this is where capoeira was most heavily persecuted. In fact, there is a widely held perception that its persecution in the 1900s forced capoeira so deep underground that the tradition was lost, but this is not entirely true, and there is a thriving capoeira scene in Rio today (see Talmon-Chvaicer 2008). Incidentally, one group I have worked with on this project traces its lineage back to Mestre Leopoldinho (1933–2007), a Rio hustler turned master who was beloved by the community. The group's members identify as angoleiros, but their style is markedly different from that of the largest angola lineage in the United States, which originated in Bahia.

In the northeastern state of Bahia there are no records of anyone being arrested for playing capoeira (Assunção 2004). However, Mestre Bimba (Manoel Machado, 1889–1974) recalled at least one occasion in the early 1900s, prior to the opening of his academy, when he had to bribe the Bahian police in order to hold a two-hour roda (Fontoura and Guimarães 2002). The relatively lax enforcement of the anticapoeira law in Bahia allowed for unbroken continuity in practice, which is why the region is now known internationally as the "cradle" or "font" of capoeira. Over time, capoeira in Bahia developed a ludic character that often co-occurred with drinking and gambling (Almeida 1986). Both its continued practice in Bahia and its shift away from overt violence created a context in which legitimate capoeira academies could eventually be established in the capital city of Salvador. This would not happen, however, until intellectuals and government officials saw how capoeira might align with their own agendas.

Like many postcolonial nations in the first half of the twentieth century, Brazil sought to establish itself as a modern nation with a distinct national character. Even while capoeira was still technically illegal, it was celebrated by intellectuals who saw it as a unique manifestation of Brazilian identity (Downey 2002). When folklorist Edison Carneiro helped organize the Second

Afro-Brazilian Congress—held in Salvador in 1937—it brought attention to the unique contributions of Afro-Brazilians (Assunção 2004), but it also paved the way for white Brazilians to co-opt Black culture without acknowledging the extent to which Afro-Brazilians suffered from persistent inequalities (Joseph 2006). Afro-Brazilians continued to be marginalized and oppressed postemancipation, even as their arts were being appropriated by the state as symbols of national identity (see Vianna 1999). The shift toward acceptance can also be seen in Bahia's premier newspaper, *A Tarde*. Though the newspaper's editors were outspoken critics of capoeira in the first three decades of the twentieth century, by 1936 they were advocating for the development of capoeira as Brazil's national fight (*A Tarde* 1936). A decade later, the paper was romanticizing capoeira as part of the region's "picturesque" and "traditional" culture (*A Tarde* 1948).

When president/dictator Getúlio Vargas (1882–1954) came into power for the first time (1930), one of his plans was to better integrate lower-class citizens into the fabric of the nation by valorizing their folk traditions (Talmon-Chvaicer 2008). Although capoeira's discourse of resisting oppression didn't necessarily align with the mission of Vargas's Estado Novo, which was characterized by nationalist propaganda, the physical art itself could be made to fit by downplaying its ideology and instead stressing the morally uplifting aspects of physical discipline (see Taylor 2005–7, vol. 2).[2] The capoeira of Mestre Bimba was ideally suited to this mission.

Despite capoeira still being illegal in 1932, Mestre Bimba was the first of two key figures to open an academy in Bahia. By establishing a formal academy, Mestre Bimba created a space for white, middle-class Brazilians to participate in the art of capoeira, which had been almost exclusively the domain of poor Afro-Brazilians (Fontoura and Guimarães 2002). Bimba's efforts at modernizing capoeira removed the taint of slavery and made it palatable for Brazilians of all races and classes, thus setting the stage for his capoeira regional to become the more popular form both domestically and abroad (Willson 2001).

Mestre Pastinha (Vicente Pastinha, 1889–1982), popularly considered to be the father of capoeira angola, opened his academy in Bahia in 1941. Mestre Pastinha was less invested in developing specific training sequences than Mestre Bimba was, and although he did introduce certain rules that would make capoeira safer for training, his modifications to the art were minimal. Pastinha was a philosopher rather than a pedagogue. His charisma and temperament contributed to his academy becoming popular among intellectuals like the painter Carybé (1911–97) and the modernist writer Jorge Amado (1912–2001) (Fontoura and Guimarães 2002). He was also skilled at creating unity for the capoeira angola community by bringing many famous players together under his school (Griffith 2016).

The story that has been told in numerous academic papers and books (e.g., Sansone 1999; Talmon-Chvaicer 2008; Assunção 2004; Aula 2017) is that Mestre Bimba "whitened" capoeira by placing restrictions on who could join his school and by incorporating movements from other martial arts to create a more sportified form that appealed to the Brazilian elites, who wanted Brazil to be seen as a modern nation; Mestre Pastinha, on the other hand, revitalized the more ludic and supposedly traditional form of capoeira (capoeira angola) in order to save it from extinction. There are elements of this story that certainly make sense. In the 1930s, when Mestre Bimba was establishing his school and formalizing his system, there was an impulse to cannibalize foreign styles and incorporate them into Brazilian art forms in an act of synthesis that mirrors the discourse of racial democracy. Indeed, this was perfectly aligned with Vargas's Estado Novo project (Aula 2017). And yet, during this same period, there were intellectuals that had a vested interest in preserving folk traditions as they imagined them to have been in some premodern era.

While it is fair to say that these two factions—the syncretizing modernizers and the traditional purists—existed in Brazilian society when Mestre Bimba and Mestre Pastinha were teaching capoeira, the discourse surrounding the ways in which each style of capoeira fit into these two camps is almost too neat. Many American capoeiristas, having bought into this narrative, come back from their pilgrimages to Brazil surprised to have seen just how little animosity exists between mestres of the different styles in Brazil. Furthermore, this dichotomization of the field obscures other variants of capoeira that have survived into the present, such as the capoeira angola *são bento grande* lineage, which comes from Rio. Some ideological issues associated with angoleiros' strong affinity with the Afrocentric origin story of capoeira, which Mestre Pastinha promoted, will be unavoidable; however, my intention is to focus on the common ground shared by capoeiristas in the United States, regardless of their stylistic affiliations.

INSTITUTIONALIZATION

In the twentieth century, official attempts at domesticating or institutionalizing capoeira took a number of different forms. Greg Downey (2002, 2) has classified these approaches as "combat sport, national calisthenic, tournament competition and cultural game." During the early 1900s, programs of national gymnastics were already well known in European nations like Germany and Sweden, and Brazilian schools at the time used European-style gymnastic instruction to instill discipline in students and build a healthy citizenry. Some individuals (e.g., folklorists, nationalist educators) argued that replacing these foreign forms with the Brazilian art of capoeira would make students more patriotic as well. This method of domesticating capoeira downplayed conflict between opponents and focused almost exclusively on physical conditioning and patriotism. What its proponents sought was "a particularly Brazilian form of physical education to generate deeper nationalist sentiment" (Downey 2002, 10).

Ultimately, the attempt to develop a national (and nationalistic) calisthenics program based on capoeira failed, in no small part because it stripped away the elements that make capoeira special (e.g., play, music, theatrics). Although some have continued to champion a sport version of capoeira, these efforts have not gained much traction. By 1975, formal capoeira tournaments were being organized, but there continued to be a great deal of disagreement within the capoeira community regarding how such competitions should be run and whether it was even appropriate to have such competitions (see Downey 2002). Even the judges had trouble adjudicating these competitions, and the players themselves often recognized that this was not capoeira at its best.

Given the appeal of capoeira as a spectacle, it has unsurprisingly been incorporated into folklore shows. Although folkloric performances of capoeira are often criticized for watering down the art, the elements emphasized in folkloric shows (e.g., theatricality, ritual, and historicity) are precisely the ones missing from the sportified version of capoeira (Downey 2002). In fact, the reason these staged performances are criticized is that relegating capoeira to the realm of folklore, often associated with museums or commemorative performances, renders it "innocuous" and downplays its potential to catalyze political change. Furthermore, it locates capoeira in the past, negating its power as a tool in the contemporary fight for justice.

Have these attempts at institutionalization failed because practitioners actively resisted the transformation of their beloved art or because they simply weren't viable ideas? Downey (2002) argues that capoeiristas were largely disinterested in these innovations, and that boredom with the processes of institutionalization led to their failure. Wesolowski (2012), on the other hand, points to flash points at which mestres loudly criticized these efforts on what can only be considered political grounds. For instance, federal law number 9,696, which was enacted in 1998, requires that capoeira teachers be certified, either by obtaining a degree in physical education or by completing a yearlong course. The monthly tuition for this course is more than many Brazilians make in a month, putting it out of reach for the people who could most benefit from capoeira as an avenue of financial and social mobility (Wesolowski 2012). Loudly criticized by capoeiristas, this law has not been widely enforced, but it nonetheless indexes the often-rocky relationship between capoeira and the state as well as the tension between capoeira as cultural heritage and as commodifiable sport.

GLOBALIZATION

Capoeira's future now balances precariously on the double-edged blade of globalization. Laurence Robitaille (2010, 1) captures the complicated nature of capoeira as a global commodity by writing that it "can be understood simultaneously as a commodified product that is exchanged in a capitalist market and as the cement of a transnational community providing networks of solidarity and reciprocity for its participants in a globalized world." As of the mid-2010s, the International Federation of Capoeira estimated that there were eight million capoeiristas in the world, with 25 percent of these being non-Brazilians practicing in more than 150 countries (Rocha et al. 2015).

Though they appear to only focus on capoeira regional/contemporânea, Angela da Rocha and colleagues (2015) present an extensive list of capoeira franchises that are truly global in scope. Abadá-Capoeira, for instance, which was established in 1988, has 338 affiliated groups in forty-eight countries. In comparison, Filhos de Bimba Escola de Capoeira (run by Mestre Bimba's son Mestre Nenel), which was established in 1986, seems almost modest with its eighteen affiliated schools in ten different nations. In addition to these large franchises, numerous independent teachers have established their own schools abroad. Many of these teachers are Brazilian, which becomes a mark of distinction and legitimacy in an increasingly competitive market (see Rosario, Stephens, and Delamont 2010). However, an increasing number of non-Brazilians teach capoeira as well, sometimes facing discrimination for doing so.

Rosenthal (2007) identifies the beginning of capoeira's global phase as being a 1966 visit by Mestre Pastinha to Dakar, Senegal, where he and several students demonstrated their art at the First World Festival of Negro Arts. Shortly after Pastinha's demonstration, Brazilian teachers started settling outside of Brazil and establishing their own schools abroad. The majority of teachers who took up the challenge of teaching abroad during this period represented the contemporânea style. Nestor Capoeira was teaching in Europe at the early date of 1971, while Jelon Vieira and Bira Almeida (Mestre Acordeon) started teaching in the United States not long after (Rosenthal 2009). Mestre Jelon's case is particularly interesting because he runs a lauded dance company (DanceBrazil) in addition to a successful capoeira franchise (Capoeira Luanda). In no small part due to his influence, many dancers have turned to capoeira to augment their training, not only because it encourages physical conditioning but because it teaches them to be comfortable with improvisation and to utilize vertical space more completely and fluidly (Stuart 2013). Modern dance choreographers have even drawn inspiration from capoeira, incorporating elements into their productions. Both Mestre Jelon and Mestre Acordeon have used their success and influence to raise money for and support economically disadvantaged Brazilians, and have transmitted these values to their students in the United States.

The growth of capoeira abroad in the 1980s coincides with a period of economic crisis in Brazil that led many capoeiristas to look for employment opportunities outside of their home country (Rocha et al. 2015). Despite the official endorsement of capoeira as Brazil's national sport, it was hard to make a living from teaching capoeira at the time, and the two leading figures of the day—Mestre Bimba and Mestre Pastinha—both died in poverty. Traveling abroad to teach capoeira also gave young Brazilian men (and later women) a chance to see the world and gain recognition for something that was not considered all that extraordinary back home in Brazil (see Wesolowski 2012). In addition to the financial situation, which pushed many Brazilians to find creative ways to make money, the rise of the conservative military dictatorship in Brazil (1964–85) may also have encouraged some capoeiristas' emigration (Rosenthal 2009).

Capoeira angola was slower to make its global debut. Mestre João Grande was born in 1933 in a small town in the interior of Bahia. After moving to Salvador, he began learning capoeira under the tutelage of Mestre Pastinha, and he was one of the individuals that accompanied Pastinha to Dakar in 1966. In the 1970s, he traveled with the performance group Viva Bahia, putting on folkloric shows throughout Europe (Castro 2007). Capoeira angola went into a period of decline in Brazil at this time, and so upon his return to Brazil, he found employment as a gas station attendant. Mestre Moraes (Pedro Martinez Trindade, b. 1950) eventually enticed Mestre João Grande to return to capoeira. Mestre João Grande spent three years teaching with Moraes's Grupo de Capoeira Angola Pelourinho (GCAP) in Brazil, and was then invited to participate in the National Black Arts Festival in Atlanta in 1990, after which he was asked to teach capoeira classes in New York (Castro 2007). Ninety years old as of 2023, he continues to be one of the most influential capoeira angola teachers in the world. He has received an honorary doctorate and even the US National Heritage Fellowship for his artistic excellence. One often-noted aspect of his instruction is that despite the length of time he has spent in the United States, he refuses to speak English with his students, encouraging his students to learn Portuguese instead. He has created a truly cosmopolitan capoeira center, where people from all over the world come to learn and play.

Throughout the 1990s, capoeira remained little known relative to other martial arts (Fuggle 2008), but the inclusion of capoeira in several movies, video games, and advertising campaigns in this decade hastened the growth of this art in the Global North (Rocha et al. 2015). Eddy Gordo and Christie Monteiro, popular characters in the *Tekken* video game series, debuted in the late 1990s and use capoeira as their signature styles. Both characters were created from video captures of Mestre Marcelo of Capoeira Mandinga, located in Oakland, California. While game developer Bandai Namco Studios clearly took some artistic license in animating these characters (e.g., unrealistic body proportions), Mestre Marcelo used this platform as an opportunity to ensure that at least some cultural and ritualistic aspects of capoeira would be circulated within this virtual form ("Tekken," n.d.). Capoeira has also been featured in a number of television programs, including the sci-fi series *Stargate SG-1* (1997–2007), in which the Jaffa people practice a martial art they call Mastaba, performed by actual members of Grupo Axé Capoeira; and movies like the 1993 film *Only the Strong* (dir. Sheldon Lettich), which features fight choreography by Mestre Amen and is credited by more than a few of my interlocutors as having been what drew them to capoeira in the first place.[3] Regardless of whether spreading capoeira as a tool of resistance factored into his decision to participate in the making of the film, Mestre Amen, by contributing to that movie, not only inspired countless Americans to study capoeira, but planted the idea that it could be used for social justice. In other instances, capoeira influences the development of a film character's way of moving, such as the signature style created for the late Chadwick Boseman in his role of Black Panther (Thorp, n.d.). Arguably the best known African or African diasporic martial art, capoeira when used in this way often signifies a character's affinity for Africa or the diaspora, aesthetically marking the character's resistance to (complete) assimilation.

That capoeira has become part of global cool is hard to dispute. Like many global trends, it has infiltrated our consciousness slowly and subtly. But this slow and easy spread does a disservice to the art when it is only utilized for its "exotic" flavor. Capoeira is sometimes included in television programs focused on Brazil, such as when the BBC covered the 2014 World Cup and journalist Jason Mohammad was filmed taking a capoeira lesson (see Delamont, Stephens, and Campos 2017), or when Henry Louis Gates Jr. (2011) explored the concept of miscegenation and racism in Bahia for a PBS documentary and capoeira provided the colorful backdrop for one segment. While coverage like this may increase audiences' familiarity with capoeira, it does little to explain its historical or contemporary significance. In the closing ceremonies of the 2012 Olympics, when responsibility for the games was being passed to the Brazilian delegation, it was clear that the South American nation wished to highlight its immaterial cultural patrimony rather than its exports or natural resources (Delamont, Stephens, and Campos 2017), and yet the lack of explicit framing around the capoeira segment of these closing ceremonies again rendered it a beautiful spectacle disassociated from the role it plays in practitioners' lives.

The ways in which global audiences first encounter an art matter. Rosenthal (2009, 158) remarks that in the early years of the twenty-first century, the idea of people learning capoeira from the internet, imitating video clips they found online, "seemed like apocryphal tales of ethnographic science fiction." And yet, as I have demonstrated elsewhere (Griffith 2017), this is indeed happening and often serves as a gateway to face-to-face instruction as prospective students build up their confidence on their own before taking the plunge with an in-person class. Capoeira appeals to a wide range of people, and today, "a capoeira group can be found in the most improbable places, those with the largest psychic distance to Brazil, with low-income populations, and in some of the most remote areas of the planet" (Rocha et al. 2015, 415). People in down-and-out circumstances find themselves attracted to capoeira because of how it has been used by other oppressed people to physically and psychologically survive their circumstances. Being part of a capoeira group links individuals to "distant places and cultural settings, such as Brazilian groups and mestres . . . other filial groups in Brazil and in other countries, and capoeira lore connecting capoeiristas with Afro-Brazilian heroes, adversities, and a mythical Africa" (Aula 2017, 68).

The global popularity of capoeira has affected the way capoeira is perceived back in Brazil. The financial contributions that satellite groups make to the original Brazilian group should not be underestimated. Also, these domestic groups receive a significant amount of money from foreign capoeiristas, who travel to Brazil to train there for weeks and even months at a time. Elsewhere (Griffith 2013, 2016; Griffith and Marion 2018), I have discussed the phenomenon of apprenticeship pilgrimage, the practice of traveling to the source or major hub of practice in order to augment one's legitimacy in the social field. Capoeiristas engage in this kind of travel regularly. After I returned from a trip to Brazil, my mestre told the group that I knew how it "really was" in Brazil now that I had been there. Regardless of whether my skills had actually improved during my time in Brazil, I was afforded a new level of respect because I had been to the mecca of our community.

In 1994, Mestre Moraes and the members of GCAP held the "First International Encounter" for capoeiristas, which brought North Americans and Europeans together with Brazilians in capoeira's heartland (Assunção 2004). Since that time, such international encounters have become almost commonplace. In several capoeira schools, one can only be promoted to the rank of teacher at a ceremony in Brazil, making travel there obligatory for individuals who want to progress within their school's hierarchy (Griffith 2016). Many teachers organize regular trips to Brazil for their students, and my interviewees who have not yet visited Brazil are often apologetic or almost ashamed, acting as if this is a deficit in their development. More than just financial benefits to the Brazilian capoeira community have come about as a result of the art's globalization. Wesolowski (2012, 83) argues that "the global commodification and consumption of capoeira as an exotic, hip, multicultural activity has influenced the tone and direction of the internal politics that have long been a part of this practice." Indeed, the enthusiasm with which capoeira has been received abroad has elevated its status back home, where many elites had long disparaged it because of its connection to slavery and poor Afro-Brazilians.

In 2008, Brazil's Instituto do Patrimônio Histórico e Artístico Nacional (IPHAN, Institute of National Historic and Artistic Patrimony) added capoeira to its list of immaterial cultural patrimony. Capoeiristas across the country celebrated, and the next day the newspaper was full of pictures of impromptu rodas that had broken out in the streets. Most capoeiristas were happy about the announcement, but a few were skeptical, worrying that official endorsement might also entail a folklorization process in which capoeira's natural dynamism would be curtailed for the sake of preservation (see Collier 2006). Having arrived in Brazil just a day after the pronouncement, I was intrigued by the discourse I heard. Many people thought that this only came about because foreigners had exhibited such an interest in capoeira, that without their valorization, capoeira would have continued to be a marginalized practice associated with poor vagrants. Some also thought that it was an overdue attempt at reparations.

Considering the complex relationship capoeira has had with the state, can a gesture like this make up for the years during which its practice was illegal and its practitioners persecuted? In 2014, capoeira was added to the UNESCO Intangible Cultural Heritage of Humanity lists. IPHAN and UNESCO have pledged to protect capoeira, but from what and from whom? I do not believe capoeira as a physical form is under threat. Quite the contrary, these pronouncements mark its popularity. The thing that remains less certain, to me at least, is what principles will govern capoeira as it continues to grow and incorporate new practitioners. I, like many of those I interviewed for this book, believe that capoeira without some degree of social engagement is hollow. In the next chapter, I examine the ways in which, according to certain mestres' and US-based capoeiristas' interpretation of the history of capoeira, being a capoeirista demands active engagement with contemporary issues of social justice.

2

SOCIAL JUSTICE AND RESISTANCE
AS ANALYTICAL FRAMES

Lá na Bahia
Terra de São Salvador
Besouro era valente
Tinha o corpo fechado
Mas a traição o matou

There in Bahia
The land of San Salvador
Besouro was brave
He had a closed body
But betrayal killed him
—popular capoeira song

Besouro (Beetle) is perhaps the best known of the legendary ruffians commemorated in capoeira songs. Manoel Henrique Pereira was given this nick-
name because of his supposed ability to transform himself into a beetle and
fly away from the police (Zonzon 2014; see also Acuña 2016). In the 1920s,
this cowhand frequently fought with people in the rural Recôncavo city of
Santo Amaro, often acting in defense of others (Castro 2007). His final conflict was with the son of a powerful ranch owner. According to legend, the
owner had Besouro carry a message to the administrator of a large sugar
factory. Unbeknown to Besouro, the message contained an order to kill him.
The administrator told him to wait until the next day so he could prepare
a reply. When Besouro went back the next day, he was surrounded by forty
men who tried to kill him. He avoided all their bullets but was ultimately

felled by a magical wooden knife used in Candomblé (Willson 2001). Another version of the story, told by Mestre João Grande, is that the woman with whom Besouro spent the night stole his protective amulet, and the next day he was decapitated with a wire (Castro 2007).

One reason this tale has become so popular in capoeira is that it seems to support the notion that capoeiristas can magically close their bodies as a means of defense, a theme that finds resonance in the legends of many ancient martial arts. Yet there is something more: whether or not Besouro had magical abilities, he is commemorated in capoeira lore both for being an extraordinary virtuoso of the art *and* for the way he inhabited this gray space between legality and illegality, using his skills in capoeira to subvert the laws of an unjust ruling class. Based on what we know about him—much of which is shrouded in myth—he was a scoundrel and womanizer, not exactly the role model I would choose for my sons. While most of us wouldn't consciously emulate his behavior, he remains a larger-than-life figure who is admired for his ability to stand up for himself and weaker members of his community (on Besouro, see Pires 2002).

While associating oneself with vagrancy or mischief might be seen as antisocial, in the context of capoeira, it is not. Rather, embracing these values has helped capoeiristas "construct a second reality opposed to Western notions of rationality and efficiency" (Aula 2017, 74). The vast majority of capoeiristas are law abiding, but many capoeira songs commemorate folk heroes who committed crimes in service of the poor or in defiance of state power. Lampião, for example, born Virgulino Ferreira da Silva, was a bandit that roamed the northeastern countryside in the 1920s and 1930s. Though his attacks were often vicious, he is widely thought of as a Robin Hood–type figure whose raids rectified gross imbalances of wealth and power (see Habjan 2015). Multiple capoeira songs celebrate his exploits. Like individuals and groups that use the word *malandro* (rogue) in their names, this should be taken not as a glorification of lawlessness or antisociality, but as a recognition that playing by society's rules is not always beneficial, especially for marginalized peoples.

Greg Downey (2002) cautions academics against seeing "resistance" in any situation where the will of the subaltern appears to triumph over the efforts of a more powerful entity like the state. Anthropologists in particular are quick to champion the rights of the underdog, so he is right to warn us against seeing what we want to see when there may be a more prosaic answer. But at the same time, even if an actor was not motivated by a desire to resist the hegemonic structures of society, their actions may later be interpreted as having been acts of resistance, and the circulation of that retrospectively constructed discourse can become an important aspect of contemporary praxis.

I have yet to meet a capoeirista unfamiliar with their art's reputation as a "secular ritual" or "narrative drama" that celebrates the creativity and perseverance of the enslaved Africans who ultimately triumphed over oppression (D'Aquino 1983, 6). But how much stock do they put in this origin story? Some take it quite literally. Others have doubts about the veracity of certain details but still see it as a compelling tale that can be used as a road map for resisting oppression in the present. Still others personally conceive of capoeira as an apolitical space but repeat the story simply because it has worn such deep grooves in the art's public face. In the previous chapter, I provided a brief overview of the form of capoeira and the history of its development, as well as some of the academic controversy that surrounds its origin stories. Here I am concerned with how that history is utilized in the present.

Social justice is a term that gets thrown around liberally in contemporary culture, and there is a great deal of variability in how people use it. In this chapter, I explain how I use the term and why I think many actions of capoeiristas can be classified as forms of social justice. I demonstrate some ways in which famous mestres have encouraged in their students a justice orientation, even though this stance is not endorsed by all capoeiristas. Capoeiristas are also more apt to use the term *resistance* than *social justice,* but I frequently use the two terms interchangeably because in my view, resisting oppression *is* a form of social justice. This is why after outlining my own views on social justice and the way many mestres' actions fit into this paradigm, I return to the resistance narrative contemporary capoeiristas have constructed. Finally, I explain how these beliefs contribute to the phenomenon of performative resistance, bringing about in members of this community a new state of being.

SOCIAL JUSTICE

All art, as a form of human agency, is inherently and necessarily political (see Boal 1993). Even when art is not being used intentionally for political ends, the artist's decisions about what to include, what to exclude, or how to present something are shaped by the artist's place in society. The formative experiences that artist has had are in no small part a result of how structures of power affect them based on their race, class, gender, immigration status, and more. That is to say, as Carol Hanisch (1969) wrote—quoting an axiom of second-wave feminism—"the personal is political."

Art is a common avenue through which people who lack political and economic power make their voices heard. Being able to speak directly about one's circumstances is a privilege. People in subordinated positions do not have "the luxury of transparency, the presumptive norm of clear and direct communication, free and open debate on a level playing field that the privileged classes take for granted" (Conquergood 2013, 24). This is why performance, art, and play in general are ideal arenas in which to seek examples of social justice efforts.

When we encounter difficult situations, play is not an escape but an opportunity to work through that trouble. Play allows us to enter into a subjective mode and imagine "what if" (see Schechner 2002). What if I were a superhero? What if I could challenge my oppressor? Such forms of play can be transformative, and under the right circumstances play can translate into social justice action. Drawing from the work of George Theoharis (2007), I associate social justice with any number of caring and compassionate efforts to disrupt and subvert social structures that perpetuate inequality, working for the equitable distribution of wealth, opportunities, and well-being across all segments of society. Social justice is any intentional action people do to help underserved communities or raise awareness about something that they deem unfair.

Capoeiristas, then, might do well to reclaim the term *social justice warrior*, which has been used pejoratively to describe individuals with a holier-than-thou desire to spread unquestioned liberal values. That the term *social justice* has acquired such negative connotations in certain circles is disappointing, for at its core it is characterized by a deep concern with the right to live an authentic, meaningful life (see Faubion 2016). This and other universal rights should be available to all, particularly those whose marginalized and non-normative identities have endangered their lives and liberty.

The fight for universal rights might be construed as radical, but the rights themselves typically are not. They are things that other citizens take for granted: access to clean water, control over one's own body, or the assurance one will not be shot in a traffic stop. In certain contexts, asserting the right to normality is a political act, which is why our analyses of social justice cannot be restricted to organized protests and activist organizations (see Ahmad 2016). Many of us in the United States, particularly those in privileged positions, have not had cause to really understand the enormity of this, though our recovery from the traumas brought on by the COVID-19 pandemic will certainly underscore how victorious and perhaps radical a return to normality can feel. We must not forget that for some individuals, those whose very bodies mark them as Other, the most innocuous acts may have deadly consequences. Ahmaud Arbery was out for a run; Philando Castile was on a drive with his girlfriend and her daughter. Simply taking up public space as a person of color, a woman, or a trans person can be an act of resistance. This is similar to what Barbara Browning (1995, 167) noted when she wrote that "the insistence of Brazilians to keep dancing is not a means of forgetting but rather a perseverance, an unrelenting attempt to intellectualize, theorize, understand a history and a present of social injustice." To take up public space in the act of performing an art created and safeguarded by an enslaved people is radical.

I take an intentionally broad approach to social justice. Cymene Howe (2016, 163) explains that "analytic attention often—perhaps always—centers on a suite of signature events that, in turn, serve to qualify a set of actions as social justice activism." These moments are often spectacular and will typically be the events remembered as being instrumental in bringing about change. But this is to focus on the performance proper, the glory of opening night, without attending to the daily grind of rehearsals. And yet without those rehearsals, the show would not go on.

Some capoeiristas I have met through this project do take part in actions that are readily recognizable as social justice initiatives. They teach free classes in underserved communities; they organize marches; they engage in acts of civil disobedience. These intentional acts of social justice are worth analyzing, but so are the activities that inform and sustain organizations and individuals in between these signature events. The quotidian practices of activists create a foundation on which action can occur. This is why I also include things like the private act of researching song lyrics, the internal debates over how to handle the power dynamics of capoeiristas' romantic relationships, and the efforts to reduce single-use plastics at capoeira eventos as forms of social justice. Even the seemingly innocent act of playing capoeira in public may be a way to decolonize space.[1] Capoeira contains a great deal of raw material that can be forged into weapons for social justice under the right circumstances.

JUSTICE-ORIENTED MESTRES

Being a mestre is about more than simply teaching capoeira moves and song; it is something that does not end when class is over. One's legitimacy as a mestre rests on ratification by the capoeira community. This kind of mestre is someone who takes responsibility for "the formation of people as citizens" (Machado 2018, 123). Mestres do not take one single position toward the use of capoeira for social justice, but a few well-known leaders have served, through their attitudes and actions, as touchstones for justice-oriented capoeiristas.

Because mestres are leaders in the social field, the stance they take on these issues matters, and it is common for an activist's group to develop a strong social justice ethos. A mestre who grows in power may even ban people from the group if they are not committed to this vision (an irony I address later). In my experience, this is quite rare, but it does happen. Those who remain are often enculturated into the discourse of capoeira as an art of resistance and may even be compelled to take actions in support of various causes championed by the mestre. The actual strategies that are used to cultivate this orientation are the focus of chapters 3–5. Here, I provide examples of the orientations toward justice/activism taken by a few notable mestres as a way of explaining how the social justice mentality manifests within capoeira. These orientations range from subtle to overt; what unifies them is the way in which the capoeiristas' actions are an extension of what they believe to be the fundamental values of capoeira.

Though I have never seen Mestre Bimba described as an activist or social justice warrior, his actions were aligned with these modern-day orientations in at least two distinct ways: he rehabilitated the image of the capoeirista so that its potential for resistance could be realized by more people, and he used his power in society to advocate for and intervene on behalf of more vulnerable people. Mestre Bimba has been criticized by some modern-day capoeiristas for his requirement that one had to be employed or enrolled in school in order to enroll in the academy (this would have excluded many Afro-Brazilians who lacked the means to pursue an education or who were unable to find work due to prejudice or other reasons), but Bimba's son Mestre Nenel explains that this requirement was a way of ensuring that a capoeirista would demonstrate at least a baseline of responsibility, thus "[strengthening] the role of capoeira as an element of social shaping" (Machado 2018, 121). This decision may have alienated some potential students during Bimba's lifetime, but, as argued in chapter 1, it also enabled capoeira to come out of the shadows and gain legitimacy. This does not mean that lessons about resistance were stripped away from instruction. Mestre Bimba's advanced students, for instance, had to ward off *emboscadas* (ambush attacks) in the forests, recalling the conditions experienced by freedom seekers (Marriage 2020, 14). The presence of exercises like the emboscada in the capoeira regional pedagogy is but one point of reference instructors can use if they want to activate the latent theme of resistance as they teach.

Mestre Bimba's quotidian behaviors also demonstrated a commitment to fairness, if not social justice per se. Bimba was known as being someone that anyone in the community, capoeirista or not, could turn to if they needed help (Machado 2018, 119). There is an oft-told tale of Mestre Bimba defending a Black boy because he was being harassed by the police. This was not done within the context of capoeira, but, according to legend, his training as a capoeirista enabled him to defend the boy and escape capture or retaliation from the police. Capoeiristas aren't necessarily taught to ready their bodies in case they are called on to defend their families or communities, but there nonetheless seems to be an impulse to help others embedded into the framework of the groups I have encountered in both the United States and Brazil.

Several interlocutors expressed an assumption that angoleiros—practitioners of the capoeira angola style—would be more likely to have an activist orientation than would players of the regional or contemporânea styles. This is not necessarily the case, but there are historical reasons for a close association between capoeira angola and activism, at least forms of activism that support the African diaspora. The popularity of capoeira regional/ contemporânea outpaced that of capoeira angola, particularly in the 1970s, and angola might even have faded away if not for the intervention of a few key individuals. The revitalization of capoeira angola is attributed primarily to the efforts of Mestre Moraes, who trained at Mestre Pastinha's school as a young man before moving to Rio.

Moraes established Grupo de Capoeira Angola Pelourinho (GCAP) toward the end of his twelve-year residency in Rio, in 1980. When he returned to Bahia two years later, moving the headquarters of his group along with him, the status and popularity of capoeira angola had seriously deteriorated. The mestres that had been most active in the first half of the twentieth century were either deceased, ill, or no longer actively teaching and playing. Capoeira angola tended to be "presented as a museum piece" (Mestre Moraes, quoted in Castro 2007 [my translation]). Mestre Moraes believes that capoeira is a form of cultural, historical, political, and philosophical resistance and that capoeiristas have to resist the co-optation of their art lest their passivity contribute to the culture being lost (Castro 2007). In this view, not only is capoeira itself an art of resistance, but the preservation of capoeira is an ideologically informed act of resistance. Mestre Moraes's training sessions double as "a forum for political debate," and he "[incorporates] Black consciousness into his teaching" (Marriage 2020, 17).

It is significant that the revitalization of capoeira angola began in the 1980s, as this was a critical time in Bahia with regard to identity politics. Thanks in large part to the narrative Mestre Pastinha promoted about capoeira being an African art (see chapter 1) and the trip he took to Senegal with several students in 1966 to showcase capoeira at the First World Festival of Negro Arts,[2] capoeira angola attracted individuals with a burgeoning Black consciousness. By bringing Mestre João Grande out of retirement to teach capoeira, and by promoting capoeira (and specifically capoeira angola) as an art of resistance, Mestre Moraes helped establish a context in which capoeiristas could align themselves with the Black Power movement, which was becoming popular in Salvador (see Dettmann 2013).

Several of Mestre Moraes's students have gone on to establish their own schools. Mestre Cobra Mansa (Cinézio Feliciano Peçanha, b. 1960) is particularly notable for the role he played in spreading an activist orientation to capoeiristas in the United States. In 1993, OC—an African American man then in his twenties—accompanied a friend to New York to look for Mestre Cobra Mansa. The local chief of the Ausar Auset Society, a pan-African religious organization, had told OC that Mestre João Grande's "grandson" was visiting. By grandson, he was not referring to biological kinship; rather, he meant that Mestre Cobra Mansa was two generations below Mestre João Grande in terms of lineage. After driving around Manhattan all day, OC and his companion found Mestre Cobra Mansa, who was staying in the home of Mestre Jelon, another popular capoeira mestre and dance choreographer, who is known for using his success to help others escape poverty.

OC told me he had been fairly apathetic about this trip, up until Mestre Cobra Mansa generously welcomed them into the apartment and he realized that this was the same man he had seen playing on a videotape recording years before, a man whose way of laughing while playing conveys utter joy. OC turned to his friend and said, "We gotta get him! That's the guy!" And so they set about negotiating with Cobra Mansa, asking what it would take to get him to go to Washington, DC, where they were from. Arrangements were made, and by 1994 Cobra Mansa had opened a branch of GCAP in DC; however, within a few years he and his students broke away from GCAP to form their own group, the Fundação Internacional de Capoeira Angola (FICA). With satellite groups in the United States, Brazil, Costa Rica, France, Mozambique, Russia, and elsewhere, FICA's influence is more than vast. Having met several mestres within this organization, which now counts several African Americans among them, I have yet to meet any that are unconcerned with issues of social justice. They advocate for racial justice, openly support immigrants including undocumented migrant laborers (a group often maligned in US politics and media), and have hosted an annual women's conference for more than twenty years (as of 2023). There is evidence of critical consciousness at all levels in the organization.

In addition to individual mestres whose own commitments to activism and social justice can be seen as leading the way for their students, capoeiristas have a long history of working with other organizations in their communities to support individuals, particularly children, in positions of precarity. Mestre Nenel, for example, was engaged in a project in the early 1990s geared toward teaching kids capoeira (Machado 2018). Similarly, Projeto Axé, with which Mestre Moraes is associated, was established in 1990 and teaches capoeira and dance to the unsheltered youth of Salvador. In addition to learning cultural arts, these kids, whom OC described to me as the "who's who of the streets," also get a hot meal and lessons in political literacy. Classes at the Pierre Verger Foundation, which I visited in 2008 with Mestre Iuri Santos, serve a similar function. Other mestres may encourage outreach in less formal ways. In 2008 I was training with FICA Bahia, under the direction of Mestre Valmir, and we were asked to donate gifts that would be distributed at a special Children's Day roda in a nearby *favela* (shantytown). It was made clear that anything would be appreciated, whether that might be a toy that one's younger siblings had finally outgrown, or something newly bought by the students who had the means to do so (by which it was fairly clear Mestre Valmir was referring to us, the students visiting from abroad). The fact that Valmir quoted Karl Marx in the course of soliciting our participation was probably not an accident.

The link between these mestres' actions and abstract notions of resistance is not always clearly articulated. In the words of Mestre Nenel, capoeira "is conceived according to the needs of each individual and can *serve* as fight, play, leisure, spectacle, resistance, folklore, dance, physical therapy, therapy, sport, religion, culture (and what else comes up)" (Machado 2018, 127 [original emphasis]). Sometimes capoeira is "just" play. Sometimes it is a spectacle performed on the street that puts money in one's pocket. But the mestres mentioned here have all found something else in the art, which in turn has influenced the ways in which they presented it to their students.

HOW PRESENT-DAY CAPOEIRISTAS CONCEPTUALIZE RESISTANCE

Floyd Merrell (2005, 23), whose sophisticated semiotic analysis of capoeira and Candomblé has become a touchstone in capoeira studies, has argued that within capoeira, "conformity is appearance, while resistance is what is actually going on." I share much of what is known about capoeira's history in chapter 1, but not all elements of this history are given the same weight in capoeiristas' day-to-day engagement with the art. Capoeiristas stress certain aspects of the historical narrative in order to convey what they think is most essential to their art's ethos. For instance, while Princess Isabel is commemorated in some capoeira songs for ending slavery, many capoeiristas feel that her 1888 act came too late to be truly meaningful. International support for the institution of slavery had already crumbled, the Catholic Church's condemnation of it just the year before being the final straw. Furthermore, by this point, many plantation owners had realized they could net greater profit by paying workers a pittance for their labor instead of shouldering the cost of housing and feeding enslaved workers. Therefore, folk heroes that actively resisted slavery play a bigger role in the capoeirista's historical understanding of Brazil and Brazilian slavery than does Princess Isabel.

Zumbi was the last military leader of the Quilombo dos Palmares, a Maroon community that lasted from 1597 until 1694 and had perhaps thirty thousand residents at its apogee (Fontoura and Guimarães 2002). Zumbi's legacy is commemorated in capoeira song, in the naming of eventos, and in plays that several groups have performed. Many socially conscious capoeiristas celebrate the date Zumbi died rather than the date of Princess Isabel's emancipation proclamation (Assunção 2007). He fought for the liberation of Black people; she signed a document that is historically important but that did little to free Afro-Brazilians from extreme poverty. The idea that *quilombeiros* (quilombo residents) used capoeira to defend themselves has added to the art's reputation as an efficacious form of personal defense (Fontoura and Guimarães 2002), even in the absence of contemporary documents that confirm enslaved Africans or quilombeiros successfully used capoeira to defend themselves against the guns of the enslavers and their enforcers (Marriage 2020). Again, however, I am concerned with how the dominant discourse informs the belief that capoeira is an art of resistance, regardless of whether the specific stories told are factually true. In fact, some elements of popular stories seem dubious from a practical or historical standpoint yet serve an important rhetorical function for modern-day capoeiristas.

The dominant discourse about capoeira's origins holds that enslaved Africans used music to disguise their fighting as dance. In addition to providing a rhythm for training, the berimbau was apparently used as a signal, a warning that someone was approaching and they needed to downplay the martial aspects of their play and highlight the dance and ludic elements so as to avoid their rebelliousness being detected (Fontoura and Guimarães

2002). However, if one's goal is to train in secret, a martial would be "better hidden by silence and secrecy than by an indexical noise and publicity" (Mason 2013, 7). I have also been told that capoeira utilizes kicks and acrobatics rather than hand strikes because enslaved people's hands would have been bound. Yet this makes little sense considering that the manual labor being performed by enslaved Africans would have necessitated the free movement of their hands. Furthermore, many early capoeiristas would have been *escravos de ganho* (enslaved wage earners), meaning that they earned money in urban areas as physical laborers, domestic service workers, vendors, and so forth and paid a portion of their earnings to the enslaver. This afforded them greater mobility than their counterparts who were confined to plantations and also provided a means for them to buy their way out of slavery. And yet both of these stories—about the use of music and types of movement in capoeira—continue to be an important part of how capoeiristas talk about their art and are some of the easiest narratives to share with audiences and prospective or novice students.

Stories of individual capoeiristas resisting the state's power—like Mestre Bimba saving a boy from being arrested by the police or Besouro evading capture—speak to the importance of the resistance narrative in the capoeira community (Marriage 2020). They hold messages about social justice that make this transference not only possible but, to the people engaged in capoeira, seemingly inevitable. In fact, when I asked people what they thought the link between capoeira and social justice was, several looked flummoxed that I would even ask such an obvious question. Tlaloc simply said that capoeira "*is* resistance" and that "so much of it has to do with freeing yourself and freeing your people." Doug is of the mind that a person who understands the historical roots of capoeira would have to actively work to *not* see the connection with contemporary social issues. Bram, a Black capoeira teacher whose path in the art has been circuitous thanks to a career that has required him to be highly mobile, told me that "the two go hand in hand, in the sense that because [of capoeira's] roots, it's built off of systemic oppression, it's built off of social injustice. . . . I think that very naturally it's designed, in my personal belief, to fight against it." And while this resistance doesn't have to be focused on racial justice, it often is. As OC explained to me, "it's very intertwined, the African identity and the marginalization, the social justice pushback, the response." In this view, capoeira was marginalized *because* of its African roots, and any pushback against that marginalization is a form of resisting racial discrimination. Extending this logic out a bit, we can hypothesize that if capoeira had been created by Europeans or even a minoritized ethnic group that was not stigmatized, it would not have been repressed and therefore might not have developed into a tool for justice.

Whether or not a particular teacher expands on popular tales about Zumbi or Besouro, or makes the connection to fighting inequality in the present explicit for students, these foundational tales create a baseline understanding of what it means to be a capoeirista, an understanding that may be activated later depending on the situations one faces and the relationships one builds through capoeira. There are legends that celebrate the exploits of larger-than-life figures who were able to directly challenge their oppressors (e.g., Zumbi), as well as stories that fall under the umbrella of what James C. Scott (1985) has called "weapons of the weak" (e.g., a song about an enslaved individual who claims to have spilled some butter instead of admitting he dumped it out in protest). Both types of stories play a role in capoeiristas' conceptualization of resistance and, seen collectively, hint at the ambiguity with which capoeiristas view resistance. Ray, a budding teacher with dreams of creating a school for children in the historically Black, West Coast neighborhood where he grew up, compares capoeira to a "duffle bag [full of] tools and values." He recognizes that capoeira can be used for physical resistance, if one is put into a situation where violence is necessary, but in his life, resistance means finding joy and bringing it forth in others.

PERFORMATIVE RESISTANCE

Early ethnographers often relegated performance to a footnote or a colorful detail rather than making it the focus of their investigations. Thus, the role of performance in resistance and social justice, from an anthropological perspective, has long been undertheorized. Finding more common ground with performance studies than with structural-functional anthropology, today's humanistic anthropologists working in the Turnerian tradition have called attention to performance as an index of power, as evidence of agency, and as the voice of the subaltern. When participation in a form of performance commonly catalyzes a shift in performers such that they become more inclined to resist oppression or fight for social justice, that genre is characterized by performative resistance.

Although Judith Butler (2015) traces the rise of renewed scholarly interest in public assemblies to the 2010 Arab Spring, anthropological treatment of rebellion goes back at least half a century, if not more. In his foundational work on rituals of rebellion, Max Gluckman (1954) described a category of rituals in which individuals who inhabit subordinate social positions (e.g., peasants, women) are compelled to perform their disdain for the authority wielded over them. In a structural-functionalist argument that fit with the prevailing theories of the time, he explained that these performances do not destabilize the oppressive system itself. Rather, they reinforce and renew the system through permitted and institutionalized protests. In essence, rituals of rebellion are pressure release valves that prevent the oppressed from overturning the system. They are allowed, sometimes even encouraged, precisely because they do not alter the prevailing social order. If religion is the opiate of the masses, rituals of rebellion are the opiate of (would-be) revolutionaries. The taste of freedom they get through such performances is satiating enough that they begrudgingly continue wearing shackles until their next opportunity to ritually act out against their oppressors.

Victor Turner (1980), a student of Gluckman's, was also interested in the dynamics of aggrieved factions in society. He, however, brought more of a dramaturgical lens to these events, tracing the rising action and redressive processes intended to either put things to rights again or forge a new path forward. Turner studied social movements that aimed at remaking society in a utopian vision that embraced communitas as normative; however, he found that structures reappear within the spaces of antistructure created by revolutionaries, and that hierarchical relations tend to be reasserted (see Schroter 2003). By eschewing the structural-functional lens, Turner laid the foundation for what would later become performance anthropology. Even his chosen terminology—*social drama*—implies either that these events have a theatrical structure or that they will be characterized by performance. Both are true. As Dwight Conquergood (2013, 27) notes, "performance flourishes within a zone of contest and struggle."

Turner's tripartite structure of ritual—separation, liminality, and reincorporation—has become the primary model for thinking about rites of passage within anthropology. During the liminal phase, individuals who were formerly well ensconced in the structure of their society, whatever that may look like, become ambiguous beings, unable to be constrained by the rules that formerly governed them, stripped of their former status, and ready to be remade into someone new. When individuals experience this transition among others, no matter how homogenous the group, they may form bonds that would be unlikely or even impossible outside of this sacred no-man's-land. This intense bonding and transcendence of difference is known as communitas. This is also the phase characterized by the most ritual (i.e., performance), making the link between performance and communitas key for understanding how performance works in society.

Normative communitas describes the unity that people are *supposed* to feel during a ritual because tradition, doctrine, or an authority figure claims that it is so—even if the individuals involved do not feel particularly unified or transcendent. Spontaneous communitas is less predictable, occurring when a group is caught up in the moment, enraptured by someone or something (see Schechner 2002, 70). The latter is far more interesting to me as a performance anthropologist, both because I want to understand what conditions encourage spontaneous communitas and because I am interested in how spontaneous communitas might encourage social action. It may be one of the most pressing issues for performance anthropologists today to address.

As a scholar of capoeira, I am not just studying a performance form; I am adopting "a performance paradigm" that Conquergood (2013, 17) argues "prevents the reification of culture into variables to be isolated, measured, and manipulated." Richard Schechner (2002, 38) differentiates between what performance *is* and what can be approached or studied *as* performance. The former includes a relatively narrow set of activities that are legitimized by specific cultural and historical definitions (e.g., a play, songs, dances, rituals). The latter is a much broader framework for understanding almost every facet of human life. To muddy his own dichotomy, Schechner argues that "from the vantage of the kind of performance theory [he is] propounding, every action is a performance" (38), and yet he recognizes that not everyone views things thusly and that to say what a performance is demands knowledge of local and historical cultural norms. As useful as this framework is, a comprehensive understanding of how performance can become an act of resistance demands also attending to how things are done *through* performance, which in turn requires differentiating between the terms *performance* and *performative/performativity*.

The term *performative* goes back to lectures J. L. Austin gave at Harvard University in 1955, in which he argued that certain speech acts are also actions: they *do* something (see Schechner 2002, 123). For instance, a couple is *pronounced* husband and wife in a wedding ceremony, and a man *becomes* a knight when the queen dubs him Sir So-and-So. In each instance, the person doing something with words must have the authority to enact that reality, and the words must be said in sincerity rather than in jest. Butler (2015, 28), whose writings brought about the understanding (now taken for granted) that we are constantly in the process of constituting gender categories through our performance of gendered norms, describes performativity as "a way of naming a power language has to bring about a new situation or to set into motion a set of effects." Yet it is not just words that have this power. The body, whether in motion or in a state of stillness, also has power. This recognition has allowed the concept of performativity to shape scholarship outside of philosophy and linguistics.

Performance studies scholars have identified different kinds of performativity at work in different genres and social settings. Tami Spry (2006), for instance, discusses the "performative-I," a researcher positionality that emphasizes copresence, empathy, and an embrace of the fragmentary nature of ethnographic research. With her concept of the "dialogic performative," D. Soyini Madison (2006, 320) wants performance to move beyond the reification of hegemonic norms, and instead create opportunities for alternative ways of being to emerge through the engagements of performers and audiences. In this vision, performance is a type of metaphoric friction. Sometimes pleasurable, sometimes chafing, it can be productive or destructive, but it never lacks some outcome. Yet I find the most interesting use of performativity to date in Jill Dolan's work.

Dolan (2005, 5) defines "utopian performatives" as "small but profound moments in which performance calls the attention of the audience in a way that lifts everyone slightly above the present, into a hopeful feeling of what the world might be like if every moment of our lives were as emotionally voluminous, generous, aesthetically striking, and intersubjectively intense." It is a beautiful but fleeting concept, much like Turner's notion of communitas. Dolan argues that "attending and creating theater is an act of civic engagement that can illustrate other ways to 'do' local and global politics" (90). In this sense, the utopian performative is not (only) about attending plays that deal explicitly with justice issues or create imaginary worlds in which the characters experience a more just (or more dystopian) social world. Rather, it is the experience of attending (to) theater in the company of others, encountering those rare and heady moments of spontaneous communitas, and practicing the art of really listening to other people—training exercises for the performance of democracy itself.

Theater and performance can be "transformational cultural practices" through which we catch glimpses of utopia (Dolan 2001, 456). Dolan realizes that we will not reach this utopia as a society—at least in our lifetimes—because harmful stereotypes and prejudices are too deeply embedded in our social framework. And yet, even though she admits that her vision is idealistic, that doesn't mean it isn't worth striving for. Time and again I have been wrapped up in the magic of Dolan's writing, but the problem that keeps me from endorsing it wholeheartedly is that outside of the academy, I don't know that many people who attend the theater regularly. When they *do* attend, it is often simply to see the annual production of *The Nutcracker* or to catch a touring Broadway hit. These performances are wonderful and hold an important place in many individuals' and families' lives, but these are not the kinds of performances Dolan writes about. Most people I know are not going to the small playhouses on the outskirts of the city to watch a one-woman show about queer feminism. If we aren't expanding the demographics of people attending the theater, how can we hope to lift them up and give them a taste—however fleeting—of what a more utopian society might be like?

Guerrilla theater is certainly one option: give people no choice but to attend to revolutionary social ideas by staging disruptive scenes in public settings. Augusto Boal's actors no doubt created a stir when they surreptitiously staged a scene at an upscale restaurant and one diner loudly argued with the unsuspecting waiter about the bill and the means through which it could be paid. They most certainly drew the regular diners' attention to disparities in wages and the devaluation of labor, but one would imagine there are limits to how often such a scene can be played. A less direct way of presenting a utopian vision for the general public may be the seemingly simple act of continuing to take up space.

Given the destruction wrought by European colonialism, the fact that African diasporic arts have persisted across generations and continue to be performed today is a victory. In the face of discrimination and, in many cases, criminalization, "Africans responded not only with resistant continuity but also with resilience, constantly seeping in and invading the boundaries of racism, colorism, classism, and postcolonial coloniality" (Welsh, Diouf, and Daniel 2019, 14). Kariamu Welsh, Esailama G. A. Diouf, and Yvonne Daniel (2019, 13–14) argue that when dance operates as a form of resistance, it "does not involve immobility, laying barriers, boycotting, or ending certain practices; it concentrates on continuing, producing, and documenting practices of memory." At a certain level, I agree. Just showing up—ensuring intergenerational continuity by embodying the legacy of one's ancestors and forging bonds with diverse Others who are similarly drawn to an art form—is an act of resistance. It is an act of resistance against colonialism (see Browning 2013), against white supremacy, and against the capitalist and neoliberal mandate that every moment of our time be used productively. And yet I believe it can be more.

Adding to the proliferation of ways in which scholars have used the term *performativity*, I use the term *performative resistance* to refer to the process through which performance of certain arts leads to the embodiment of social justice ideals and activism. In Welsh, Diouf, and Daniel's (2019) important contribution on African dance in the United States, a compilation that pays tribute to the immense effort it has taken to persist and gain recognition in a society that reserves its greatest respect and monetary rewards for European-derived arts, it is assumed that the dancers understand how their embodiment of these traditions is an act of resistance. Such an assumption does not attend to the transformations experienced by dancers as they come to embody the ethos of the arts. This is what I mean by performative resistance. Ideally, performative resistance will not only touch the person embodying the art but ripple outward to affect the other social fields in which performers are embedded.

Performative resistance is decidedly not what has come to be called, in popular parlance, performative activism: putting on a show of caring about social causes but not doing much about it. Performative resistance is visceral, and it is productive. Performative resistance can be felt in the quickening of one's heartbeat when she learns to recognize the *cavalaria* rhythm (played on the berimbau as a signal that the police are coming), or in the bittersweet sense of satisfaction one gets when he delivers a *benção* (lit. blessing; kick to the stomach), knowing in the back of his mind that he is animating the irony of a plantation owner pushing his religion onto the people he keeps in captivity. This *conscientização* (development of a critical consciousness) does not happen magically just by practicing capoeira or any other art of resistance. If that were the case, we could simply adopt a program of teaching capoeira in every school in the country and call it a day. I, like the capoeiristas I have interviewed for this project, see in capoeira a great deal of source material that provides the context in which performative resistance can occur. It is then up to the capoeiristas themselves, especially those in leadership positions, to forge it into a tool (or weapon, if you prefer) of social justice.

CONCLUSION

Playing capoeira reanimates the fierce resistance of the ancestors, or at least what present-day practitioners conceptualize as resistance. We do not know the degree to which the capoeiristas of the past thought about their actions as a form of resistance. We can look to recent history and conclude that by the early to mid-1900s, some at least were engaging in this resistance discourse. It is this discourse that provides the basis for performative resistance, which is activated when students train in the company of diverse Others under the guidance of leaders and peers who make explicit connections between the struggles of peoples in the past and the struggles of people in the present.

Circumstances have changed, such that capoeiristas can now practice their art in the full view of society. Some may still wish to train in secret or at least keep the depth of their knowledge to themselves so that they retain the upper hand in encounters with their adversaries, but that is not the reality for most of the capoeiristas I have encountered in my years of study. They are proud of being capoeiristas, and many take pride in openly embodying an art that oppressed Africans fought to preserve. That being said, there is still plenty of secrecy, of hiding in plain sight, within capoeira. In fact, the social justice aspects of capoeira may be so well hidden that some practitioners are not even aware of the ways in which they embody these principles. Whether a student—particularly one in the early years of training—is aware of the social justice elements of capoeira is largely related to how that student's teachers present the art. The process through which teachers use capoeira as a means of catalyzing a social justice orientation in students is the focus of the next chapter.

3

BECOMING A CAPOEIRISTA

You never know who's going to come and what could happen on any given day. That's why Deacon—the leader of the local branch of an international capoeira contemporânea organization—doesn't like to close the academy when he's away, whether that's for work, personal reasons, or an evento somewhere else. He typically asks at least one student to stay behind and keep the classes running. There are of course practical reasons to recruit more members to the group. More tuition dollars help keep the doors of the academy open, and more people to play with enriches the experience for everyone. Yet Deacon hints at something deeper: an opportunity to touch people's hearts through capoeira.

"Capoeira is about character, and discipline," Deacon said. But what does it mean to be a disciplined student of an art that celebrates loafing, or a person of character in a community that celebrates the ruffian? Who are these people that flock to capoeira, and to what degree are they changed by their experiences? Paul—a white man whose city has a reputation of being a liberal sanctuary in a conservative state—says that "capoeira kind of attracts more radical activist people to it." Barrett, who was an antiracist skinhead in his youth, delightfully describes capoeira as the most "punk" of the martial arts.

As with any leisure community, capoeiristas are a self-selecting group. While practicing capoeira, particularly in the company of diverse Others, does have the potential to open an individual's eyes to issues of injustice and cause them to rethink both their explicit and their implicit assumptions about race, inequality, and more, the social field may simply winnow out those who do not change their attitudes.

There is a reason that I have yet to find a white nationalist capoeira group in the United States. Most capoeiristas are at least nominally on board with the valorization of a Black art form rooted in resistance. If their beliefs are significantly out of line with the dominant ideology of their group, then they probably will not stick around for long. Or at least one might expect this to be the case. I have encountered a few individuals whose worldviews have been significantly changed by their participation in capoeira. A woman in Grupo de São Miguel used to date a fellow capoeirista whose family made racist remarks when he brought her home. He himself was never vitriolic or extreme in his conservatism, but he became more open minded as his engagement with the capoeira group deepened.

What is more common, however, is for individuals that are already sympathetic to social justice causes to move slightly to the left on the political spectrum, or to become more actively engaged in activism than they were previously, as a result of their participation in capoeira. Or they take their engagement in a new direction, like Rene, who says he "was raised under [his] mother's rain poncho, outside of a nuclear plant, shouting, 'Hell no, we won't glow!'" but who now channels his activist energy into more direct, capoeira-related interventions.

In this chapter, I address the chicken-and-egg question. One potential weakness in my argument that capoeira and other arts like it become the catalyst for social action is that they tend to attract people who are already inclined to support these causes. Perhaps they would be out marching in support of Black Lives Matter or volunteering with youth in underresourced communities regardless of whether they had ever heard of this once-obscure Afro-Brazilian martial art. But they *did* find capoeira, and there is a dialectical relationship between their involvement in capoeira and their engagement in social causes outside of capoeira.

This chapter addresses the diverse ways in which practicing capoeira can result in personal growth. This growth may be political or activist oriented, but it need not be. The cases I discuss here are not unusual; rather, I chose them because they exemplify the kinds of experiences many capoeiristas have. In addition to surveying these cases, I present the notion of affective habitus as a complement to the predominant way in which martial arts scholars have to date conceptualized the changes an apprentice undergoes as a result of training.

PERSONAL GROWTH

A new student isn't likely to grab a berimbau and immediately march down to city hall, agitating for social change. Overt activism tends to be preceded by a period of personal growth, and it would be shortsighted to suggest that social justice is the *only* kind of awakening that people have as a result of their involvement with capoeira. I had a mestre tell me that capoeira is a powerful catalyst for growth because so many people start doing it in their twenties, "the age that you are abusing your id after you come out from your parents' influences . . . [when] you start to become who you're going to be in the thirties and the forties and the fifties." New capoeira students tend to be young, but plenty of people start later, and even these individuals can experience a profound transformation as a result of their involvement in capoeira. Imani has had several such students.

I first met Imani in 2008, when we were both training at a Brazilian capoeira academy. Though she plays contemporânea, she was taking classes at the same angola school where I was based. We both found the days when our school was closed to be quite lonely and enjoyed getting to know the city of Salvador together. In the years since, we've both had children and our respective relationships with capoeira have changed. Whereas I've become squarely rooted in academia, she is a full-time teacher and practitioner of the art, running her own school.

Imani isn't prescriptive about the kinds of work she wants her students to do. She doesn't require that they go to protests, and she is rather reserved about sharing her personal beliefs about social issues because of how her various identities are read or interpreted by others. However, she structures her classes in such a way that students cannot help but be transformed.

Imani issues challenges to her students on a regular basis. They are even gamified for the children. When the kids complete their challenges at home, they get to move their marker on a game board and eventually earn rewards like movie tickets. The adults, too, have challenges: whoever makes the most progress might win something like a free açaí bowl when the class goes out to celebrate. Some challenges are physical, like doing twenty kicks on each leg every day for a period of time. This is about more than one's performance in the roda; Imani is explicit about how this also builds discipline. Fitness and character grow in tandem.

Once, Imani issued her students a gratitude challenge. Every day for a month, they had to write down fifty things they were grateful for. Even if they wrote down the same fifty things every day, it inspired growth. One student that did this challenge was a fifty-two-year-old African American dad whose mother had just been diagnosed with cancer. Imani could see that he "was a little bit overwhelmed." But participating in the challenge "transformed his life." Imani explains that this is "not about getting this move, or getting another move. This is just a man in his fifties, making new friendships . . .

and making changes to his life that directly are going to affect the livelihood of his family."

Imani had another student do a meditation challenge. This woman had just turned forty and only did capoeira for a year, but the meditation experience stuck with her. "It changed my life," she told Imani. And while she doesn't meditate every day, she still does it a few times a week. So, when Imani thinks about capoeira as a form of social change, *this* is what she means. She said, "this is social change because this is people that all of a sudden are changing their eating habits [to ones] that are better for the environment. These are people that are walking in the world differently. When you do meditation, if this is the thing for you, you're more aware. You're not going to honk [at] somebody on the freeway . . . you're making the world a better place by changing first yourself." Even if she only has twenty or thirty students in her school, she knows that she can use her influence to help them influence others.

Using capoeira as a tool to help others is not necessarily going to happen immediately. More than one interlocutor told me that it is a process. If someone is coming to capoeira out of their own personal interests—to get fit, to relax after work, or whatever it may be—they are not necessarily thinking about how they could help others. But in time, that transformation occurs. In July 2019, I was interviewed on the *Capoeira Connection* podcast. I spoke with Cory, the host, about a donation-based evento I had recently attended where the mestre told us, "don't be a parasite." Capoeira, as an art form and as a community of practice, has so much to give, but this mestre's comment suggests that this gift comes with strings attached. One must repay the debt by serving others, whether that's by helping out inside the academy or by doing outreach, service, or activism.

Cory agreed with this sentiment, but also argued that "before you make that transformation, there's a lot that has to happen, where you have to take from capoeira a little bit to develop your own identity within the art and then you can start helping people. Basically, you can't help someone else if you can't help yourself first." In his organization, there is a general expectation that as students advance they will take on more responsibility. It isn't like a gym membership, where one can belong for years and years and remain single-mindedly focused on their own individual development. These responsibilities might include teaching during class or doing outreach in the community. Students who don't meet these new expectations won't be thrown out, but "they kind of flatline, or they make their exit intentionally or unintentionally." Taking on greater shares of responsibility moves one closer

The author being interviewed about capoeira and social justice on the *Capoeira Connection* podcast in 2019. Photo courtesy of the author.

to the center of the community in the centripetal process so well described by Jean Lave and Etienne Wenger (1991). That movement is accompanied by personal growth and change.

AFFECTIVE HABITUS

Within martial arts studies, Loïc Wacquant's (2004) work on the boxer's habitus has become a foundational piece of scholarship that is often used to explain not only the importance of researchers' participating in the arts they study, but also the vast ways in which an individual is shaped through involvement in a community of practice. Greg Downey (2005) has done an excellent job of demonstrating how a capoeirista's senses are altered by training. Having used his own body as an instrument of data collection, he writes vividly about the experience of catching his foot in a subway train door but being able to calmly extract himself because of the ways in which his body and his perceptions of space had been molded by capoeira. I argue that something similar happens at the level of an individual's affective engagement with the world. Just as there is a physical habitus—a set of embodied dispositions one acquires by virtue of enculturation—so too is there an affective habitus.

Capoeira has the power to alter an individual's affective habitus, an underlying emotional orientation toward the world that one acquires as a result of engagement with a particular social field. Emotions are a constitutive force that must be given serious attention if we are to understand how, in practice, people produce and reproduce the structures that shape social life. That emotions have the ability to flow around and through people, without definitively residing inside any one person, is what gives them a binding power, forging individuals into collectives that can be mobilized (Ahmed 2004, 119).

Mona Lilja (2017) argues that emotions are performative in the sense that they cause us to act in certain ways, particularly in relation to others within our social worlds. The circulation of emotions among people (as well as among animals, places, and various things) helps constitute our subject positions. The love I feel for my sons, the uneasiness and fear I feel in seeing a Nazi symbol carved into a picnic table at our local playground, and the joy I get from spending time with friends all shape the person I am and the actions I take on a daily basis. This understanding of emotions is similar to the way in which Zinzele Isoke (2011, 119) defines affect: "the force that drives us toward movement, toward thought and extension." Affect is not just a feeling or the act of feeling something; it is the agentive power of feelings.

Here, I follow Daniel White's (2017, 177) interpretation of Brian Massumi's distinction between affect and emotion, with the former referring to "nonconscious intensities variously activating and deactivating bodies," and the latter referring to the "feelings that fix into place through a variety of discursive practices." Affect sets bodies into motion; emotions are talked about. When my friend Riser says that he is "frustrated" when he hears about another Black man like himself being murdered by the police, he is using the language of emotion, but it may not—and likely does not—accurately convey his visceral response to these events. Riser contacted me at the early stages of this project. When someone you've never met contacts you out of the blue and says, "I heard about your project and you'll want to talk to me," you can bet that things are probably going to go in one of two ways. Either this person knows nothing about the topic and is seeking attention or validation, or they are actually incredibly knowledgeable and will likely change the course of your work for the better. Fortunately, Riser was the latter. He is an ideal interlocutor: generous with his time, reflexive about his own practice, and incredibly skilled at putting his thoughts into words. Physically and intellectually he's sharp enough to put you on your backside before you sense what's coming, but he'll do it kindly enough to leave you thanking him for having had the pleasure. The way Riser paused before settling on the word "frustrated," the way he drew out its syllables and took a breath upon completing its utterance, indexes the disconnect between his visceral reaction to these atrocities and the ways in which he has been socialized to talk about them (particularly with a white woman he did not yet know well). In this work, I am not probing the gap between affect and emotion, which White (2017) rightly argues is productive ground for further research. I simply wish to explain that I chose the term *affective habitus* rather than *emotional habitus* because I believe capoeira shapes not just the way in which practitioners talk about their feelings, but the underlying responses to social situations that give rise to action *and* talked-about feelings.

Focusing on affect in all its messiness rather than trying to explain the world through fixed academic categories allows us to "describe what precedes and exceeds the categorical in the labors of living through historical presents" (Stewart 2017, 195). In using the term *affective habitus*, I point to the ways in which membership in particular communities leads to individual members' adopting similar emotional orientations to the world. That doesn't mean that we will all feel the same way about every issue. No two boxers move in exactly the same way, and no two capoeiristas will have the exact same beliefs about the art's history, its contemporary uses, its potential for fighting injustice, or the responsibility they have for taking on that injustice. Yet in much the same way that Wacquant was able to document the boxer's habitus and its cultivation, so too can we identify some general features of the capoeirista's affective habitus and the way it comes to be.

Capoeira "is understood to transform the disciple, bringing about a deep-rooted change in character" (Downey 2002, 13). This in and of itself is not unique; most martial arts make similar claims, which is the hook that gets many parents like myself to commit significant amount of time and money for their kids to take classes at the local dojo. The form of the affective changes a capoeirista experiences is what I find to be of particular interest. Margaret Willson (2001, 25) describes the *mentalidade* (mindset) of the capoeirista but limits her discussion to the street smarts and survival skills one needs in order to get ahead in an unjust, unequal social system such as that found in Brazil. She describes this as "a quality of deception, a certain way of being, an alertness to one's environment." However, this quality is more than just a mindset or mentality. Being *malicioso/a* (getting one's way through trickery or deceit) is an essential part of the capoeirista's habitus.

Several authors have discussed *malícia* (trickery or sneakiness) and *malandragem* (a roguish quality) as defining features of capoeira that transfer over into real life and the way one walks in the world (see, e.g., Downey 2005; Robitaille 2010). Recognizing the power differentials that govern relationships in the roda and in the world at large alters the ways in which capoeiristas move through those spaces. Sophie Fuggle (2008, 205) argues that capoeiristas unconsciously demonstrate "a Foucauldian understanding of how power [operates] within society," particularly in terms of how power is constantly "in flux and is always transforming itself into new relations, new operations and discourses." Inside the roda, this might look like a smaller woman staying out of her male opponent's reach because she knows he might pick her up and physically place her outside the roda, something that violates the formal rules of capoeira but is nonetheless known to occur. Or it might manifest in a player marking rather than fully executing a leg sweep against a mestre if the player senses that such a move might result in the mestre holding a grudge or retaliating in some way. Outside of the roda this might take the form of wariness toward those who hold power in society and a calibration of one's actions in response to that differential. When someone who has begun to experience the world in terms of power differentials hears about a Black man being murdered during a traffic stop or in the course of dealing with a minor infraction, they are inclined not to ask whether the victim "complied" with the officers' orders. Rather, they're more likely to focus on the officers' use and abuse of the power they held relative to the victim.

Some aspects of the capoeirista's affective habitus go hand in hand with their physical habitus. Trying to completely separate them would be as foolhardy as trying to separate the mind from the body. In fact, experiencing the literal manifestation of these principles in the roda can facilitate their incorporation at a deeper, affective level. Idris is a younger Black man whose social media posts about authors like James Baldwin speak to his studiousness and his emerging Black consciousness. He belongs to a contemporânea group that is overseen by a Brazilian mestre who came to the United States in the 1980s, but his local chapter in the upper Midwest is led by a strong Black woman whose leadership he reveres greatly. In comparing his group's style of capoeira to what he sees in other groups, Idris says that his group has "more humility" and that "you can't be an arrogant capoeira player in [their] style." In my own experience, people tend to take great pleasure in seeing an arrogant player fall.

The importance of humility extends beyond the roda, as OC—the angoleiro who played a role in bringing Mestre Cobra Mansa to the United States—made clear to me. "You have to humble yourself," he said, but he didn't mean physically. Rather, he was talking about the need to practice humility in conversation and daily interactions with other members of one's group. The members of his group have had some vocal—legendary even—disagreements over whom they should accept as students. Rather than making hard-and-fast rules about who could join, they have taken the approach of "just [checking] that people humble themselves and come to this African expression as a humble student . . . with an open mind." Groups that value this orientation are apt to include roundtables at their eventos and encourage dialog in other ways as well so that members are constantly learning and reflecting on their own practices.

In addition to humility, another important element of the capoeirista's habitus is self-control. Again, this has both physical and affective dimensions. Twenty years ago, if someone had kicked Barrett in the roda, he would have lost his cool. Today, he's more apt to say, "Good job, man. That was awesome." Some of that may just be part of maturation; he went to college and professional school, had a successful white-collar career, and then transitioned into teaching capoeira full time at a clean, modern studio in a midsize southern city. He also became a father. But the way he talks about his own maturation is inseparable from his beliefs about capoeira.

If someone has managed to land a kick on you, he says, they've already controlled you once. "If I lose my shit because of it, they've controlled me twice." Of all the people I interviewed, Barrett is among the least likely to explicitly connect capoeira with activism or social justice, but he strongly believes that training in capoeira helps students build their "emotional control and mental control." That, in turn, makes them "more dangerous as a human being . . . whether it's defending yourself or fighting oppression or whatever you want to do with it." And that is something he attributes to the enslaved Africans who created capoeira, who "had no control, and they were fighting [for] any kind of control they could." In terms of the capoeirista's affective habitus, this might mean enduring the ups and downs of social projects without letting rage deter them from the larger goals of resistance.

CONCLUSION

Joining a leisure community entails submitting to that group's explicit and hidden curricula. Becoming a capoeirista is a process of personal growth. Regardless of where an individual started in terms of their personal relationship to justice work, the people I talked to often recall a moment when the relationship between capoeira and social justice became clear for them. Reflecting on how he thought about capoeira when he was still a student, Tlaloc—a Xicano man who was in his late twenties when we spoke—said that he had "never really [seen it] be politicized . . . [he] just thought of it as a way to work out, as a cool thing that burns also." Eventually, however, his commitments to social justice and capoeira began to merge. "This can't be separate," he said to himself. "Because I can go to the gym and burn anytime. I can go and lift anytime. But it doesn't do it for me, doesn't do the same thing."

The capoeirista's affective habitus includes an acute, embodied sense of how power operates in society and how one can navigate those power structures. It also involves humility and self-control. This is not an exhaustive accounting of the capoeirista's affective habitus. I have said nothing here of the carefree joy one feels during a roda, which makes the hours of training worthwhile. Instead I have focused on those themes that emerged organically from the socially engaged capoeiristas I interviewed for this project. In the next chapter, I provide more detail regarding how class sessions and capoeira eventos, including the pedagogical choices made in these contexts, work on the capoeirista's affective habitus.

CAPOEIRA'S PEDAGOGIES OF RESISTANCE

In the previous chapter, I put forth the idea that an individual's participation in the capoeira community results in personal growth, tending toward an affective habitus that is characterized by an acute understanding of power differentials as well as humility and self-control. Students begin to acquire this affective habitus just by being exposed to the stories and songs of capoeira during class, but it generally takes more intentional intervention on the part of a teacher or other leader within the group for someone to experience a fundamental change in their orientation to the world. In this chapter, I elucidate some strategies that teachers use to help open their students' eyes to the social applications of capoeira and its utility as a tool of resistance. Sometimes these take the form of intentional interventions, when a teacher uses their position as a platform for social justice. In other instances, this socialization happens less intentionally but is still a result of the teacher's leadership.

SONGS OF RESISTANCE

The lyrics of capoeira songs are a main channel through which information about capoeira's potential for resistance is communicated to students, and when I asked the teachers in my sample why capoeira was so well suited to social justice work, many of them referenced the songs. Rene, for instance, told me: "We sing about it all the time, when we sing about Rei Zumbi dos Palmares, when we sing about Ogum, the *orixá* [god] of steel, of warriorship, of justice." However, because most capoeira students—especially casual ones who are coming for fitness, fun, or friendship—do not speak Portuguese and cannot understand the importance of the songs without some guidance, these songs' ability to "galvanize [capoeiristas] to be a force for change," as Rene says, typically depends on how teachers frame the songs for their students. Capoeira songs often reference historical events, but the details communicated through the songs themselves are sparse, requiring that a student learn the full tale by conversing with a mestre or someone more knowledgeable in the art (Assunção 2007). Rene, who had an international upbringing but encountered capoeira via a touring folkloric show in California when he was a teenager, is intentional about helping his students see these connections.

Not unlike the "Negro spirituals" sung by enslaved Africans in North America, many of which have persisted into the present, capoeira songs can be appreciated at a surface level for their beauty, or they can be mined for deeper meaning. Although it is sung in many academies without people necessarily seeing a greater significance in it, the song titled "Folhá Seca" (Dry Leaf) may be a reference to the danger posed by even the slightest sounds when an enslaved person was trying to escape captivity (see Marriage 2020). Other songs celebrate what James C. Scott (1985) calls "weapons of the weak," tools that marginalized individuals and groups can use to counter the hegemony of more powerful parties without having to engage in direct confrontations, which would almost certainly worsen their situation. In the song "A Manteiga Derramou" (The Butter Spilled), an enslaved person plans to tell the enslaver that the butter spilled, got wet, and was ruined. The story is told in passive voice, with the enslaved person never admitting to having purposefully spilled the butter, though this possibility is likely. Butter, being a delicacy intended for the enslaver's daughter, represents the riches of life that the enslaved person will never taste. Denying the enslaver's daughter this little luxury may seem petty, but capoeiristas who understand the meaning of the song also understand—and perhaps feel—the outrage of someone whose labor is stolen from them for the benefit of someone else.

Of course, no hidden meaning will have any effect on students who do not know what they are singing. So, as Imani points out, singing these songs *can* filter into a student's consciousness and affect their worldview, but only if they understand Portuguese or are provided with translations. An accomplished musician whose talent is greatly respected in the capoeira community, she talks to her students about the meanings of the songs. But she also cautions that it isn't like reciting a mantra. There is a limit to how deeply the songs themselves affect an average student without intentional intervention on the teacher's part.

Inkeri Aula (2017, 71) explains that "practitioners sing in the first person about the hardships of slavery, because, as capoeiristas, it is now their history too." I understand this line of reasoning and have heard similar comments among my contacts, so I do not dispute the accuracy of her observation. However, I am slightly uncomfortable with taking this justification too far. As many interlocutors for this project were quick to point out, we may experience struggles in our contemporary life, but none of our present experiences really compare to the injustices suffered by the enslaved Africans about whom we are singing. We may claim them as our ancestors, at least in a metaphorical way, but their pain is not the same as our pain. In fact, there may be a risk to overstressing the painful facts of slavery.

On a conference call that I participated in during the summer of 2020, a white female teacher said that she wanted to have her students play some restorative music to help them recover from the trauma of not only George Floyd's murder, but the unjustified killing of so many Black people, which was at the heart of the season's protests. Unfortunately, she wasn't really sure what that would look like or how to initiate it. She said she could think of lots of capoeira songs celebrating resistance and the strength of enslaved people, but she couldn't think of many that were about the beauty and strength of Black culture apart from slavery. Furthermore, she noted that many songs about slavery are written by white capoeiristas. She wanted to make sure she wasn't playing into the "trauma porn" of constantly revisiting the perils of slavery. Knowing the history of capoeira is important, and the conditions of slavery in Brazil directly contributed to the particular form capoeira took, but just repeating this history—whether through stories or through song—is not enough to promote resistance or healing.

TEACHERS' INFLUENCE

Whether someone is a mestre or a lower-ranking teacher, whenever they stand in front of their students, they assume a degree of responsibility for the well-being and development of those individuals. This, of course, includes the students' physical well-being. A good teacher will keep their students as safe and healthy as possible while helping them develop their skills. Equally true, though perhaps less obvious, is that the teacher implicitly assumes responsibility for students' moral development within the art. Students learn what is considered fair play, and what is not. The academy may also become a locus for learning about how to navigate the world in a moral fashion. As

I heard one teacher say, part of keeping students safe is making explicit what white supremacy, sexism, or homophobia looks like in capoeira class or in the roda and shutting it down. Uncomfortable though such occurrences may be for some, she isolates and elevates these incidents so that they become an object of study for her students.

Some instructors I met through this work feel like they have to walk a narrow line in discussing the ongoing marginalization and oppression of Black people. They want to be authentic and honest about these uncomfortable topics, but, as Riser says, they also want "to do it in a way that is not off-putting to some people." Others are so up front about their commitments to social justice, and infuse it so thoroughly into their regular classes, that anyone willing to stick around for more than a few classes is either going to be like minded or, at least, tolerant of strong, progressive rhetoric. If you ever take a class with OC, "from day one, [he's] explaining to you, 'okay, this is not just movement and [songs] . . . there's a social justice element to this. There's a transformative element, personal development aspect to this.'" OC was a martial artist before he found capoeira. Looking back, he describes his former approach as "kick and punch, whatever whatever." But as he became more deeply involved in capoeira and saw the intentionality with which his own teachers infused their teaching with a commitment to social justice, he began to see "capoeira as a vehicle for social justice, . . . social change, and personal development."

Many teachers require their students to turn in written reports before they can advance to the next level. In this way, students may be exposed to the foundational beliefs about capoeira's origins even without the teacher emphasizing these beliefs during class. The parameters of the assignment will shape the narratives students learn about capoeira's history and the degree to which elements of resistance, power, and oppression come up. Barrett, for instance, requires his students to turn in a report every time they test for a more advanced belt. Asked what that report looks like, he said: "Three pages, double spaced, Wikipedia is not allowed. You have to actually go to page 3 of Google, I tell them. Especially the young ones. There is more than one page in Google. I mean, you don't think there is, but I promise you, you keep clicking, there will be other pages with other shit down there; you just got to go find it."

Similarly, an Afro-Brazilian mestre who has been teaching in the United States for several decades is frustrated with what he interprets as a lack of dedication among his students. He not only demands a three-month financial commitment up front, but also makes prospective students write a seven-page paper. Essentially, he requires proof of their willingness to study capoeira's history and the larger history of colonialism that shaped capoeira before he will accept them as students. He isn't requiring that his students be activists or ascribe to any particular belief system. In fact, he is one of the few individuals I spoke with who is opposed to participating in protests and discourages his own children from doing so. Yet by only accepting those individuals who are willing to write a fairly detailed research paper on capoeira, he is constructing a group that is thoughtful and perhaps, as he claims, open minded.

Notably, requiring students to write a paper reflects a colonial way of demonstrating knowledge; there certainly could be other ways for teachers to assess students' understanding of history. And yet, the writing requirement is currently used by mestres/teachers of various ethnic, racial, and national backgrounds, not just white or US teachers. In some ways, this makes it even more interesting in terms of demonstrating how colonial values may have seeped into capoeira, unintentionally undercutting the message of liberation espoused by teachers. Hypothetically, this requirement might bar some of the people most in need of capoeira's liberatory messages from joining or remaining in a group.

The teacher's influence also extends outside of the confines of weekly training sessions. Elijah is a white man in his late thirties who has trained in capoeira for more than a decade. He has spent a significant amount of time with his mestre, not just in capoeira classes but in other artistic and social settings as well. He recognizes that this is something that not everyone will experience, especially in countries outside of Brazil, where opportunities to develop this kind of relationship may be more limited. This, he believes, is "where you're actually going to get the transmission of just stories, after stories, after stories and things to research to where it's something that you're not learning for the first time, but you're taking a step on a marked path." Elsewhere (Griffith 2016), I have talked about the importance of proximity to one's teacher as a way to benefit from the more subtle aspects of instruction, aspects that are not always available to the casual student in a large-class setting. There, though, I was focused on the transmission of physical knowledge. For Elijah, being among his mestre's inner circle allowed him access to the affective dimensions of capoeira. Simply *knowing* the stories of capoeiristas from eras past, which one can gain from reading a book, is not what matters. Rather, for Elijah, experiencing the emotional weight of these stories in the company of his mestre contributes to the development of his affective habitus, which he would call steps along a marked path.

EVENTOS

A few different kinds of happenings bring large swaths of the capoeira community together at semiregular intervals. In the regional and contemporânea traditions, annual batizados are ceremonies in which the accomplishments of students are recognized and celebrated, though the regional batizado differs somewhat from the contemporânea batizado because Mestre Bimba did not award belts. Angoleiros do not have batizados, but do periodically hold workshops or multiday eventos. Prestigious mestres or contra-mestres are typically invited to offer master classes at all of these gatherings. The eventos are open not just to students of the group hosting, but to others as well, who pay a fee for participation. The participation fee typically covers classes, at least one roda, and an evento T-shirt. Sometimes, the evento will also include a lecture, roundtable, or film screening. Depending on the inclinations of the organizer and participating mestres or contra-mestres, these additional components can take on a politicized flavor.

In May 2019, an African American mestre flew halfway across the United States to offer a free, daylong workshop in a lower-income neighborhood of

A film screening at a capoeira evento in 2019. Photo by the author.

a major metropolis. The evento was open to capoeiristas who had trained for years with the local chapter of his group, Os Provocadores,[1] as well as community members with little or no experience. The neighborhood in which the evento was held is stereotyped as being dangerous and crime ridden, but the capoeiristas who train there feel perfectly at home. Asking whether the wheels of one's car are going to be stolen is a quick way to mark oneself as not an ally. The community center where the workshop took place is devoted to preserving and promoting African contributions to world culture, making it an ideal setting for capoeira classes. Nearly all participants that day were Black.

I was chatting with the two or three people I knew before things got started, stretching my muscles so I would be ready for class. Instead of starting with movement, however, we found ourselves cooling our heels and listening to the mestre talk. He did talk about capoeira, eventually. But his lecture interwove the history of capoeira and information about his own lineage with a commentary on the prison system that could have been taken directly from Michelle Alexander's 2012 book *The New Jim Crow*. He said that if people remain ignorant, they won't realize that being "chattel of the state" (i.e., a prisoner) is the same thing as being enslaved.

The mestre then broached the topics of segregation and gentrification. He asked where the "nice homes" in the city were located. Although there were initially some confused looks, the locals easily answered: the north side. "And who lives there?" the mestre asked. "White people" was the obvious answer, though it took a while before people would say this. "It's because they have income like this," he said, stretching one hand up high, "and you have income like this," he said, lowering his hand toward the floor. And their neighborhoods look nice, he said, but then they start moving into your neighborhoods, and then your rent goes up, and you have to move out. Even old people who have paid off their homes have to move out "because they're paying rent too . . . it's called taxes."

Students sometimes joke about their teachers' diatribes or the tangents they go off on whenever they get the floor (quietly, of course, because an outright challenge of the leader's right to hold court would violate the norm of respecting one's mestre). Jokes aside, these lectures—whether planned or impromptu—are an important tool of enculturation. Students sometimes think of their teachers' propensity to lecture on seemingly anything and everything as an idiosyncratic quirk, but such discourse during class or at public eventos needs to be seriously analyzed. These teachers are not just teaching movement but instilling in their students a certain worldview.

In some instances, the workshop organizer intentionally creates space for this kind of discourse to occur. In November 2019, Riser held an evento that stretched over the course of three days. His mestre and three special guests from Brazil were featured presenters. There were capoeira classes, classes on samba and orixá dance, formal evaluations of students' progress, and a large roda that brought together many members of the local capoeira community.[2] There was also a film screening. This particular film focused on the discrimination women experience inside the capoeira community and prompted some difficult questions from attendees. Although Riser told me it was a coincidence that he chose this particular film to show at the evento, he couldn't have picked a much more appropriate one had he been trying to do so.

Even while capoeiristas' discourse tends to stress resistance and rebellion, the hegemonic maleness of capoeira spaces leaves little room for feminist challenges to the status quo (see Owen and De Martini Ugolotti 2019; Joseph 2012). At this single evento, I lost track of the number of people—male and female—who brought up the issues of sexual harassment and gender-based discrimination with me. I address the topic of gender-based discrimination in chapter 8, where I discuss ongoing injustices within the capoeira community, but I mention it here to show how certain songs, topics of discussion, films, special classes, and so on can raise awareness and perhaps spur action around key social justice issues, particularly at eventos that are marked as being special and therefore of greater significance than a typical training session. Lucha—a grant writer now in her early forties who discovered capoeira in college—was pleased with how people responded to the film Riser screened. She told me the discourse was far better (i.e., critical) than what she typically witnesses in her capoeira community. She wasn't necessarily pleased with the mestre's response, however, and neither were several of the other women there. They felt that he missed the point. Instead of engaging with the real and symbolic violence women experience in capoeira, he told the attendees about a roda he had taken a group of students to several years before, where a violent confrontation appeared to be brewing. With a chuckle, he told us he pulled his students away before the fracas started. Without a doubt, a teacher should be able to sense when a roda is reaching a boiling point and latent violence threatens to become real, but that was not the issue at hand. The question the audience wanted answered was the degree to which the mestre had witnessed gender-based discrimination in Brazil and the steps that people at all levels within the capoeira community could take to put an end to it. This disconnect shows how the meanings of stories, lectures, and films may be contested by the different individuals involved; however, the fact that such supplemental elements are included in eventos such as this one speaks to an intention on the part of the organizer to affect students at a level beyond the physical. It is part of a holistic approach to developing capoeiristas as people, not just players.

In other instances, opportunities for mestres and other leaders to encourage critical reflection on social issues arise spontaneously. During Os Provocadores' evento, a man dressed in a formal, double-breasted, navy blue jacket with gold buttons swaggered into the room where we were training. He said something to the mestre, and then he spoke to the whole room. The rise and fall of his voice approximated conversational English, but I was unable to make out a single distinct word. He kept up his utterance while moving to the back of the room. At first, I thought this was an old friend of the mestre who was trying to be funny (I later learned that the first time they had encountered each other was the night before, when the man had wandered in from the streets). Then I began to wonder whether he was drunk. Slowly, it dawned on me that this man had a mental illness.

After about a minute or two—during which time some people were staring, and some were nervously giggling or smiling like someone waiting to be let in on a private joke—the mestre calmly but assertively told the man, "you're going to have to leave because you're playing too much." The man walked away without a complaint. As soon as he was gone, the mestre stopped what he had been doing and took a serious tone. He said there are two things in our society we don't want to talk about: AIDS and mental illness. He said that mental illnesses like depression, bipolar disorder, and schizophrenia are serious issues. He explained that schizophrenia doesn't typically manifest until someone is eighteen to twenty years old. If it were to manifest before age eighteen, that person's parents could help them seek treatment and develop a management plan. But if the disease doesn't manifest until later in life, there is no way to mandate that they get help. He said that if you become a capoeira teacher, you will encounter this. He said you might wonder why we don't just change the laws to make it possible to mandate treatment, but as Black people, he cautioned, you don't want the state to have that kind of power over Black bodies. Once that happens, the mestre argued, it's a slippery slope toward things like forced sterilization.

This was such an unexpected moment. The way the mestre handled it spoke volumes about his commitment to people who are victimized by our social systems and the duty he has to enculturating the next generation of capoeira teachers. In this completely unscripted encounter, he gave life to the principles he had been lecturing about at the beginning of the day. He could have moved on with class as soon as the distraction was over, but he chose to elevate it so that it became an object of study.

AFTER CLASS DISCUSSIONS

Every class has the potential of being a "brave space" if the teacher chooses to use it in this way. Rene uses this phrase in contrast to the idea of a "safe space." He wants capoeira to provoke, and he is committed to helping his students work through these provocations so they can grow as human beings. This does not always feel safe, and it demands bravery. Many teachers regularly carve out time for discussions at the end of class. Sometimes these discussions focus on the physical component of capoeira, such as a debriefing session that followed a highly unusual class I experienced in Brazil, during which we turned off all the lights in the room and played by candlelight. The mestre wanted us to learn how to sense our opponent without having to rely so heavily on our sight. These conversations can also take a more abstract turn.

Over the years, as he himself has experienced a personal transformation and come to understand how damaging it is to repress one's feelings, Rene has become more intentional about encouraging these discussions:

> I've heard many teachers say, "Come into the roda, come into the school, with good axé [energy], leave your bad axé outside so we can have something good inside." And to me, that's so difficult to hear people say that. I want people to come into my school as a whole person, with everything. Because now, if whatever has bothered you out there . . . is manifested, [or] comes out in the roda, then we can deal with it there. We can say, "Well, what was happening there? Why did you go straight forward when you should have escaped? We should have changed levels, we should have gone around. That's not like you, that was an emotional response, what's going on emotionally?" We can then talk about it, because the roda is a diagnostic tool. It's not just a space where we're playing a game. We're not playing games while we're playing our game.

His last sentence sticks with me. It speaks to the seriousness of play and to the way that especially with specific interventions or in particularly charged social contexts, play can have ramifications far beyond the parameters of a game. Nothing is out of bounds.

I know what people mean when they say a person should check their baggage at the door. They mean that a person should not let outside events influence what happens within the academy, as if that somehow keeps the space sacred, untainted by the messiness of "real" life. But one thing that came up unprompted in several interviews is that we *should* bring these real-world problems into capoeira. Not so that we can use them as fuel for hyping ourselves up and preparing to fight, but so that capoeira might be used as a tool to process those experiences we are having in the real world.

In Idris's group, "if anybody sees their human rights violated, of course we're going to probably talk about it." In telling me this, he said, "every group is a little different in [doing] that," but among those with a developed social consciousness, this is actually the norm. "We're always discussing, we're always trying to encourage people to speak up," said Bruno, a Brazilian who has become a mestre since moving to the United States and training extensively with an internationally recognized group headquartered here. This group has been inclined toward activism since its inception, but Bruno told me that he has learned so much from one particular individual who joined the group and "started exposing [him to] more things like that." By creating space within the context of capoeira for this student and others to talk about current social issues, Bruno has become much more of a social justice warrior than he initially was. When their group becomes aware of social injustices, either locally or on a national or international scale, he says, "we do discuss and talk and we try to see . . . if there is a way that we can make a difference."

Tlaloc's group also has a faction that intentionally seeks opportunities to make a difference. This subset of the group began informally. Even though Tlaloc claims that its members try to keep politics away from training, there is clearly overlap:

> Even though it's a subgroup, it's not a separate group. We don't have meetings of capoeiristas for justice. When we go and train capoeira, we do our thing, and then those of us who are more prone to that or more attracted to that conversation will just meet afterwards and plan stuff, or talk about it. But a lot of times we're just there in the group, and the group itself, even though it's not an official part of the [subgroup], we say they are. If anybody has any input, of course, we're not trying to be separate from anybody. And some of us are more politically inclined, and some want nothing to do with it. So they might just have an idea, and we take it. We want to hear everybody's voice, but no we don't have an official separate meeting or anything like that. It's just kind of intertwined in our already-built family.

Initially, these individuals just shared information with one another on topics like avoiding burnout in social justice work. At that point, the people involved were primarily academics, but they intentionally brought others into the conversation because they "didn't want it to be elitist, or [use] language that's very academic that people might not understand." They wanted to stay grounded, to keep their "feet in the roda," so to speak, which is how dialog transformed into social action.

CONSCIENTIZAÇÃO

Janet MacLennan (2011, 149) writes that capoeira is "the counterdiscourse of an oppressed people." The teachers I have written about in this chapter would likely agree, but there are other groups that intentionally shy away from singing songs that focus on slavery or marginalization and oppression. People in these groups probably won't become social justice warriors without some sort of intervention. "You still have to purposefully invoke those themes in the practice of the art," said Doug, a medical doctor who has experience training in all three of the major capoeira styles. If a teacher is not promoting these themes, a student may not know they are there, unless the student takes on a course of self-study. I have found many capoeiristas to be voracious readers of the literature that has been written about them, and reading such texts is an important way that members of less politically active groups become aware of capoeira's history and begin to draw connections with present-day social issues.

"When I first started," Geoff said, "I just devoured everything that was capoeira." With his sun-streaked blond hair pulled back in a "man bun," Geoff doesn't look like he is in his mid- to late forties. He is not new to activism, but his reflexivity has increased with age. He first encountered capoeira on a beach in Bahia in 2008 or 2009, when he was a voluntourist at an orphanage there, something he now questions in terms of its ethics. When he heard the berimbau for the first time, he "just felt it in [his] soul" and knew he would seek out classes when he returned to the United States.

So many people I talk to describe feeling a similar insatiability at some point along their journey, sometimes describing capoeira as a thing they grew "obsessed" with. Many capoeiristas I have encountered in the United States are quite scholarly, whether or not they hold advanced degrees. Lowen, a Black man in his late forties, leads a dizzyingly diverse group in a major southern city comprising college-educated professionals as well as former inmates. Even those who aren't college educated, he says, are "very astute. They're readers." Seeking out information wherever they can, capoeiristas read books, articles, magazine stories, websites, and blogs. They watch documentaries and listen to podcasts. When I asked specifically what they read, a few books top the list, particularly those written by capoeira mestres (e.g., Mestre Acordeon's *Capoeira, a Brazilian Art Form: History, Philosophy, and Practice* [Almeida 1986]), but they may also read monographs geared toward academics like Floyd Merrell's *Capoeira and Candomblé: Conformity and Resistance through Afro-Brazilian Experience* (2005). Doug had something like twenty-five capoeira books on his shelf at the time of our interview, and more than one interlocutor learned Portuguese in order to read untranslated books, magazines, or dissertations on capoeira. Twice now, individuals that I have gone to interview have pulled my own book off of their shelf as a way of demonstrating their familiarity with my ongoing work.

And of course, it's not just material about capoeira that informs these individuals' beliefs about social justice, and the ways in which their lives as capoeiristas might intersect with a broader commitment to justice. They read books on the African diaspora. Idris's Facebook feed is often peppered with his own reflections on the writings of scholars like James Baldwin, and he analyzes everyday life through a Marxist lens with great facility. Riser draws inspiration from Maya Angelou and her ability to stand up to daily acts of injustice. He also reads Malcolm X. Elijah directed me to books on the Klan's involvement in the city where he was arrested for allegedly defacing a Confederate statue, and said that he planned to use his jail time, if convicted, for reading and studying. At a time when readership among the American public in general is declining, this is notable, and when capoeira is practiced alongside these other acts of *conscientização* (consciousness raising), the practices can't help but inform one another.

Whereas Geoff jumped headfirst into reading about capoeira, others don't necessarily start reading literature about capoeira right away. Instead, they might find themselves drawn to do so following something that was intriguing or even bothersome in their practice. Jordan's interest in reading about capoeira's history came about as he reflected on his own identity as an African American and on the identity of his teacher, who was Black but neither American nor Brazilian. Jordan hadn't initially made a connection between capoeira and his own African heritage. He was young when he started studying capoeira, and it was presented to him as a Brazilian art. He just didn't have the understanding, at the time, to appreciate how heavily influenced Brazil was by African cultures. It wasn't until he started studying under an African-descended teacher from another part of the diaspora, the Caribbean, that it "clicked" for him. He realized that there was something about capoeira that appealed to and connected African-descended people throughout the diaspora. The curiosity engendered by this moment is what led him to read more on capoeira's history. "It was seeing another Black person from somewhere else in the diaspora," he said, "which made me wonder what was the story behind these Black people down there [in Brazil]."

Reading the capoeira literature seems particularly important for people who may not have steady access to a mestre. Bram, for instance, went through a period during which he traveled almost constantly and would drop in on groups wherever he happened to be. But he lacked the continuity that being part of a stable group provides. So, when he would visit a group, he would chat with the teacher and ask about any suggested reading. "All right. Well, I got a lot of homework to do," he would think to himself after these meetings. And since many books that were suggested to him were in Portuguese, he had to work on his language abilities. Personal tutors, Rosetta Stone, and Duolingo are all ways that the people I talked to prepared themselves to dive more deeply into the Portuguese sources they felt compelled to read.

Today, the sheer amount of material that has been written on capoeira is overwhelming, and information literacy is needed to be able to evaluate the quality of different sources. But those capoeiristas who started their journey with the art in the 1990s or early 2000s were often frustrated with the lack of information about capoeira published in English. Therefore, their desire to learn more about capoeira often pushed them even more forcefully to learn Portuguese.[3] Now in his very early fifties (as of 2023), Francis remembers the days of having to send money orders to Brazil in order to get books and magazines on capoeira sent to the United States (and he remembers some of those funds getting "lost" en route). He would go to events hoping that the visiting teachers had brought along books to sell. He wanted to familiarize himself with as much history as possible because otherwise he believed that he "wouldn't be taken seriously by Brazilian capoeiristas," or might be seen as just another American who expected to be accepted but who hadn't put in the effort to really understand capoeira. Learning Portuguese was both a marker of his dedication to the art and a means through which he could become more informed.

Doug initially began learning Portuguese because he didn't ever want to "lose sight of what the songs were about." He was bothered by the hypocrisy of people singing songs without understanding what they were singing, or even being able to recognize when their tone was out of keeping with the mood of the song's subject. However, "as a side effect . . . or as a secondary benefit" of learning Portuguese, he was able to access original writings on capoeira that he could not understand before. He admits that he still has to use Google Translate to get through certain sections, but his reading abilities are now quite strong.

Seeking out additional information—whether as part of the emerging capoeira canon or on adjacent topics—gives an individual a broader perspective on what capoeira is or can be. So while the group Doug first trained with wasn't particularly active in social justice issues, he describes himself as studious, having read things like doctoral dissertations on capoeira. Through his research, he "started seeing that this . . . is indeed a cultural expression, but it definitely is a cultural expression rooted in resistance and enslaved peoples' angst to get out of that mindset." He also became more aware of how enslaved Africans had seen their cultural expressions ripped away from them. These realizations, which were a direct result of his taking the initiative to read widely on capoeira in both English and Portuguese, paved the way for transformations in other areas of his life.

CONCLUSION

Certain values are built into the structure of capoeira itself. Alejandro, a capoeira teacher in Southeast Asia, recognizes that capoeira will change over time; its original purpose may become unclear "as society and people who come into capoeira begin to change it a little bit." But when he thinks about what capoeira fundamentally represents, and what happens in the roda, he says, "inherent . . . are these values that talk about having to work together, to cooperate with each other." Students will learn some of these lessons, he believes, even if their teacher isn't putting them "right in front of their face." Just think about the berimbau. A student can be virtuosic and perform beautiful variations on the basic rhythm, but if the student isn't attuned to how the rest of the orchestra sounds, then it is "all going to sound like noise in the end," Alejandro says. Even the actions of the two capoeiristas squaring off inside the roda are a physical manifestation of the value of cooperation and collaboration. Opponents are most certainly trading attacks and seeking to get the better of each other, but they are also instructed to build a beautiful game together. Capoeiristas do not dismiss individual differences inside the roda. They learn to use what they have to create the best possible scenarios for themselves while also bringing joy to the collective.

Some students may intuit the connection between how to play capoeira in the roda and how to enact this philosophy in the world at large, but the internalization of this message is often aided by teachers who are explicit about how capoeira aligns with a program of social engagement. The narrative of enslaved Africans using capoeira to resist oppression is a powerful foundation for the contemporary social justice work that many capoeiristas—teachers and students alike—are doing, but groups don't suddenly become antiracist or active in their communities because they sing a song or two about slavery, especially if more than half the students don't understand the lyrics they are singing.

Capoeira teachers have an extraordinary opportunity to shape how their students conceptualize the link between this art form and contemporary social issues. They have a captive audience, and during the course of regular classes, they can frame everyday occurrences in such a way that students become more aware of structural inequalities, implicit racism, toxic masculinity, and so forth. The choices these teachers make, like having students write reports on colonialism and slavery, contribute to how students think about capoeira and their commitments to other people. Whether teachers are unabashedly bold in their commitments to justice or choose to work more subtly, students pick up on these orientations, and we can see how they flow through different generations of teachers and students.

Mestres like the one who discussed gentrification, taxes, the disproportionate incarceration of Black men, and the nation's mental health crisis all in the course of one daylong workshop refuse to "stay in their lane." They use their positions of power to socialize students into a particular worldview. And while we could contrast his boldness and perhaps outspoken advocacy for a pro-Black agenda with the words of someone like Deacon, whose equally powerful leadership is gentler—or even Barrett, whose belt test requirements socialize students into an antiracist worldview even as he claims to check politics at the door—a similar current runs throughout their teachings. When teachers are willing to make space for the hard conversations, change happens. In the next chapter, I consider what that change looks like when it spills outside of the academy's doors.

5

THE CAPOEIRA COMMUNITY

On May 29, 2020, Lucha invited a handful of other white capoeiristas to join her in attending a web-based training course on weaponizing white privilege to dismantle white supremacy. I was among this group. Approximately three hundred people from across the country participated in the Zoom event, at least one-third of whom were taking their first course on antiracist organizing. After the training ended, the ten capoeiristas switched to a second Zoom room, where we spent an hour and a half debriefing and discussing the types of injustice we see in capoeira and the ways we, as white capoeiristas, can show up for and support our Black *camaradas* (comrades or colleagues). Still reeling from the senseless deaths of George Floyd, Breonna Taylor, Ahmaud Arbery, and others, we all wanted to see the capoeira community take concrete action of some sort, but our collective energy was tinged with a bit of skepticism, our having seen how quickly hot, righteous anger can cool and dissipate. Nine of the ten participants were female. One woman said she was only three days into her journey with antiracist activism. She later said that she wished she had been on board twenty years prior, or five years prior, or even a week prior, but that what happened in Minneapolis (George Floyd's murder) really shook her; she hoped she wasn't one of those new activists that overcommits or gets overzealous in the early days and then quickly burns out. Certainly, she was not alone in having her eyes opened to the insidious nature of racism by this incident. Perhaps the events of 2020 would have turned this woman on to activism no matter what, but context matters, and she happened to be part of the capoeira community when these historic events transpired. She was in the right place at the right time not only to see a connection between her practice of capoeira and contemporary social issues, but to benefit from the guidance and leadership of her fellow capoeiristas with more experience in antiracist activism.

There are at least two different ways of thinking about the relationship between social justice and capoeira. Using capoeira as a tool for overt activism in the world at large, which is the subject of the next chapter, is one way. Treating capoeira as a site where one can build the kind of community they want to live in is another way. Dalia—a relatively privileged woman whose family raised her to believe that supporting her community was just the right thing to do—eloquently captured this idea when she said, "capoeira is a microcosm of the world, and we have the opportunity in our different groups, and our capoeira communities at large . . . to create the capoeira we want to see, and have that be a representation of the world we want to see." By fighting for inclusivity and justice at the level of their own group, these capoeiristas are creating a template for a more utopian society that we might work toward in society at large.

The concept of prefigurative politics holds that the outcomes of a social movement are shaped by the methods used to achieve those outcomes; therefore, actors seeking social justice should take care to ensure that the strategies they use in their struggle are themselves just. As David Graeber (2014, 85) puts it, prefigurative politics is "the defiant insistence on acting as if one is already free." The way in which capoeiristas construct their communities around values like cooperation, collectivism, and reciprocity rather than the individualist and capitalist norms of mainstream society is a case in point. This chapter focuses on how the capoeira community functions as a site of resistance, making it more likely for an individual to adopt the affective habitus that I associate with socially engaged capoeiristas.

CULTIVATING COMMUNITY

Imani tells her students, "really when you practice capoeira, you practice vulnerability." All martial arts, she believes, require intensive participation for such an extended period of time that participants cannot help but make connections with their training partners. This, she continued, makes martial arts different from other sports like tennis or running. As a runner myself, I cannot wholly agree with this latter statement, but it speaks to a widespread belief that capoeira is somehow special in terms of the affective habitus it produces. To explain this, Imani said, "I think with capoeira there's an extra element of community."

Imani's understanding of the capoeira community fits within David W. McMillan and David M. Chavis's (1986, 9) definition of community as "a feeling that members have of belonging, a feeling that members matter to one another and to the group, and a shared faith that members' needs will be met through their commitment to be together." According to Imani, one reason the capoeira community is so intensely connected and linked by feelings of mutual obligation is the complexity of the different elements required to have a roda. "It's not like a spinning class. It's not like a yoga class, where you roll your mat and leave," she said. The berimbaus have to be strung carefully before class and unstrung again afterward. In many cases, the room needs to be cleaned before and after class because there isn't a janitorial staff to do it, as would be the case at a posh gym. In fact, willingness to clean the space was one thing that distinguished the foreigners who would ultimately find warm acceptance at the Brazilian academy where I did my fieldwork in 2008 from those who would remain on the margins, accepted as students but not embraced as part of the group (see Griffith 2016). So much of what is required for a roda depends on collaboration. There must be enough people to fill the orchestra and to sing the songs or the roda will be missing the *axé* (energy) that is necessary for it to feel satisfying. Plus, as Imani pointed out, this is all done in a circle. While she didn't delve into the Foucauldian implications of this arrangement, where all participants are subjected to the gaze of everyone else and thus discipline themselves in accordance with the norms of the group, this was implied: "I always joke and I say, 'You can't be an asshole [in] capoeira; eventually you'll stop.' Because really at the end of the day you need to do it with other people."

Imani didn't go into detail regarding how an "asshole" might find their way out of the group. Barrett was more explicit:

> If somebody's an asshole, they weed themselves out usually over time, so I don't have to be an ass. But if they're an asshole . . . they need to be asked to leave and not come back. I've done it lots of times, and I'll do it again if I have to. If somebody's disrespectful to other people here, or any one person here, it's a family, and everybody has to get along, and everybody have to be on the same page. If one person, or if one or two or three or four, ten people can't get on board with that, then I'll ask them to leave. It means you can't come back here anymore. If you're a dick, I don't want you here. Because if you get one person who's like that, they'll attract others. One bad apple in the barrel, you know what I'm saying, right?

For Barrett, it isn't just about tolerating one or two people that aren't very nice, it's about protecting the group as a whole. From the limited time I spent with him, I could see in the way he had the kids sitting quietly against the wall, waiting for class to start, that discipline was important in his school. Even if he relishes the "punk" nature of capoeira, he also values structure and order and won't let any "assholes" ruin that.

Barrett's school is something of an outlier in that it is run very much like a business, and he is proud of this fact. Others, in contrast, have a relaxed feeling, more akin to a family. I participated in a class with Grupo de São Miguel two days before the Martin Luther King Jr. march that I discuss in the introduction. Since the group has its own space, members come and go pretty freely whenever the leader is there or the space is unlocked. A kids' class was scheduled to last until 2:00 p.m., but adult members of the group started trickling in at 1:30. Even though they had just seen one another for a community performance the day before, most of them hugged or touched in some way as they entered and said hello.

When people spend so much time together training, they often begin to socialize outside of class, and other aspects of their lives become intertwined. The group I was part of during graduate school, for example, held a roda at my wedding rehearsal dinner. We had a roda at another member's wedding reception. Babies often follow on the heels of capoeiristas' weddings. The experience of capoeiristas who are also parents is not something I have focused on explicitly, nor am I aware of any specific research on this topic; however, anecdotal evidence suggests that becoming a parent may result in an individual's pulling back from their commitments to capoeira or being unintentionally marginalized by their group (e.g., criticized for not training as regularly or for not attending eventos). This is more pronounced in the case of mothers, who have historically borne more of the parenting burdens than do their male partners, and it is a pattern I have seen both in Brazil and in the United States. However, I have also encountered capoeira groups where children were welcome to be in the space while their parents trained. When I took a class with Os Provocadores, a heavily pregnant woman whose *bananeira* (handstand) put mine to shame took a break from class to breastfeed her older baby while the rest of us continued training, and no one raised an eyebrow. At Grupo de São Miguel, two parents took turns in the roda while their toddler wandered about, grabbing anything he could get his hands on as toddlers are wont to do, without anyone getting upset. It may not be causal, but it is also not coincidental that the groups that are structured like a family and respect the intersectional identities of members are also the ones that tend to be actively agitating for a more just society.

Lowen's group offers another example. Unlike most groups, which tend to move repeatedly in search of a room to rent, his group has been hosted, essentially rent free, by the same community center for approximately twenty years. He describes this organization as "a powerhouse in the Black community here," in a highly diverse, major metropolitan area in the South. Training in this location puts the capoeiristas in proximity to other kinds of activists (e.g., a group seeking to abolish the death penalty, and volunteers that organize reentry programs for formerly incarcerated people). Such proximity can lead to the sharing of ideas and collaborative projects.

Sometimes, the right people seem to come together at the right time and the community just clicks, but in other cases the cultivation of this community ethos is intentional. Ray is not very old—only in his midtwenties—but he takes his role as a leader and role model in his community seriously. He prides himself on how the youth in his capoeira classes have really taken ownership of their community: "The idea is that they just have a space that they know belongs to them. It's filled with people that they know are part of their community. They know that when new people come in, that they're coming into something that belongs to them and is welcome for others to join in too." He is passionate about passing capoeira on to Black youth in particular, but the way he runs his group brings in all kinds of people.

A young woman who had trained in capoeira for eight years but had been training less frequently as of late, was due to have surgery, so Ray and a student went to be with her beforehand, and they had a roda to support her and "just to kind of be with her." He said to his students, "the point of this is because we're supposed to . . . look out for each other and we want each other to know that we've got each other." This ethos of caring is woven deeply into how Ray runs his group, but he doesn't want to make too big a fuss out of it because he wants this to be normalized and expected, not something to be self-congratulatory about.

When the community aspect isn't there, people feel its absence. I spoke with Ray about gentrification and about the changes in his city. Thinking about what makes capoeiristas special, he said, "a lot of us come together, not just to move, but . . . movement within a social context as well as the hanging out before and after." When I was studying capoeira in Bahia, the teacher told me that if someone just paid their money and said bye immediately after class, he would intentionally withhold knowledge from that student if they asked for clarifications or additional information. At the time I thought it was a bit harsh to deliberately subvert the advancement of a student who treated class strictly as an economic exchange, but to hear Ray talk about the importance of just being together helped me see things differently. Ray laments the fact that people in his city seem to not have as much time to hang out anymore. He says, "the after-parties"—meaning parties that happen after eventos like batizados—"aren't even close to the same anymore." It isn't the parties necessarily that he's really concerned about; the lack of participation in after-parties is a signal that the community is changing and perhaps becoming less close knit. "I feel like that's the glue that we may not even know is missing right at the moment," he said with some sadness.

Students may leave one group and join another if they feel like it isn't serving their needs. Briana left her first teacher because she felt like he wasn't looking out for his students appropriately. Her new group has the "kind of bonds [she] was looking for." They have a "like-minded mentality" and a willingness to stand up and say when something is wrong. Saltão used to train with a different group in the same city where he currently resides, but he left after seeing Grupo de São Miguel give a public performance. He immediately felt that this group was a better fit for him than was his previous group, whose teacher struck him as more interested in making money than in cultivating community. In Grupo de São Miguel, Saltão told me, everyone has become friends because they spend so much time together. Several people from his former group have also made this switch; no one has gone in the opposite direction, or at least that is what I was told. Saltão attributes this to the fact that no one in Grupo de São Miguel is making money from capoeira.

That is not to say that classes are free. All these groups need money in order to function. The weekend I was visiting Grupo de São Miguel, in fact, it was launching its annual fundraiser. But Deacon—its primary teacher—holds a job in addition to running capoeira classes, and there is a sense of collective responsibility for the group and its activities. In no way do I mean to glamorize poverty or romanticize the real struggles that many capoeira teachers experience in order to keep their doors open, a situation only exacerbated by the COVID-19 pandemic, when many had to turn to Zoom or stop offering classes altogether. However, something in the struggle for financial viability is relevant to how the community ethos in capoeira is established. When Imani began explaining to me the importance of the capoeira community in differentiating it from other sports or martial arts, she took what I initially thought was a tangent, talking about awkward conversations she has had with parents who balk at paying tuition even if they happily pay hundreds of dollars for their kids' participation in other activities. Capoeira is "always underfunded," she said, "and I think because it's underfunded, it requires a community to lift it up on its feet." The necessity of pitching in to keep a group alive binds people together, creating a foundation that Imani and others can build on through their poignant interventions.

At the beginning of this project, I tended to think about resistance as an intentional action undertaken to challenge a specific injustice. It provides such a nice parallel to compare present-day capoeiristas in the streets agitating for police reform with colonial-era quilombeiros using capoeira to protect their freedom. Lucha disabused me of my romanticism. In Lucha's conception, "[the] parts of capoeira that are . . . resisting oppression, colonization, and all that stuff, are the parts that we actually don't recognize as being such." Most people I interviewed simply told me that capoeira *is* social justice, implying that because capoeira is rooted in resisting oppression, any fruit it bears will have a social justice flavor. I don't think they are wrong, but it is striking how easily that narrative is spread, without an interrogation of what aspects of capoeira's present-day practice challenge the systemic oppressions under which people live today. Lucha further explained that "the idea of community, of spending time together, of enjoying each other's company, of making personal connections, of singing, and making music, and playing together is anticapitalist." She recognizes that of course there is money involved in capoeira. Instructors must be compensated for their time and expertise, and the frequency with which Black teachers in particular are asked to perform or teach for free indexes the effects of white supremacy even within the capoeira community. But much of what goes on within the capoeira community cannot be quantified and is based on generalized reciprocity. It is fairly well known within the capoeira community that someone who is traveling can call on fellow capoeiristas almost anywhere in the world and find a place to stay. "To me," Lucha said, "that is actually an anticapitalist way of being, and that is much more like resistance to oppression than the f—ing slave narrative, which doesn't make sense to me."

Tlaloc locates the origins of his school's social justice subgroup in the experience some Muslim members had of being afraid to leave class. I spoke with Tlaloc in 2016, not long after a highly contentious US presidential election and the institution of travel bans on citizens of certain Muslim-majority nations, but he felt like Islamaphobia had already been on the rise in his city. When Tlaloc and others in the group heard that their Muslim friends had been followed in the streets or verbally harassed, they decided to take action. "Even if it's something small," he said, "we're gonna stand up as a community. We're very close knit in capoeira, you know?" But this ethic of caring extends beyond the bounds of their local group. When something makes national news, like the 2016 mass shooting in an Orlando nightclub, members will reach out to capoeiristas local to the tragedy and ask, "Did your group know anybody?" or "How can we [be helpful to the] community?"

Building community, for Tlaloc, is a form of resistance. He argues that "resistance doesn't just mean going up against" someone or something. Unlike with Lucha, when Tlaloc talks about the link between capoeira and social justice, he *does* root it in capoeira's origin myth; however, in much the same way that Lucha identifies capoeiristas' couch surfing as an anticapitalist form of resistance, Tlaloc believes that proactively building an alternative to oppressive social relations is a form of resistance.

Cultivating a strong, inclusive capoeira community can be an end in and of itself. It can be a way of resisting the hegemony of capitalism in US society, and can support a proactively antiracist agenda. The capoeira community makes these things possible, even if individual capoeiristas are not necessarily attuned to the process through which this is occurring. Even without individuals being consciously aware of it, the expectations governing this community support small, everyday acts of resistance.

When my interlocutors talked about the capoeira community, they tacked back and forth easily between discussing the community or family feeling of their home training group and discussing the global capoeira community. Being a capoeirista is like having a passport that permits entrance into these smaller, local communities and ensures that the bearer will be cared for while there, regardless of who that person is. Ray said that capoeira brings together "the outliers that are misfits." Speaking of himself, he said that he fits in across many different places, but because of that, he also doesn't fit in; he is simultaneously Other. He thinks that capoeira attracts a lot of people who are like him in that way. "We have to figure how to get along, because everybody's so different that if you see us all sitting together, it's like, 'How the f—does that work?' You try to figure that out." When someone is immersed in the world of capoeira—and he does feel like it is a world unto itself—"it just feels normal." But at the same time, he knows for sure that growing up he never could have guessed he'd be involved with the people he's gotten to know through capoeira. This structural diversity is also part of what allows the capoeiristas' discourse about historical resistance to find new life in the present.

STRUCTURAL DIVERSITY

Francis and Riser are African American men nearly a decade apart in age who used to live in the same city and train in capoeira together before Riser moved about two thousand miles away. A few years ago, they decided to meet up in Bahia. It was Francis's first, and to date only, trip to Brazil. The two of them were talking with some local capoeiristas, and the conversation turned to the issue of racial profiling and interactions with the police. In Francis's telling, everyone walked away from that interaction having learned something about their counterparts' experience of Blackness. It reminded me of a meeting I attended in 2008 where some Brazilian activists and community organizers expressed incredulity that the Klan still exists in the United States. "But how could they [know]?" Francis prompted me. "I mean, they're not here, we're not there. So, it's good to have those conversations." These kinds of conversations could theoretically arise anytime people from two different cultures meet, but they don't always. This is where Francis finds capoeira to be a particularly useful tool. "Capoeira is a vehicle for that type of stuff if people are interested because it seems to lend itself to community," he said. The connection people have because of their shared interest in capoeira, the vulnerability they need to have in order to learn in the company of others, and the background of what capoeira is all contribute to making the capoeira community a brave space where these conversations can occur. "It kind of does that naturally by force," Francis said.

How can something be natural if it is also done by force? This poignant observation speaks to both how natural it feels to have these kinds of conversations if one has been involved in the capoeira community for a long time and how improbable it is that all these different people from different places with different ideas could come together and find common ground. There is a lot going on under the surface that makes the capoeira community feel natural.

Back in 2008, I was in a plaza in Salvador's historic district, not far from Mestre Bimba's old academy, talking to a local capoeirista who was interested in my research. With his voice full of reverence for the power of capoeira, he told me that he had seen an American and an Iraqi play in the roda. "It was great," he said, "inside capoeira they forgot about the war." I've been told similar stories about Palestinians and Israelis in the roda. The unofficial representatives of warring factions engage not in mock battle but in collaborative play that transcends difference and gives hope to the onlookers, who interpret the interaction against the backdrop of international politics.

This example demonstrates the different frames that get used to talk about diversity and transcendence of difference within capoeira. At the most basic level is the game itself, the bounded interaction between the American and Iraqi or the Palestinian and Israeli. Then there is the frame that encompasses both the fellow players and the spectators, who bring their knowledge of larger social forces to bear on their interpretation of the game. Finally, there is the frame surrounding my interaction with this capoeirista completely outside of the academy, well removed from the immediacy of the game, in which the game and the spectators' interpretations are each reanimated to make a greater point: capoeira has social power. This is where the discourse about capoeira has an opportunity to reach people outside of the capoeira community itself.

When I asked people why they thought capoeira was particularly useful as a tool for social justice, they often came back to the theme of community. Yet my conversations with them and my own experiences in capoeira make clear that it is a particular kind of community. White nationalists also constitute a community, but they don't engage with social issues in the same way as do capoeiristas, which leads me to ask what it is about the capoeira community that makes it so unique in the eyes of its members. One distinguishing feature is its racial and ethnic diversity, which creates a context in which capoeiristas—particularly those who may not have experienced much diversity of this nature in the past—overcome subconscious prejudices and become concerned about how people (including their training partners) are disproportionately affected by things like institutional racism.

That capoeira is a physically demanding art that requires intimate contact with others, who may also be Other, is key to understanding why a structurally diverse training environment aids in the development of a socially engaged orientation to the world at large. At a basic level, learning any new skill requires the learner to be vulnerable. Learners make mistakes and, if they want to improve, need to accept critiques. In a martial art, critique may take the form of getting kicked, thrown, or knocked to the floor. Curupira is a Black man in his late thirties who spent several years of his adolescence desperately looking for capoeira classes before a chance encounter in his high school weight room led him to his first class. His formal training has been sporadic at times, but he remains passionate about the art and engages with the community whenever he can. Curupira believes, "when you open your eyes to something, when you're learning something new about anything, more often than not, you're gonna accidentally lift a couple other filters." That might be the racist filter that we acquire from being raised in a racist society, or a filter of toxic masculinity. It could be anything that prevents us from seeing others in an empathetic light. Most of the time, he believes, this is something that happens subconsciously, but "when it happens and you know it and you realize it, you're like well damn. Where the hell was my head at this whole time?"

Status markers are stripped away both physically and metaphorically, the former when students are required to wear uniforms, and the latter when, as Quinten said, "you see everyone at their grimiest and worst." Quinten is now the product director for a large, well-known, international aid organization, but he started training in the early 2000s. At that time, he was out of shape and not particularly athletic. After he first saw capoeira, he was so nervous that it took him three months to work up the courage to start training, but then he was hooked. Interacting with such a wide swath of people in a setting that not only eliminates the material markers that have meaning outside of the roda but also strips away performances of status has led to numerous "epiphanies" for him. For example, he was surprised to learn that a training partner was a researcher at a leading international think tank. "Okay, I had no idea," he thought, "because we just kick each other all day." Situations like these have allowed him to stop making judgments based on stereotypes and "dismissing people who I shouldn't be dismissing."

Quinten told me, "the first few games you play are worthless. You're working through your own ingrained, kind of like rote movements, and only once you become absolutely beyond exhausted, when you are destroyed as a person and broken down into nothing, [does] your real creativity emerge." This is more than just taking some time to warm up or get into a groove. It's about stripping away the artifice in which we cloak ourselves as we interact with other people. We are constantly engaged in various presentations of self, consciously and unconsciously tailoring our performances to match the masks we wear: professor, wife, mother. Erving Goffman (1959) differentiated between front spaces, in which these performances must be carefully calibrated and kept up, and back spaces, where we can let down our guard and be, more or less, who we really are. Quinten's comment suggests an alternative. Back spaces are not the only place that we can reveal this elemental self. It can happen in public settings when an individual's body and mind are taxed to the point that keeping up any sort of pretense is virtually impossible.

Franca Tamisari (2006, 49) argues that the "intercorporeality" of performance allows performers and spectators "to enter into an empathic space where the other person is encountered at a deeper level of intensity." In the Australian Yolngu ceremonies she studied, this intercorporeality does not lead to the complete identification between performer and spectator, but it creates an opening for the development or consolidation of a deep relationship with the Other. Quinten's talk of exhaustion, destruction, and the experience of being broken down sounds awful, but is probably recognizable to anyone that has pushed their body past the infamous "wall." There is no energy left to maintain a facade. This vulnerability and nakedness invite empathy and lay the foundation for communitas.

Quinten believes that when this work is done collectively, as is the case in a roda, exhaustion and brokenness give way to a special experience of togetherness. It "opens all these channels of thought . . . that don't normally exist." Recalling a conversation he had with Mestre Nenel for his podcast *Capoeira Connection*, Cory said that one of Mestre Nenel's biggest points was that "when you're in the roda, and it's the music, and you're clapping, and you're singing, and all these things, you're putting this energy all in, nobody remembers where they're from. You just don't. You just don't want to get kicked in the face." In that moment of adrenaline-fueled intensity, the focus required to avoid being kicked precludes thinking about an opponent or their various identities. Inkeri Aula (2017, 82) similarly describes the roda as "a potential moment of union, overcoming the differences that separate people in a complicated society." I believe this is true; however, this in and of itself is not a comprehensive explanation for how training in capoeira leads to the transcendence of difference. That is because capoeira is about much more than what happens during the roda.

Like Ray, who expressed with wonderment the wild diversity of outliers and misfits that he has met through capoeira, Curupira told me that thanks to capoeira, he has become close to "people who [he] wouldn't even associate with were it not for capoeira; [people he] wouldn't know to associate with were it not for capoeira." In other words, being involved in capoeira brings together people who never would have met otherwise and provides common ground on which friendships can flourish. Bram said something similar: "I think capoeira is really, really good for bringing people together who would never ever in a million years even cross paths let alone get along or become lifelong friends. . . . I have countless friends from capoeira that I know for a fact if we didn't do this art, I wouldn't know you. And it wouldn't even be that I wouldn't like them, but I feel like we just have nothing in common. We'd have nothing to really talk about, nothing that we could talk in depth about."

Talk between capoeiristas occurs, of course, not just during class but before and after the class, in the dressing rooms, on car or plane rides when they are traveling to performances or workshops, outside of class if group members happen to socialize together, and on social media if they happen to follow one another. Imani has heard that "some of the most meaningful talks about politics and gender happen, surprisingly enough, on sports forums. . . . Because . . . this is somebody that is rooting for your team. And you can't just dismiss them." She says that the first real conversation she had with someone from a different religious background was in the capoeira studio. When you have something in common that you both love, it is easier to see the other person as an equal. She says, "you're going to listen because you have to bridge this, you have to find commonalities because you are in the same group, you love doing this thing."

Consider what was shared with me online by a white man who has now become a capoeira teacher in an upper Midwest city:

> I grew up in a place with very few African Americans or anyone of African descent. My first capoeira teachers were black men from Detroit. They spoke different than me and it was one of the first times I had significant interactions with black people. These two became role models to me that I still admire today. I was only a teenager when I began training capoeira. The more I participated in the art the more people I met who had different backgrounds than myself and the more I had to question a lot of the things I believed about race, people of color and my own place in society. I would see and hear black people share things about their experiences with prejudice that I had always been taught were in the past, things I had believed didn't happen anymore. Additionally these people became mentors and friends so I found myself having to take what they said seriously. I had to re-evaluate what I thought of my understanding of "other" because [we] were now all capoeira. How different could we be?

In this narrative and in Imani's musings about the difficult conversations that can emerge on sports forums, recognition of common ground breaks down the feeling of otherness that separated people and requires a reevaluation of previously held beliefs. It is significant that in both cases, they use the word "listen." It cannot be assumed that just being together or sharing a common interest will lead to a visceral understanding of another's experiences; rather, these experiences are filtered through the narratives people share.

Increased sociability between group members may also lead to situations in which students experience acts of injustice together. One night, Briana was riding in the passenger seat while her friend, a Black man, was driving. They got pulled over, and the first thing the officer did was ask her, a white woman, whether she was okay. Meanwhile, we've seen enough incidents of traffic stops turned deadly to imagine that her friend may genuinely have been in fear for his life. "That's what you call driving while Black," her friend later said to her. Before capoeira, she wouldn't necessarily have been exposed to or understood the reality of what it's like to be racially profiled. "Once you've become aware of these things," she said, "you have to change the way you act, otherwise you're being a dick." It's just common sense in her book.

These conversations are not always easy. In fact, sometimes they are down-right painful and can cause groups to splinter. OC said that early on in his group's history, around the time that members were contemplating the question of integration, "it was nothing" for people in the group to use blatantly derogatory language (e.g., anti-Asian racist slurs). Whether this was due to ignorance or malice, the effect was the same. It hurt people. Over the years, through a lot of hard work and carefully constructed opportunities to learn from one another, the group as a whole has progressed and healed. Now, someone can look back and say, "hey, I've made some mistakes. But . . . thank God that I've grown."

Riser told me that pretty much everyone in his group is, for lack of a better term, "woke." In other words, they all have at least a basic understanding that the society in which we live is plagued by inequalities and structured by power differentials that make life harder for some groups than others. I asked him whether they were all already woke when they joined the group or whether this was a process he witnessed in his students as they became more deeply involved in the community. "It's a process of awakening," he told me, one that is affected by the interactions students have within his group. "[Whatever] level of wokeness you are, then the more you interact with people of different ethnicities, then you're gonna become more aware of their struggles, of their culture, and things like that." His group is diverse in terms of ethnicity and nationality. "What will happen is we will get together for celebrations and things like that. So . . . Lunar New Year, or someone's birthday, or someone's quinceañera, you know, and things like that. So then we get to develop deeper relationships with people." Riser acknowledges that the degree to which these cross-cultural engagements affect someone's orientation to the world, or their wokeness, depends on their consistency in attending classes and participating at the school. Again, it isn't that capoeira is somehow magical in its ability to transform people, but the leaders of these groups are consistently creating a context in which exposure to difference leads to empathy, allyship, and activism.

Ray teaches kids in several different locations throughout his city. At their belt ceremonies, there might be one hundred kids that gather. This is one way that he thinks capoeira can "create proximity." Having a shared interest in capoeira brings people together, physically and metaphorically, but it also goes beyond capoeira. "They recognize each other in the streets. They follow each other on Instagram. They hang out." If coalitions that transcend difference are going to be formed, something must happen in order to make this possible. Several authors have pointed to proximity, intimacy, and the circulation of emotion as just such a facilitating force (see Alexandrakis 2016). But for this facilitating force to work, there must be structural diversity within the group. Structural diversity is a necessary precursor to interactional diversity, which my interlocutors consistently brought up as one way they think capoeira contributes to a social justice orientation. In order for capoeiristas to reap the benefits of engaging with people who come from different backgrounds, those people must all, somehow, be brought into the capoeira community in the first place. Achieving the right balance of members from different demographic groups is difficult, particularly because capoeiristas are self-selecting. At least two individuals I interviewed were disappointed in the small number of Black students training in their groups. Ironically, both live in cities that have traditionally had large Black populations. One city in particular has a high concentration of historically Black colleges and universities (HBCUs) and was crucial to the civil rights movement of the 1960s. What these cities also have in common, however, are areas of gentrification. Jordan explained it to me in this way: "I think [it] is because of the location of where we are. It just so happens that there are more white people who live in the area than others. And since the group is white, it most likely attracts more white people." Neither individual expressed any negative feelings toward non-Black capoeiristas. While my own whiteness should not be discounted, based on the openness of our conversation I did not feel that either individual censored himself for my benefit. As Jordan put it, "Black folks kind of feel . . . more comfortable when they see more Black faces."

At the same time, however, some teachers want to see more white students among their group. Imani's group is interesting in that almost all her current students are, "to some extent," immigrants. There used to be one white girl in the group, and Imani says she wishes that student was still involved, "because I think that the power of [capoeira] is to create a diverse community." That power stretches to include members' families as well. Think about what happens when parents gather to wait for their kids to finish class: there is "this one lady that cleans houses [who] is talking to this lady who her husband owns his own company or whatever." There is nothing staged or artificial about the interaction between these parents; the structural diversity of Imani's class created the context in which two women from very different class backgrounds could meet and interact. De facto segregation often prevents us from seeing the struggles experienced by other groups of people. Proximity leads to empathy. Training in the company of diverse others opens individuals' hearts to struggles they may have been blind to in the past.

CONCLUSION

Tlaloc's mestre has a nephew who attends a local elementary school. As this Black boy walked home from school one day, he was harassed by a bunch of white teenagers, "not even half a block from the school." The boy called his mom right away, crying, telling her what had happened. They yelled slurs at him that Tlaloc wouldn't even repeat to me, and "threatened his life, [just] for walking home." The boy's mom called the school, demanding to know whether anyone had been outside to witness what happened. Apparently, no one else saw it, not even any crossing guards. The school officials said they couldn't do anything about it until they investigated. Frustrated that the school was not going to be more proactive, someone in the group said, "Why don't we walk him home? We can even bring some of our instruments, some of our berimbaus. And we'll walk down the street and make it a big deal. And bring up not only his self-esteem but show the school that if they're not gonna do something about it, the community will." This particular incident "hit close to home because it was family, but it could have happened to any-body." In the end, there were community members, parents, and teachers involved, in addition to the capoeiristas. They turned a hateful incident that made a child fear for his life into a celebration of community. One might say this is an example of organized activism, or it might just be what people do when they are part of a community that cares.

One lesson capoeira teaches is how to "embrace difference rather than erase it or assume its undesirability in efforts of dialogic processes, all the while building intersubjectivity on a foundation of expanded conceptions of conflict, quality, inclusion and connection" (MacLennan 2011, 148). But how does it actually accomplish this? What does it mean to transcend difference in the roda or in our groups? Does it mean ignoring differences or seeking to understand them? The latter can be transformative. The former is dan-gerously close to a "color-blind" mentality or the myth of racial democracy. Sometimes, downplaying difference *does* work to create a more inclusive and just community. Uniforms are a case in point. Yet other differences, like race, ethnicity, or social class, need to be engaged. By engaging with difference and the question of what specific kinds of difference mean within the con-text of our societies, the teachers who do this can create a climate in which students, especially wealthier, white students, recognize their privilege and understand what lack of privilege means for their training partners who have now become friends. The ways in which that affective change gives rise to action are explored in the next chapter.

6

GROUP ACTIONS

Dong-ding-dong, dong, dong. Dong-ding-dong, dong, dong. Faster and faster the rhythm is played, emulating the sounds of horse hooves as the mounted police arrive. It was intended as a warning for one's fellow capoeiristas. Watch out! The cavalry is coming. Run away before you get caught playing capoeira. On this day, it is a different kind of warning. The summer sun shines down on a few hundred capoeiristas marching through the streets of this West Coast city. The axé (energy) is palpable, even through the mediation of Facebook's livestream. Rarely before have so many of us come this close to apprehending the intensity and complexity of emotions that may have animated those early rodas of enslaved Africans in Brazil. On this day in June 2020, there is joy at finally being together, in person, after months of isolation and pandemic lockdowns. There is anger, rage really, at the blatant injustice of yet another Black man being murdered in broad daylight by someone whose job it was to ensure his welfare. And finally, there is the hope engendered by *doing* something about it.

Dong-ding-dong, dong, dong. This time it isn't a warning that the police are coming, though the marchers are alert to that possibility. No, it is a warning that the people are coming. "Não é agressão," I remember my teacher in Brazil saying. It isn't aggression. It's having an objective, a purpose in our movements. He was talking about a kick. These capoeiristas have a different objective. Watch out! Here come the people, and they won't passively comply when the state sanctions violence.

The details of every case are unique, but many socially engaged capoeiristas follow a general pattern as they become more deeply entrenched in this

Still taking precautions against the COVID-19 pandemic, hundreds of capoeiristas took to the streets in June 2020, playing the cavalaria rhythm as part of their protest against George Floyd's murder. Photo shared with the author by Lua Negra.

community of practice: (1) the act of performing capoeira encourages an individual to subjectively identify with an oppressed Other (namely, enslaved Africans in colonial Brazil); (2) becoming close to diverse Others within the physically demanding context of training increases the individual's empathy and awareness of injustice; and (3) the recognition that today's social problems are not unlike those that capoeira was designed to fight against compel the individual to take a more active role in protesting or fighting against inequalities. Whereas the previous chapters focus on the ways in which participating in the capoeira community alters a practitioner's affective habitus, this chapter looks at the diverse ways in which capoeira groups around the United States enact this philosophy of resistance.

PUBLIC PERFORMANCES

When capoeiristas play in public, they assume responsibility for embodying a symbol of Brazilianness and Blackness. Most rodas are attended only by other members of the group. Eventos like batizados typically have an open roda that attracts capoeiristas from the nearby region as well as family and friends of the people who are graduating to the next level. Sometimes a group or collective of individuals representing multiple groups will hold an open roda in a public setting like a park or on a college campus, which tends to attract spectators with varying degrees of familiarity with capoeira.

On particularly nice days, the capoeira group I trained with in graduate school would have a roda near the campus gates. Passersby would stop and watch, sometimes tossing a few dollars into an upturned *pandeiro* (tambourine) to thank us for our performance. A few might inquire about taking classes. So while for most of us it was an exciting opportunity to play in the fresh air instead of training in a dim and musty gym, it was also a way for our mestre to recruit new students and perhaps put a small amount of money into our group's account. In other instances, we might do the exact same thing but put a sign out saying we were collecting money to donate to a particular cause, like supporting victims of a natural disaster, which we did multiple times.

Our outings were mostly spontaneous, but my interlocutors consistently reported public rodas being held in commemoration of two different holidays: Martin Luther King Jr. Day and Juneteenth. There is no tangible link between capoeira and Martin Luther King Jr.; however, the references made to Dr. King or the holiday dedicated to him speak to at least a tacit connection in some capoeiristas' minds. Riser was probably the most explicit about this connection, likening Dr. King to Mestre Bimba insofar as both recognized that society comprises diverse peoples but that we can nonetheless "join in together in support of one another, but with respect to the roots." Bruno contrasted the absurdity of doing a Halloween-themed roda or a Christmas roda with the appropriateness of a roda dedicated to someone like Dr. King, Malcolm X, or Marcus Garvey, whose work supported the African diaspora. Of these, Dr. King is probably most synonymous with civil rights for most US Americans, many of whom do not know much about his legacy aside from small, whitewashed snippets of the "I Have a Dream" speech. It's not surprising that references to Martin Luther King Jr. Boulevard were used as shorthand for "Black neighborhoods" in one of my interviews.

Lucha—the phenotypically white activist who celebrates capoeira's anticapitalist ethos—described one particular roda that her friend Riser organized for Martin Luther King Jr. Day. The goal was to reclaim the more radical aspects of Dr. King's legacy, which are often swept aside. Martin Luther King Jr. *did* present a utopian vision of communion between people of all races, but what doesn't get as much airtime are the anger, the callout, the insistence on recognition for the injustices experienced by Black people at the hands of the white people in the United States who held power over them. Making sure that people understand the full scope of capoeira—its utility in a fight and the role it played in resistance against the injustices of Brazilian slavery—is akin to restoring the image of Dr. King as a real revolutionary whose message was dangerous enough that it resulted in his assassination. The Black capoeiristas in attendance led the evento, and the non-Black supporters who were there participated but without centering themselves or their emotional needs.

Riser has also organized a number of Juneteenth eventos. Slavery is the most obvious point of connection between capoeira and Juneteenth. Riser characterizes this connection thusly: "Juneteenth is a celebration of the final group of Black people being notified that they're quote, unquote free, right? And with capoeira, it's something that was used to liberate people, but also something that was forced to be done in the dark, in the shadows. And now the African descendants can celebrate their freedom in the open, and also with capoeira because of the efforts of Mestre Bimba, an African descendant, we can celebrate in the light what was forced to be in the shadows." This holiday originated in Texas and was for many years little known outside of the US South (Hamer, Chapman, and Osbourne 1998), and yet a seemingly disproportionate number of capoeiristas not only are aware of the holiday but have celebrated it with a capoeira roda for several years. I expect to see this connection not only continue but become more prominent following the events of 2020. Because very few face-to-face gatherings were able to happen during the COVID-19 pandemic, capoeiristas became accustomed to connecting with one another via internet platforms like Zoom. Widespread anger over George Floyd's murder in late May 2020 combined with the unprecedented level of virtual connection between geographically distant capoeiristas set the stage for a number of pro-Black capoeira eventos that were scheduled to coincide with Juneteenth. Juneteenth is a celebration of freedom, but one that is tinged with the recognition that freedom is often partially and incrementally gained. That is a message that resonates with many capoeiristas.

These two holidays are not the only times that public rodas take on a political or activist orientation. In a West Coast city I visited, several groups came together to have an evento in support of Women's March, the grassroots organization for women's rights that coalesced after an inaugural gathering in 2017. Dalia remembers that women from local angola and contemporânea groups were present at the evento she attended. The *bateria* (capoeira orchestra) comprised all women, and when she had the opportunity to lead, she was mindful of choosing songs that represented the current moment. She felt honored to be among such strong women who were also strong capoeiristas, and the onlookers felt it too: "I could just see people's faces light up to see, you know, at this women's march, a woman-led bateria."

In addition to these instances of playing in public, capoeira groups are occasionally invited to give more formal performances, for which they are often paid. While not necessarily undertaken with political aims, formal performances are moments of heightened saliency during which the capoeiristas' actions, comportment, dress, and more are evaluated by any onlooker that happens to stop and watch. Even though capoeira has become more popular and more widely known than it was even a decade ago, it is still common for the organizer of a public performance to feel the need to give some history and context either at the beginning of the performance or at various points throughout it. If a leader is politically inclined, this may be an opportunity to advance the narrative about capoeira being an art of resistance. These leaders use the entertainment aspect as a hook to draw spectators in and then promote their perspective.

Some instructors have a more-or-less standard script that they follow during these presentations, or at least a few key points that they regularly emphasize. Imani says that for her, "what's important to tell people is it is one of the earliest forms of art activism. It was a way of people getting together around joy in a time of darkness, celebrating and keeping the culture alive. Because once all documentation was burned by the Brazilian government once slavery was abolished, this was a way of celebrating ancestors and telling stories. So, it was such a revolt against trying to erase the culture."

Others speak more extemporaneously. Sitting cross-legged on the floor, waiting for our mestre to signal us to begin the performance, I looked across the circle and caught my friend's eye. We simultaneously broke into grins, the anticipation of the performance mixing with our uncertainty over what our mestre would say. We knew that he would always preface our performances with the standard discourse of how enslaved Africans resisted the colonists' ban on fighting by disguising their martial art as dance, and he often talked about the quilombos as part of this history, but we never knew what else he would add to his speech. He might compare what happened to Africans in Brazil to the experience of slavery in the United States, or he might explicitly condemn the sitting president. The term *charisma* might as well have been invented for this man, and his audiences always appeared rapt. I don't recall us ever having any conversations as a group about our political stances or the degree to which we agreed with our mestre's left-leaning, progressive politics, but by our sitting in that roda while he condemned conservative politicians and urged solidarity across the diaspora, our bodies not only consented to these messages but reinforced them.

I asked my mestre later about these presentations and whether his political discourse was intentional and premeditated, though I didn't use those exact words. Of course it was intentional. As an Afro-Brazilian man, he finds that these presentations are a valuable opportunity to help his audience see the common ground shared by Afro-Brazilians and African Americans. It's not just about teaching the audience the history of capoeira; it's about encouraging them to make these connections and think critically about why such similarities exist. Even when a public performance is economically motivated, it is also an opportunity to spread awareness of enslaved Africans' ingenuity and resistance to oppression. Whether each individual present in the performing group has a vested interest in spreading this information is immaterial. Their bodies become instruments in the teacher's performance of justice. It is certainly true that individuals could walk away from a group if they found it too political, and surely some have done so, but in the moment of these performances, every willing body becomes part of the teacher's narrative.

PROTESTS AS GRACEFUL RESISTANCE

Thirty-two-year-old Philando Castile was a cafeteria worker in Minnesota who often bought lunch for children who couldn't afford it. In July 2016, he was driving in a Saint Paul suburb with his girlfriend and her four-year-old daughter in the car. Castile was pulled over because his brake light was out, and the officer asked him for his license and insurance. Castile informed the officer that he had a gun in the car, which he was licensed to carry. He was told not to reach for the gun, and Castile said, "I'm not pulling it out." But as he reached for his wallet to retrieve the identification the officer had requested, the officer fired seven shots. Castile's girlfriend, Diamond Reynolds, recorded what happened next on her phone. Understandably upset, she is yelling, and the police handcuff her. Reynolds's four-year-old daughter says, "Mom, please stop cussing and screaming 'cause I don't want you to get shooted."

When this happened, Bruno knew he couldn't just carry on with his class as planned for that evening. He said, "there's no way to have a [regular] class, to ignore that . . . to be like, 'oh yeah, another Black person got killed, let's do our thing here.'" Bruno is not of African descent; he is a white Brazilian, but he believes strongly that capoeira should support the African diaspora. His group has gone through a number of internal struggles over the years regarding what role white students could have in the group, and how to incorporate them without sacrificing the sanctity of this cultural space for Black students. All of this is to say that the members of this group are no stranger to identity politics and, for the most part, follow Bruno's lead on issues like this. Instead of holding class as usual, he told the students to grab their instruments and hop on the train because they were going to use their normal class time to support the local protest that had been organized in honor of Castile. One student later confessed to him that she had thought about skipping class that night because she wanted to be at the protest, but she ultimately decided to attend class because she thought practicing capoeira and being with her group would be a comfort. Therefore, she was grateful that Bruno had made the decision to hold class at the protest. He knows that attending a protest won't bring a man's life back but says they cannot carry on with business as usual. They must do something: next time it might be one of them that is shot by a police officer.

Attending protests as a group is the most explicitly political action that the capoeiristas I interviewed regularly take part in. A few campaign on behalf of political candidates in their communities or undertake other forms of activism, but they do those things as individuals, not as representatives of their groups. Riser did invite a mayoral candidate to speak at an evento, something that Lucha appreciated in part because it sent a message to the visiting Brazilian mestre in attendance that capoeira could be used to promote progressive political causes, but this kind of overt endorsement of a platform is rare. Nonetheless, many groups seem to have an unspoken agreement that they support these causes, which is made visible when they attend protests in uniform or bring their instruments to organized protests/rallies.

Like Bruno, OC makes activism an explicit part of how he runs his group. I asked whether he attends protests with his students. "So much so, I don't even catalog it anymore," he said. His group has shown up to protest issues ranging from unfair housing policies to police violence. In protesting, people "are demanding a livable life" (Butler 2015, 26). Their needs could—at least theoretically—be enumerated (e.g., housing, health care), but at the same time, their demand for a livable life is greater than the sum of each individual item on that list. This helps explain why OC's students show up to such far-ranging events. They go in uniform with their instruments and make their presence known, "and just [their] presence evokes a conversation." Again, OC traces this back to the Brazilian organization his group ultimately broke away from, whose members would show up and play capoeira at events supporting grassroots causes like the Movimento Negro (Black Movement) and Movimento dos Trabalhadoes Rurais sem Terra (Landless Workers' Movement). He says their involvement wasn't particularly "rah-rah," but that they made a statement just by being there. The protesting or demonstrating bodies give tangible shape to the people who are accusing the state of injustice; they put a face on what might otherwise be too abstract to arouse support for their cause (see Butler 2015).

When people gather to publicly resist a more powerful entity (e.g., the state) or take a stand against some exercise of that power (e.g., mass detention of migrants), they become vulnerable to the same forces of power that they decry (Butler 2016; see also Foster 2007). People resist because they or those they care about are vulnerable to abuses of power, and although they are exerting their agency in the act of resisting, they are also increasing their vulnerability by exposing their stance to those with the power to retaliate. When Bruno insisted that his students participate in the Castile protest, one individual didn't want to go: an African American man from the Deep South. Apparently, this man said he didn't want to go because he didn't like crowds. Bruno said no, you already decided you were coming to capoeira and this is what we're doing today, so you come with us and stay until nine—when the class was scheduled to end—and then you can go, which is what the man did. Bruno brushed off this man's excuse, saying that the place where the protest was being held was a safe place and no one was going to be "stupid enough" to do something there, but I think it might be worth considering the man's reticence a bit more carefully.

Some bodies are more vulnerable than others and are more at risk in this kind of environment. If a teacher assumes responsibility for the safety of their students inside the academy, it stands to reason that their safety in the real world should be a concern as well. Like Rene later told me, "it's not the type of thing that you would want anybody to do unless it was voluntary. . . . Even under the best of circumstances, you're still subjecting your body to possible harm due to violence from the authorities." Even if no violence occurs at a protest, there is still the risk of exposure and potential arrest, which could be devastating for someone whose legal status is tenuous or whose ability to make a living demands a clean record (e.g., a counselor or teacher).

Bruno is unusual among the people I interviewed in insisting that someone participate in the protest. Although Riser tends not to mandate his students' participation in protests or other organized actions, he will sometimes commit his group to something because of his confidence in members' "wokeness." For the most part, my interlocutors told me that they might encourage their students to participate but would stop short of insisting. They might not want to endanger their organization's nonprofit status by politicizing participation in the group, or they might only want people to participate if it is a genuine reflection of their commitments. Bram, for instance, might require students to do community service, but he did not demand that they participate in any protests of George Floyd's murder. That was too personal. Nonetheless, many of his students did participate in a variety of efforts to support the cause.

Even though, as Bram notes, the violent death of Black people due to police brutality has become almost commonplace, he still feels it personally. Whereas Bruno insisted that the group go out to protest after Castile was murdered because, as he put it, it could be one of them next time, Bram avoids mandating students' participation because, he says, "it feels like it's happening to [him]." The difference here is slight but important. Bruno's comment is concerned with the likelihood of excessive force being used against people of color in the future. Bram's is focused on the present and his internalization of the pain brought about by the terrorization of the Black community. The different stances they take could be interpreted in a number of ways. Bruno is Brazilian; Bram is from the United States. Bruno's phenotype is ethnically ambiguous, but he is Euro-descended; Bram is without question phenotypically Black. Their unique personalities may also explain the difference. Both leaders are conscious of the power they hold within the capoeira community, particularly the influence they have over their students. Bruno uses his power to put his students—and their bodies—out in the public sphere as a way of supporting the African diaspora. This action is completely in keeping with his organization's stance on social justice. Bram's refusal to do so, however, is no less consistent with his own leadership philosophy, which focuses on the ethic of care. He expects his students to take care of one another, and this extends to supporting individuals in the community who are in pain because of what is going on in the world. Bruno's philosophy demands a visible, embodied presence so that those with political power *see* resistance; Bram's philosophy calls for individual acts of support that may never be visible to the world at large. One is not better than the other, and both align with the value system of capoeira.

The raw materials for activism exist in capoeira, particularly in groups that focus on the history of resistance and talk about this explicitly, but whether they are active in going out and doing things because of this will vary dramatically based on the composition of the group, which tends to fluctuate over time. All the conditions were right for Bruno's group to develop a strong activist orientation. The group's founding mestre had been involved in the Movimento Negro in Brazil, which in turn was heavily influenced by liberation theology and the work of Paulo Freire. The religious organization that sponsored the founding mestre's move to the United States was also highly politicized and involved in the pan-African movement. These capoeiristas have gone through a lot of soul-searching and debate over who should be allowed to practice capoeira, and how white people can prove their sincere desire to support the African diaspora. And while the group attended the occasional protest as far back as the early 2000s, the more recent efforts of a single individual who is heavily involved in activism put political engagement at the center of the group's agenda.

The political climate of the community in which a capoeira group is located will shape the degree to which its members engage in these kinds of actions. Although I received reports from all over the United States of capoeiristas attending protests, the most sustained engagement in this kind of behavior was reported by individuals who live in parts of the country where such activism is a deeply entrenched and valued part of the culture (e.g., liberal cities on the West Coast). The individuals who told me such stories sometimes grew up in other parts of the country but had found their way by choice or circumstance to cities with a history of social and political activism. That they were participating in a protest was not noteworthy, but *how* they chose to engage was influenced by their belonging to the capoeira community. Dalia, for example, loves being part of a community that has a lot of protests, and she's happy that the capoeiristas in her city come together to support them. When she hears about something happening, she or someone else in the local capoeira community will issue a call to get people together to attend. She says her goal is often, "just to bring some joy, bring some fun to each of these marches, and also to be there in solidarity."

Thomas N. Ratliff and Lori L. Hall (2014) found that the vast majority of actions taken during protests are peaceful, typically involving symbolic, aesthetic, or sensory displays. These capoeiristas aren't looking for a fight when they go to protests. Lua Negra is the African American teacher who organized the march described in this chapter's opening vignette. In preparing his students, he instructed them to adopt the nonconfrontational stance advocated by Mestre Pastinha. "Look," he said, "if something comes at us, we run. Cool? We get out." At the same time, however, he also acknowledged that fleeing is not always possible, and that if they had to take a stand, they were physically and mentally prepared for it. "But that's not the intention of what we're here for." Protests are not necessarily volcanic reactions to flash points but rather reflect a "choreography of political struggle" (Goldman 2007, 39). The leaders of these movements are not choreographers in the strict sense, but the choices they make in staging and orchestrating the bodies of protesters and utilizing other media have a rhetoric that echoes what could be found in more conventionally choreographed dance performances.

Danielle Goldman (2007) found a delightful synchronicity between the approach to dance known as contact improvisation and the public enactment of political protests, even though the former is rooted in the relative safety of dance studios and the latter takes place in the less controlled environment of the street. "At its core," Goldman writes, "contact improvisation is a practice of making oneself ready for a range of shifting constraints" (62). Capoeira has much in common with contact improvisation, as the partners constantly adjust their performance to what is offered by the other. The capoeirista's goal is to outshine and outmaneuver an opponent, all the while building a beautiful game in collaboration with this person. In contact improvisation, Goldman sees a form of bodily training that can enable a political actor to execute "calm, confident choices even in situations of duress" (62). These same capabilities are cultivated in capoeiristas.

Protests are performances. Capoeira teachers who take their students to protests make careful calculations about how they perform their identities and affiliations within the context of the protest. These decisions are made partly based on individual experiences and proclivities, and partly based on the context of the event. When Bruno and his students attend protests like the one for Castile, they often wear their uniforms and bring berimbaus and other instruments with them. They don't sing capoeira songs: "that's irrelevant to what's happening there." Bruno doesn't want his students to impose their own agenda on the protest in progress; rather, they use their presence to amplify the voices of those that are protesting. They use their instruments to make noise and draw attention to what is already in progress, chanting along with the other protesters.

Ratliff and Hall (2014) found that chanting was second only to the holding of signs as the most common type of activity to occur during a protest. Wearing symbolic clothing was the twenty-first most common activity on their list, putting it roughly in the middle; however, when capoeiristas attend protests in uniform, their clothing has little direct connection to the subject of the protest (seemingly less salient than, say, a Black Lives Matter T-shirt at a protest against officer-involved shootings or traditional Native American dress at a Dakota Access Pipeline protest). Nonetheless, by wearing their uniforms, capoeiristas identify themselves as part of a subculture that has historically resisted the oppression of Black people. Far less common on Ratliff and Hall's list were organized artistic contributions like musical/vocal performance, drumming, or dancing (appearing twenty-fifth, twenty-sixth, and forty-first on their list of forty-nine specific actions that occurred during protests).

Geoff's group has been involved in protests for as long as he can remember. Whenever its members would hear about something happening, his group would get together and ask, "Well, hey, there's this action. Do we want to go and bring instruments and support it in that way?" By bringing their instruments, they create an energy that will hopefully draw in other people and help swell the embodied presence in the streets. Geoff likens it to hearing a marching band. Something in the rhythm calls to listeners and makes them want to join in. "When there's a march, and we're drumming [along] with it, it gets those people feeling it, and that energy helps carry them further," he reflected. The capoeiristas aren't trying to "take a center-stage kind of role," but rather to be present to support the primary mission of the protesters. "To be able to participate in the giving of that," Geoff said, "has been really fulfilling."

In Geoff's city, the Occupy movement lasted for most of October and November 2011. A tent city complete with services for protesters grew as thousands of citizens as well as several high-profile celebrities gathered to condemn global social and economic inequality. The tent city had to be cleared twice by an intracity cooperative of police officers. Geoff and the other members of his group that went to support the movement recognized the strain protesters were under, especially if they were camping out for days on end as many of them did. Their way of contributing was by bringing entertainment. They held rodas in the encampment as a way of bringing joy and emotionally sustaining the people who were serving the mission in another way. To be clear, nothing in our modern-day, privileged existence can even begin to compare to what enslaved Africans experienced in colonial Brazil, but this example perhaps comes closest to our modern-day imaginings of how the joy and metaphorical liberation of capoeira might have sustained the ancestors living in the *senzalas* (slave quarters).

The Occupy movement shone a light on the gross disparities in US wealth and called for a redistribution of resources; however, while protesters relied heavily on social justice rhetoric, they failed to address the irony of demanding a more equitable distribution of wealth only made possible by the theft of Indigenous land. Eve Tuck and K. Wang Yang (2012, 3) warn that reducing decolonization to a metaphor, and too easily integrating it into liberal discourse that celebrates social justice and antiracism, may actually be a form of appropriation that excuses our complicity and "entertains a settler future." As the Occupy example shows, it is possible to be anticapitalist while still centering the interests of settlers. Lucha also participated in the Occupy protests, but she is adamant that showing up for social justice without divesting oneself of ill-gotten gains is fraudulent. The protest in which she participated is a possible exception to Tuck and Yang's generalizations about the movement, just as the strength of her commitment to decolonization as well as other social justice projects is not typical within the capoeira community, even among groups that prioritize social justice.

The visceral feeling in one's gut that something is wrong with society and demands action is part of the affective habitus I have been describing. These injustices spark anger, but there is also an undercurrent of hope. There has to be, otherwise taking to the streets and exposing oneself to risk would be pointless. Capoeira is one embodiment of this complex coupling, outrage and optimism in tension with each other, allowing for creativity to spring up from even the most seemingly dire situations. Writing in the *Guardian*, Steven W. Thrasher (2015) called attention to the spontaneous expressions of grief, anger, and resilience that burst forth when Freddie Gray died in police custody after he was wrongly arrested for possession of a knife that turned out to be legal under Maryland law:

> All of us in America owe a debt to those brave souls who protest with their bodies, day in and day out, when the state tells them not to. Martin Luther King said: "a riot is the language of the unheard" and we salute those who have used any means necessary to attract attention to the suffocation of black America. But we owe an even bigger debt to those who remind us for a moment of black beauty in the face of black death. . . . The problem of white supremacy in America can't be fixed with more cops or a techie band-aid like body cams on cops; it is, at its root, a problem with spiritual and societal causes. Protest can help us identify those roots and moments of light can help us not to get lost in the darkness along the way.

Capoeiristas were there in Baltimore, providing light to the other people in their community. In the midst of what outsiders called a riot, they held a roda. It was a public celebration of togetherness that flew in the face of the violence that had been wrought on their community. According to a member of the local capoeira community, the roda just kind of "sprang up," and he got a text or message on Facebook after it had already started, saying, "we're down here, on such and such a street." About Black protests, Nicole Schneider (2017, 21) wrote, "joyful artistic practices similarly confront state violence, lines of militarized police, and discrimination with the beauty of black lives, enacted political participation, and cultural diversity." Capoeiristas are martial artists, and they know how to fight, but they also know that resistance can be graceful.

THE BERIMBAU MARCH

Although it will take years if not decades to fully understand the effects of the antiracist, antifascist activism that characterizes the current moment, it would be folly to omit coverage of how the capoeira community responded to the events of May 25, 2020, when George Floyd was murdered by a police officer responding to a call that Floyd had allegedly used a counterfeit twenty-dollar bill at a local deli in Minneapolis. The nine-minute-plus incident that caused his death was recorded by bystanders using their smart phones. The officer knelt on Floyd's neck, ignoring his pleas for help and indications that he could not breathe. In his last moments, Floyd called out for his mother, a detail that shakes me to my core even knowing that my white sons are not likely to ever receive this kind of treatment. As a popular meme that circulated in the aftermath of his death said, all mothers were summoned when Floyd called out for his mama. Capoeiristas were summoned too.

Of all the collective actions capoeiristas took part in after George Floyd's murder, Lua Negra's berimbau march was perhaps the most show stopping. Lua Negra is no stranger to protests. He and his group were already involved in local activism. Yet something changed in the summer of 2020, and he saw how capoeiristas could be not only more involved in activism but more explicit about connecting their art and its rich history of resistance to contemporary social issues. In May 2020, an already polarized nation was further strained by the threat of COVID-19 as well as inconsistent messaging about how to best mitigate risk. While white-collar workers by and large retreated into the safety of their homes, essential workers in food processing plants, grocery stores, and the like bore the brunt of the pandemic. Black and brown people fared worse than did their white counterparts. So when Floyd was murdered by someone who had taken an oath to serve and protect the public, it is no wonder that the explosion of outrage set not only Minneapolis but cities across the world ablaze.

Seeing activists from all racial backgrounds demanding justice for Floyd's death prompted Lua Negra to reflect on the role capoeiristas should be playing:

I was like, "What are we as capoeiristas doing?" I see all these people out here, who don't look like me, who are standing up for Black lives. But as an African-based art, formed by Black people in Brazil . . . as a form of resistance, as a form for freedom, of speaking up against all the, and let's say the word, evil acts posed against them. What are we doing? We should be out there on the front lines as well too. It's fine and dandy to be in class and talk about it, get on a forum, cool. No, we need to be out there and especially with our berimbaus too. Not just marching along with everybody, but this is the symbol of that. So why are we not throwing it out there?

He discussed this with his group. Many people had ideas for things that could be done down the line, like when the COVID-19 lockdown ended. But he felt that more immediate action was warranted. When one woman suggested a march, he threw his full weight behind her idea. There is a time for quiet justice work and a time for more overt, visible action. As Lua Negra points out, his group's actions were intended not only to agitate for police reform in the local community but to inspire other capoeira groups to carry the torch and become more engaged in activism. "If we do this," he thought, "who knows, it might inspire other capoeiristas to do the same."

Once the planning began, things grew with remarkable speed. Members of the group reached out to others by calling, texting, and posting on Instagram. They marshaled their diverse talents to make flyers and print T-shirts. Initially, the group was going to give away the T-shirts for free, but people wanted to pay for them. The money the group collected was donated to other organizations working for justice and reform. "As soon as the idea came," Lua Negra said, "it just started flowing."

This may have been the first time Lua Negra brought together his experience in organizing with his passion for capoeira, but he found that they were a natural fit. From his previous work, he had learned how important it was to plan every detail and bring out every nuance. Of course, he attended to the practical details. They hoped there wouldn't be any violence—and fortunately there wasn't—but they were prepared for it just in case. They organized a security detail, a medical team, and representatives of the national lawyers' guild. They also prepared COVID kits with masks and hand sanitizer so people would feel safe interacting with one another. What made this march truly special was how every aspect was saturated with symbolism.

Most of the people marching carried their berimbaus. Together they played the cavalaria rhythm. It was a good choice for the march: it kept everyone unified and contributed to the swelling energy of the protest, but it was also intentionally chosen for its symbolic value. Lua Negra explains that it is both a warning and a way of mocking the police. That complex mixture of meanings seemed particularly appropriate for this march. Another teacher in Lua Negra's city posted information about the cavalaria rhythm on Instagram the day before the march. She wanted to make sure that attendees not only knew the rhythm and could play along, but understood its significance: "Loud and proud on the streets . . . it will ring out and any police person who cares to ask [its] significance will be told—it is the historic and current sound of capoeirista protest against police discrimination and brutality." This teacher's post bridges keyboard activism and traditional protests. She used her platform as a respected capoeira teacher with a solid Instagram follower base to spread awareness about the cavalaria rhythm and encourage her followers to join her in the streets. She also invited others to add to the collection of stories she had gathered about this rhythm, which speaks to the dialogic nature of social media. Information is spread not just by an influencer to an audience; the audience has the power to speak back, adding to a narrative that now has global reach.

Capoeiristas often bring their berimbaus to protests in order to amplify the messages being shouted by the organizers. The berimbau, visually speaking, is a striking instrument that will call attention just by virtue of its presence (not to mention that for those who don't know what it is, its bow shape may look like a weapon). When played, its distinctive but not overpowering twang contributes to the energy of a chanting crowd without drowning out their words. In this evento, however, the berimbau itself became a symbol of resistance that collapsed the struggles of enslaved Africans in colonial Brazil and the Black victims of police brutality in the contemporary United States.

Lua Negra and his team carefully weighed every decision they made in planning this march. They wanted it to be inclusive. Even in naming the evento they took care that it not be associated with a particular group, style, or geographic region. They wanted something that would speak to the capoeira community as a whole, or at least those capoeiristas who are invested in antiracist social change. Lua Negra believes that "wherever [in the world] you are, if you identify as a capoeirista, you . . . should be identifying with the roots of what capoeira is."

Their march started at the headquarters of an organization that provides wraparound reentry services for people exiting gangs and prison, including counseling, job training, and job placement. From there they passed the ICE detention center as well as a jail. Lua Negra heard some people saying things like, "why are we standing up for George Floyd? He had a record." But to him, this "doesn't make a difference. He's a person, and nobody should be treated like that regardless." Because they were marching in protest of "police brutality, crime, and racial inequality," Lua Negra felt like these institutions were essential places to include on their route.

The march culminated at city hall. Until that point, Lua Negra had no idea that a couple hundred people were behind him. He remembers a white guy that traveled all the way from Utah coming up to him on the steps of city hall. "Damn," he thought to himself. "You came all the way from Utah? Thank you, brother. I appreciate that." He had to shake himself as he gazed out on the assembled mass. He was "mesmerized," but needed to focus on keeping up the axé (energy). He switched up the chant, brought everyone to a fever pitch, and then introduced one of the most famous contemporânea mestres operating in the United States, an Afro-Brazilian man who not only helped popularize capoeira through his work in film, but also maintains a strong commitment to social justice in his personal and professional life. This is a man whose fame would entitle him to take center stage in almost any capoeira gathering he walked into, but who has made space for African American capoeiristas to take the lead in using capoeira as a tool for their own empowerment.

Capoeiristas use their instruments to amplify the message that Black lives matter. Photo shared with the author by Lua Negra.

Lua Negra asked the mestre, whom he describes as a "freedom fighter," to sing a *ladainha* (litany) as a way of rooting their contemporary act in the rich history of resistance that capoeira embodies. Then he called up an angoleiro who is also a lawyer, as well as other activists in the capoeira community. They spoke in English and in Spanish, striving to be as inclusive of the local population as possible. They spoke from the heart about what this movement represents to them. "Look," Lua Negra told the crowd, "there are people that are going to be on the front lines, and there's people who are going to be behind the scenes. But we need all people to be a part of this. It's all inclusive." That they even have to say that Black lives matter underscores that Black lives aren't valued equally in our society, he explained in his own way. But their concerns don't stop there. They were demanding justice for "anybody who's been marginalized or disenfranchised." Because this march was organized by capoeiristas as a way to explicitly connect their art with contemporary social issues, Lua Negra felt it was appropriate to end with a roda. Like their vision of the social movement, it was inclusive. It didn't matter how much experience someone had or what style they practiced, everyone's unique contributions were recognized and valued.

A capoeira evento was also held in George Floyd Square, the intersection outside of the Minneapolis Cup Foods where Floyd's fatal encounter with the police took place. This evento was not under the purview of a single individual, but represented several groups coming together. Like the berimbau march, this also occurred on Juneteenth. There are obvious symbolic connotations of where and when it was held, but rather than its having a unifying effect, at least two teachers in the region declined to participate. One, an African American man who is deeply committed to his community, opted not to participate because he felt like it would be inappropriate. In discussing this choice with me, he said, "it seemed to me at the time that it would only be right if it was more of a celebration of Black empowerment [and] ingenuity, that type of thing." He found it "distasteful" that the evento would take place on the hallowed ground where Floyd was murdered. This is a site that has since added a sign with a code of conduct, including five guidelines specifically geared toward white people so that their own emotional needs don't overburden the people of color who are in that sacred space (see Rosner and Brown 2021). My interlocutor was also bothered that one person involved in organizing the capoeira evento had not participated in any of the city's ongoing protests or even commented about the situation online. He worried that it would not be a demonstration of capoeira's potential to resist or offer refuge from oppression, or even a celebration of Black creativity and joy, but would turn into a recruitment opportunity for the teachers present. Bringing that aspect of commercialism to a sacred space seemed crass and out of alignment with the ethos of capoeira.

CONCLUSION

Bodies that resist power by protesting are characterized by Judith Butler (2015, 84) as both productive and performative, yet she also reminds her readers that "they can persist and act only when they are supported, by environments, by nutrition, by work, by modes of sociality and belonging." Deprived of these things, they may protest and, in the process of doing so, may form alliances that provide (some of) the very things they are demanding. The 2020 protests in Minneapolis after George Floyd's murder did result in stores being looted and set ablaze—whether these were actions initiated by provocateurs or an authentic if misdirected outburst of inchoate anger—but according to one of my interviewees, protesters also mobilized their resources, took one another into their homes, cooked food that was served communally in the streets, and distributed groceries to community members in need. Do these community actions excuse the state from its responsibility to care for its citizens by improving education, supporting employment opportunities, and, perhaps most obviously in this instance, rethinking the very nature of policing? No, they do not. But as Butler (2015, 84) wrote five years before these events, "in the most ideal instances, an alliance begins to enact the social order it seeks to bring about by establishing its own modes of sociability."

Based on images they see in the media, many people have the sense that protesters are an amorphous mob, looting for their own personal gain; however, the capoeiristas I have interviewed that have taken part in protests or organized their own are hyperattuned to every detail of their engagements, considering both the practical and the symbolic ramifications of the decisions they make. I asked one interlocutor what he would want the world to know about the 2020 protests in Minneapolis. He knew that a lot of people had the mistaken idea that protesters just wanted to burn the city down, that they were indiscriminately and self-destructively destroying property. But he did not find that to be the case. He and others in his circle were tirelessly working on behalf of their community. "There's so many community gardens that have popped up now," he said, giving just one example of the positivity that emerged from the crisis. "It was just so much love, and the strongest sense of community that I felt in this community in a very long time."

Capoeiristas spend countless hours training for the physical aspects of their art, which makes it understandable that the bulk of research to date has focused on what happens inside the academy or even inside the minds of individual practitioners. When we talk about the "small roda" of capoeira being preparation for the "big roda" of life, we are generally talking in abstract terms. The sway of the ginga is a metaphor for how to go with the flow and respond to life's uncertainties with grace and ease. The lack of concern with matching players based on size or gender is a reminder that in life we don't get to choose who our opponents are. We likely will have to go up against someone more powerful than ourselves at some point in our lives. As I have shown in this chapter, however, there is reason to attend to the literal ways in which capoeiristas take their games outside.

When capoeiristas perform in public, they implicitly take responsibility for embodying a tradition that reaches back into Brazil's colonial period. Their bodies also tacitly endorse the messages being presented by their teachers, unless they actively work to subvert that message in some way, which would likely have consequences either inside or outside of the roda. Some groups take their performances of resistance even further, by lending their bodies to organized protests. Just by being present, they help amplify the messages of these protests, which are almost always in service of an oppressed or marginalized group, people who are the modern-day corollary of the enslaved Africans who created capoeira in the first place.

7

JOGUE PRA LÁ

Individual Applications

A group of teenagers are paired off for their next exercise. One person is to do a *meia lua de frente* while the other does a *cocorinha*. If done correctly, the meia lua (half moon kick) will sail harmlessly over the other person's head as they squat down and block their face. In one pair, the person doing the cocorinha has been identified as a suicide risk. The partner doing the kick is quite athletic, but today his balance is off. He wobbles. It looks like he might fall. The person defending is "scared, scared to the point [of being] frozen, like . . . [a] deer in headlights." They are so scared that they are physically incapable of dropping into a squat to get out of the way of the kick. Rene stops the exercise and talks to the pair. "Just put your arm up," he explains, "so that if you do get hit, it'll just hit the arm, it won't hit your face." When it's all over, Rene asks, "So what were you feeling? You looked like you were scared?" The person responds, "Of course I was terrified! I could have gotten killed." And there is the crux of it. "What," Rene prods, "you didn't want to die?"

Rene described this incident for me as a way of explaining how he has used capoeira as a form of therapy. In this case, he was working with young adults at a facility for people with double diagnoses, meaning they have a mental health condition and suffer from substance addiction. By this point, the students were familiar with the basic exercises and accustomed to the way Rene would have them practice and then stop and discuss the issues that came up for them in the course of training. "My head hurts after doing this," someone might say. "What does it feel like?" Rene would query. "It feels like there's just like these [plants that] are growing out of my brain, that's what it feels like." Rene would press further. "Well, what kind of plant? Is it a tree, is it weeds?" The intimacy they shared enabled the participants to use the tangibility of their physical experiences with capoeira as a springboard to more abstract discussions of their mental health and overall wellness.

So, what happened when he called attention to the irony of an apparently suicidal patient being frozen by their fear of "[getting] killed" by their partner's kick? "Boom! Deer in headlights again. The person's frozen, realizing that there's another part of [them], the core part . . . that living animal that does not want to die. And that the idea of ending [their] life was never . . . is not something that they are really all in on." The experience that Rene was able to facilitate through the use of capoeira "allowed them to then come out of that state of suicidality."

The title of this chapter, *jogue pra lá*, is a phrase my capoeira mestre often sings before opening a roda as a reminder that we play capoeira here in the small circle of the roda but also out in the world at large. Sometimes this is literal, like how Rene has incorporated capoeira into his work as a therapist. Other times, it is more metaphorical. "Capoeira [is] a big part of your mindset," Tlaloc told me. "It doesn't mean I'm going around doing kicks everywhere I go," he said. Rather, it's something a person carries with them all of the time.

In this chapter, I showcase less obvious examples of how capoeira relates to the social justice work being undertaken by individuals rather than capoeira groups. They are things that happen behind the scenes, without anyone making a big deal out of them. It is the subtle way the *mentalidade* (mentality or mindset) of capoeira infiltrates an individual's day-to-day life and affects how they relate to others in their families, at their jobs, and in their communities. Oftentimes, the individuals might not recognize what they are doing as justice work at all, but in conversation they professed many of the same underlying attitudes toward marginalized populations (especially members of the African diaspora) as do the more overt social justice warriors. "Capoeira in some way galvanizes you to be a force for change," Rene told me, which I have seen to be true even if people are not aware of it in the moment.

SOCIAL JUSTICE AT WORK

"You can't sell empowerment," Quinten said to me. He was citing a phrase he often uses at work in the marketing division of a high-profile, international NGO. "You can't say, 'I'm going to make you empowered,' it doesn't work. What you *can do* [is say], 'I have a mechanism that causes people to be empowered.'" He was talking about a product his organization makes to help address a humanitarian crisis, but it applies to capoeira as well. "I don't think about social justice when I'm playing capoeira, and I don't really care about doing my capoeira through a march, but it could be that the act of playing capoeira is the mechanism that ignites this in me."

Capoeira attracts a large number of people whose professional work could be classified under the umbrella of "helping professions," which is how Saltão from Grupo de São Miguel described it. You've got doctors, nurses, teachers, social workers, and more who are all drawn to this art. It also attracts many artists, musicians, and other performers. Communities comprising people like this have a different feel than, for instance, a popular branded functional fitness gym that not only originated in the training of elite forces but perpetuates hegemonic masculinity and military fetishism through its excessively intense daily workouts and discourse of training for the zombie apocalypse (see Hejtmanek 2020). When someone like Tlaloc, who has purposefully sought out jobs "geared toward justice," devotes hours every week to training in capoeira, singing its songs, and learning its history, it is easy to see how the lessons learned inside the academy could transfer to his work with youth and vice versa. When he invites his mestre to give a demonstration at the community center where he works, the connection is quite obvious. In other cases, the connection may be less apparent to outside observers but is still palpable to the capoeirista, who carries these lessons forth into the "big roda" of the world at large.

Real change comes when people are in the trenches working to make things happen. Doug admits that he can be a bit judgmental of people who just march or engage in keyboard activism. "Okay," he thinks, "well, I'm glad that you're marching and yelling, but what are you doing about it?" Given his family's origins in Central America, he has been heavily influenced by liberation theology. That kind of grassroots organizing is action oriented, and even if it isn't as visible as a big march, it makes a significant difference in the lives of the people who are engaged through it. "We need doers," he says. "I would rather have a quiet doer than a hundred marchers. I've always had that perspective, that for me, real societal change, combating injustice, requires you to just grind, grind every day, and unglamorously. But I think if you're going to do nothing, then at least marching, I'll support that. The alternative is doing nothing. If you want to protest, fine. But, there's just more that you could do, I think. There is more that we all can do." Doug does attend protests, and like many capoeiristas, he spreads his influence by sharing his views about various issues on social media, but probably the most meaningful forms of activism he engages in happen through his professional work.

Doug was involved in activism during his youth, but this part of his life had fallen to the wayside until he started studying capoeira. Growing up, he was always encouraged "to be involved in social causes, perhaps not social justice per se, but just be of service to society." Like other people I interviewed that are now in or approaching middle age (their forties and fifties), Doug has vivid memories of the United States' first action in Iraq, when he protested alongside other students from his liberal arts college. He also recalls protesting against the anti-immigration and anti–affirmative action rhetoric that characterized the 1990s. After college, though, life got busy. Medical school and residency didn't leave much time for active involvement in social issues. He wound up "downplaying that aspect of [his] life" because he was "so focused on making [his] career happen and struggling through the rigors of medical school." During this time, he also earned a master's degree in public health. Eventually he began practicing medicine and had a family.

Doug conveyed to me the guilt he felt about not being more socially active during this time in his life, which was exacerbated by the overall politically charged climate of the post-9/11 years and life in a community that has a long history of left-leaning activism. To be clear, it wasn't that he turned against this kind of work or adopted any beliefs that were antithetical to social justice, he just felt like there was no space in his life for activism. A lifelong martial artist, Doug didn't discover capoeira until around 2013. As a particularly studious individual, he took it on himself to learn more about the history of capoeira. As mentioned in chapter 4, Doug taught himself Portuguese so he could access even more resources, like dissertations on capoeira, and researched the lyrics his group would sing, which convinced him that capoeira is indeed rooted in resistance.

Doug was bothered by the hypocrisy of US students singing capoeira songs without knowing what they meant. As he realized how difficult it would be to honor the capoeira ancestors if he didn't really understand their legacy, he started reflecting on other areas of his life:

> I saw that there were a lot of contradictions in my own life, similar [to what] I was noticing in the practice of capoeira, contradictions of here's this beautiful thing that we should be honoring all these different aspects [of], and sometimes we don't. Well, in my life, at the same time, here I am, a physician working within a society where a lot of our medical ills are due to societal things that I'm not doing anything about. . . . Now, I feel like I've been more active in being involved in social justice as a physician, and as an academic.

The medical school that he attended was "founded to address a need, to train physicians to address needs in underserved communities." His professional ancestors, so to speak, believed in a social approach to medicine. This experience he had within the realm of capoeira, recognizing the hypocrisy of paying homage to the ancestors without really understanding or continuing their mission, led him to ask: "Am I honoring the training that everybody has been giving me throughout my whole life for my profession? Am I honoring it in my day-to-day work as a physician?" He decided he was not.

Now, Doug is following a path that actively decolonizes medicine by offering his services to the community and listening to community members' needs rather than assuming he knows what is best for them because of his formal medical training. As "a midcareer person that's in the trenches," he hopes that his calls for universal health care will be taken more seriously than they are when made by medical students, "who no one listens to," or by "retired guys that have been part of Doctors Without Borders, who also nobody listens to." He also incorporates this perspective into his work with medical students.

Doug's experience with capoeira provided the gentle nudge he needed to use his professional identity to affect change in the broader community. The primary way he enacts the underlying, justice-oriented ethos of capoeira is through his work, but this goes beyond his role as a clinician. He attends community meetings and uses his power to call attention to issues like Black children's being suspended from school at higher rates than their white peers and the assumption some educators unfortunately have that their Black students will not be high achievers. Doug makes a clear connection between his practice of capoeira and the way he operates in his professional life, yet he is intentional about not bringing that back into the capoeira world because he does not need that validation.

Quinten also sees a connection between his professional life and his experiences with capoeira. At the NGO where he works, he is responsible for leading the engineering and art teams in the execution of the youth-focused, philanthropic projects that he creates. He actually studied anthropology in college before completing a degree in creative writing, so he has an interest in understanding how people work and what motivates them. He has experience with game design, too, so this coupled with his embodied experiences of capoeira and other art forms where sleight of hand is useful has helped him think about how the products the teams design can make prosocial behavior not only fun, but addictive.

To be sure, this is less of an explicit utilization of capoeira than what is on display at a march or protest. Quinten has little interest in using capoeira in those ways. I met other members of his group who do participate in protests, and Quinten says that if he were invited to go along, he might go "just out of loyalty to [his] school," but it isn't something he feels moved to do:

> It actually goes the other way, I think I lose my life as a capoeirista outside of the roda and the things I have learned and the mindset that it puts me in influence how I participate in my social justice. Or even just in my career or everything. So I'm interested in helping people in the world and I'm a capoeirista and I have taken my lessons from that world and apply it all day every day in the world. But . . . for me the act of playing capoeira isn't a social justice act.

So when he is in the roda, he is not thinking about capoeira as an act of social justice, and he doesn't feel particularly motivated to engage in justice work alongside other capoeiristas. Even so, the lessons learned in the roda transfer to other domains of his life (e.g., his job) where he more actively works for change.

THERAPEUTIC APPLICATIONS

Capoeira has inspired Doug and Quinten to advocate for social change through their professions. This is a highly metaphorical application of the mandate to jogue pra lá. Other people, like Rene and Lua Negra, apply capoeira in their professional lives in a much more literal way. Lua Negra, who organized the berimbau march featured in the previous chapter, believes that "capoeira angola is a healing art." He incorporates it in his work as a therapist, counselor, and life coach as "it all falls under the same umbrella." He believes that "because the art itself was birthed from trauma," capoeira can be used to "help people deal with trauma and intergenerational trauma."

Rene's use of capoeira as a form of therapy has become relatively well known within the capoeira community. When I started asking people about capoeira and social justice, it seemed all roads pointed back to him. He himself has experienced trauma in his life, and his recovery has led him to think deeply about how capoeira might be used as a tool to help others. Relatively early on in his exploration of capoeira as therapy, he gave a presentation at a national conference that attracted "activists, direct action people, legal scholars, clergy people." His goal was to showcase capoeira as an organizational strategy that they might be able to utilize in their own work. As he discussed capoeira with the people who attended his workshop, it was impressed on him that capoeira is akin with the work of both Paulo Freire and Augusto Boal: it "shares so much DNA with the methodology of pedagogy and theater of the oppressed. And so, people kept dropping that and bringing it up and were really heated about it and wanted to draw me into more things."

In his studies, Rene found that games like capoeira that involve both a mental and a physical component lead to neurogenesis. When he looks at the variety of approaches that fall under the umbrella term *art therapy*—things like dance therapy, music therapy, Theater of the Oppressed, movement therapy—he sees that capoeira already contains them all. Capoeira has music, movement, and dance, and it is all embedded within a framework of empowering the oppressed. "I didn't have to invent anything," he said, "I just had to be able to identify" the therapeutic elements that already existed within capoeira.

At first glance, Rene's therapeutic application of capoeira might not look much different from an average class. He begins leading the patients through the movements, builds interactions out of those movements, and eventually gets them to the point at which they can play games. But he uses the games as a diagnostic tool. It is not unlike what he would do if he were seated with his therapy patients in a room, having them talk about their concerns. He would watch their body language and try to gauge not only what they are telling him, but what they are showing him with their bodies. Using capoeira, however, opens up additional channels through which he can reach his patients. He has also used capoeira songs as inspiration for an intervention in couples therapy. The two partners each write four lines that they want to communicate to each other. If they happen to be capoeiristas, they'll probably sing these lines like a *ladainha* (the opening litany that praises the ancestors or commemorates some aspect of history). If not, they may have to draw inspiration from an R & B song. The act of singing, rather than just speaking, these lines causes the partner to hear them in a new way, even if these are things they've heard for years.

One setting in which Rene uses this therapy is the residential facility for teens with double diagnoses—mental illness and substance abuse—that features in this chapter's opening vignette. I thought it might have been a tough idea to pitch: let's take kids who are struggling with trauma and teach them to fight. Fortunately, the director of this center, a Brazilian, was familiar with social programs in Brazil that utilize capoeira and was therefore "already of the mindset that capoeira was going to help these kids." This program does not allow Rene to track long-term outcomes of the youth that pass through the facility, and he knows that relapse is part of the recovery process, but he is encouraged when he receives positive feedback and hears that someone is doing well, has finished their term at a sober living facility, or has been reunited with their family.

My interlocutors are not the only ones who have used capoeira in various forms of therapy. For instance, in her interviews with teenage offenders in Canada that had been given the option of completing a capoeira-based rehabilitation program she taught, capoeira scholar Janelle Beatrice Joseph (2015) found that these teenagers made a connection between learning how to get up in the roda, presumably after falling, and learning the more abstract values of humility and resilience. As they learned to construct a beautiful game together and take risks by jumping into the roda even when they felt intimidated or underprepared, they learned the importance of cooperation and taking initiative.

Capoeira's applicability in therapeutic situations is not necessarily unique. Katie Rose Hejtmanek (2016, 313) witnessed something similar in the residential treatment facility she studied when residents would play dodgeball and then "process" the game by "discussing how they felt during it and how dodgeball might be comparable to other difficult life situations and the feelings they might elicit." She also observed that rapping could provide a means of expressing one's feelings rather than fighting, and saw that hip-hop's you-do-you philosophy could provide courage to youth seeking to apply what they learned in therapy, even when those lessons run counter to the norms of their social environments (Hejtmanek 2015, 198). What I find notable is that Rene and Lua Negra each thought of using capoeira in conjunction with their other therapeutic methods without prior knowledge of this work. Something about the art itself—whether that was its origins within an oppressed community or the way it makes visible an individual's interior emotional state—spoke to each of them as having potential to be harnessed for therapeutic purposes.

NEVER *NOT* A CAPOEIRISTA

DaleChé told me about a conversation he once had with someone who asked him to demonstrate a capoeira move. DaleChé said if he were in a fight right now, he would probably just pick up a bottle and use it. The interlocutor objected, saying he wanted to see a *capoeira* move. But DaleChé said that since he's a capoeirista, anything he does is a capoeira move. If we follow this line of reasoning, then no action taken by a capoeirista can be completely divorced from capoeira. If capoeira really is *tudo que a boca come* (all that the mouth eats), as Mestre Pastinha is said to have argued, then not only is any move a capoeirista does a capoeira move, but any form of activism undertaken by a capoeirista might be considered part of capoeira.

Some socially engaged capoeiristas do all, or almost all, of their justice work through capoeira or as representatives of capoeira. Others belong to multiple organizations involved in justice work. In these cases, a capoeirista may take lessons learned inside capoeira and apply them to their work with other organizations. The Brown Berets is a Chicano organization that exists to protect the community. As a member, Tlaloc has attended antiracist rallies and counterprotests whenever the Ku Klux Klan holds an event in his region because the Klan events threaten the security of his community. The Brown Berets provide a first line of defense to keep other protesters safe.

Tlaloc draws inspiration from the structure of the roda to create a community-building experience for the Brown Berets. He isn't teaching them capoeira, but he might say to the people at the protest, "Okay, we're gonna make a circle. And . . . instead of playing a game of capoeira, we're gonna jump in and somebody's gonna shake out their thoughts about this. . . . So some people looking from the outside may not think it's a capoeira circle, but when I'm there, [it is]." None of the other Brown Berets are capoeiristas. A few have tried it but didn't stick with it. Capoeiristas are accustomed to having the efficacy of their art challenged, and Tlaloc's fellow Brown Berets sometimes joke, "If something happens, what are you gonna do? Dance around me?" Fortunately, he's never had to use his fighting skills to physically defend himself or anyone else. However, he has found himself "instinctively" using defensive postures of capoeira when holding the line at a protest, not because things were turning violent per se but as a measured response to the jostling of bodies in a tightly packed space. His training as a capoeirista allowed him to *ginga* (sway) in response to power, both literally and figuratively.

Sometimes it is hard to draw a line between civil disobedience and criminal mischief. In 2017, one week to the day after a violent confrontation between white nationalists and counterprotesters in Charlottesville, Virginia, Elijah was arrested for defacing a Confederate monument. This is something that was done not under the cloak of darkness, but calmly and deliberately in a public place. Video footage of the event shows a man approaching this statue with hammers in his hands, chipping away at the names of soldiers who died defending their so-called right to perpetuate an economic model that rested on the backs of stolen laborers.

Elijah is a white man in his thirties who is something of an outlier in this book because of how overt this one act of antiracist activism was. He is someone I have known for many years, though it wasn't until recently that we had an explicit conversation about racism or the relationship between capoeira and social justice. Elijah feels like his antiracist beliefs were "always kind of there." Or at least they had been "for a really, really long time," even if he couldn't put his finger on the moment when these ideas became clear to him.

Elijah grew up in what he calls "a notoriously white area." And while his family wasn't rich, he says his parents were "well enough off to not get suckered into seeing things the other way," by which he means that they had enough financial security that they didn't buy into the us-versus-them mentality that often pits poor white people against people of color. Elijah believes that "if you're a quote, unquote white male, and you're not avidly antiracist, you're gonna be a racist. Unless you're sweeping yourself constantly to make sure you're not falling into any of that, you're gonna fall into it. It's like standing on quicksand . . . if you just stand still, you're gonna be a white supremacist. You're not even gonna notice it because that's how it really works."

His family members might not support the precise approaches that he uses, but in general they understand his orientation and encourage his antiracist commitments. After all, his parents met through their mutual involvement in activism. Together, they helped stop the construction of a nuclear power plant in their state. His mom even sought out the Black Panthers in a nearby town so she could learn from them. This outlook has been so much a part of his life that when he encounters bigotry and close-mindedness, he thinks, "Are these people joking? Is this just a big joke? Do they really think this?" Unfortunately, he has learned that they do. Elijah more or less went into hiding after the incident because of the vitriol being thrown at him by strangers on the internet. He received multiple death threats after his story was featured on several ultraconservative platforms like *Breitbart*.

In some ways, this action has nothing at all to do with capoeira. Elijah undertook this action as an individual, and in no way did he link this action to his capoeira group or his identity as a capoeirista. At the same time, however, his beliefs about race and racism have been affected by his involvement with a politically engaged, justice-oriented mestre who insists that his students maintain an inclusive, open-minded environment. Thinking about this particular action, Elijah credits capoeira with "getting rid of that fight-or-flight response, like going on autopilot based on an adrenaline rush." Through capoeira he has learned that "you can temper that out and turn it into something. Adrenaline can just be a chunk of metal and then with actual tempering, make it into a sword or any type of implement you need, that works. I was able to go into an area with a notorious white supremacist population and damage something that these people hold dear." This is an idea with resonance in the broader literature on martial arts. Dedicated training can help an individual remain calm in the face of danger, or perceived danger. Although the concept of "no mind" and the importance of Zen Buddhism in many Asian martial arts have been distorted both by time and by Orientalist fascination with the East, samurai training for example did cultivate the mind and body to react to real-time threats on the battlefield without allowing fear of death to cloud one's judgment. Elijah is referring to something similar, even though capoeira is rarely described as a battlefield art. The attainment of mental clarity in the face of danger, which is a common goal of martial arts training, helped Elijah stay focused on his goal without being distracted by the bystanders who were watching, filming, and condemning his actions. To be clear, this is the only case I recorded of a capoeirista undertaking illegal action in pursuit of social justice causes, and he did so as an individual rather than as a representative of his group. Yet it speaks to the ways in which some individuals may choose to take what they learn as members of the capoeira community and abstractly apply it in more public settings.

Some people I interviewed shied away from making an explicit connection between their activism and their experiences as capoeiristas. Both of these things are important parts of their identities, but they don't integrate them to the same degree that other people in my sample do. One member of Grupo de São Miguel even framed her participation in capoeira as a necessary respite from the stress and burnout that come from a career in activism and social organizing. Yet the reason she gravitated toward capoeira rather than something like yoga is its history of resisting oppression, a position that she spontaneously offered in a class I just happened to be observing. When I followed up with her, she said that yoga has become "too bougie," divorced from its roots and done in high-end studios by upper-middle-class women in expensive workout gear. She could have chosen virtually any sport or hobby to get her mind off of work, but even her choice between the two competing capoeira groups in town reflects her value system. She intentionally chose the group whose training space was less polished and whose online photos reflected more ethnic diversity. Even if individuals like her don't think of their work in social justice as being directly related to their training in capoeira, there tends to be a dialectical relationship between these different parts of their lives.

CONCLUSION

"Don't isolate the knowledge that comes from capoeira to the roda," attendees were told during a capoeira Zoom evento held on Juneteenth 2020. "Take it into the real world and vice versa." When I spoke to my own mestre a few months later, he reiterated this idea that you need to apply what you learn in capoeira to the rest of your life. That, for him, is the hallmark of someone who really understands capoeira. He has worked with students who are excellent technicians, and who may even be good teachers of the physical aspects of capoeira, but who fail to integrate capoeira into their lives. That's something that goes beyond making time and space in one's life to train, though that certainly matters to him too. For him, a real capoeirista enacts the metaphorical aspects of capoeira in everyday life and navigates the world with the affective habitus described in chapter 3.

In chapter 2, I broadly defined social justice as any number of caring and compassionate efforts to disrupt and subvert social structures that perpetuate inequality. These efforts are undertaken intentionally to rectify a perceived wrong, an instance of injustice that exists because society has allowed it to be so. In popular discourse, social justice activism is often presented as something that is done in the public sphere. For example, attending a defund police rally is a visible action some activists—including several people profiled in this book—take in response to instances of police brutality. Yet not all forms of justice work are so overt.

Someone doesn't stop being a capoeirista when they change into street clothes. It is an identity and a way of being that is carried into one's workplace, community, and home. In much the same way that Rene wants people to bring their baggage into capoeira so that it can be examined and dissected in the roda, so too should they take what they learn inside the roda and apply it in their day-to-day lives. Lessons learned in one context can transfer into another, whether that means using the capoeirista's sleight of hand to create an almost addictive philanthropy experience like Quinten does or following Doug's example of rooting out hypocrisy in his profession.

The stories in this chapter show how capoeiristas have been affected by their participation in this art and how they take their social and ideological commitments, which have been influenced by capoeira, out into a larger arena. The link between the individual acts they perform in this arena and capoeira may be tenuous, but it nonetheless surfaced in the course of our conversations. Capoeira may not be the singular influence that causes them to take such actions, but it influences how they construct their actions and reconstruct them through narrative. Even so, however, not all capoeiristas make this connection, and the disconnects and even instances of injustice within the capoeira community are the subject of the next chapter.

8

CHALLENGES TO THE
SOCIAL JUSTICE PERSPECTIVE

It was at a poetry reading that Lua Negra finally met someone who did capoeira, this thing he'd been wanting to do since he first watched *Only the Strong* at age eleven. "Man, I can't wait to learn to do a backflip," he tells her. She puts him in contact with her teacher. He begins training and falls in love with capoeira angola. "So are we going to learn how to do backflips?" Lua Negra asks his teacher for the umpteenth time. "Yeah, yeah, yeah, yeah," his teacher responds, clearly blowing him off yet again. Finally, Lua Negra realizes he's been subjected to "some type of Jedi shit." "We're not going to do backflips. Right?" "No." They may look cool and be fun to do, but for an angoleiro, flips are unnecessary and potentially dangerous because your feet could be so easily swept from underneath you. They're flashy, but they're not where the real work of outmaneuvering your opponent gets done.

Lua Negra is all about inclusivity, in the roda and in society at large. The march he organized to agitate for police reform and accountability after George Floyd's murder ended with a roda. All sorts of people participated. Most were capoeiristas, as one would expect given that most people were carrying berimbaus, but some friends and family attended too. At the end of the march, Lua Negra asked whether people wanted to have a roda. Not only had their collective action built up the axé (energy), but people had been cooped up for months because of the pandemic. They were happy to be outside and eager to play together. There were angoleiros as well as people who play contemporânea and regional. Lua Negra thought about announcing that all were welcome, but ultimately decided it was unnecessary: "No, you don't have to say, 'this is all inclusive.' This is all-inclusive art. It's like this movement."

The closing roda was philosophy in motion. Everyone played together, regardless of level and regardless of style. Most importantly, it stayed grounded. "Meet the person where they're at," Lua Negra advises, but "yeah, no backflips."

Like with so many capoeiristas, Lua Negra's imagination was captured by the cool moves he saw in a film. Eventually, he came to realize that capoeira could be a form of therapy and a tool for social justice. Not everyone who plays capoeira—in the United States or elsewhere—is going to have this same orientation. Although there is strong evidence to support my claim that many capoeiristas in the United States utilize the art and its foundational myths as a springboard for local social action, others just want to do backflips. Or maybe they want to play the music, learn Portuguese, make friends, or lose weight. This chapter, which is necessarily broad, presents a slightly different view of present-day capoeira. Not only are some groups completely apolitical, but certain practices within even the most justice-oriented groups are downright antithetical to the ethos of capoeira as an art of resistance.

GETTING A CAPOEIRA BODY

Even one woman who is extremely vocal on the subject of female empowerment in and through capoeira jokingly admitted to me that the prospect of getting to hug shirtless men with cut abs on a regular basis was part of what motivated her to train in capoeira (see Hedegard 2013 on the fetishization of the Black male body in capoeira). Capoeira does tone the body, and in an era of rampant childhood obesity, heart disease, diabetes, and other illnesses either brought about or exacerbated by lack of physical activity, I am not going to cast aspersions on anyone's reasons for taking up a new sport. Training in capoeira can improve cardiovascular fitness, increase flexibility, promote muscle development, and support hand-eye coordination. It also contributes to individuals' sense of self-efficacy. All these are perfectly valid reasons for pursuing a new activity, and yet, for some, to disengage from the issues of oppression and resistance is to practice an incomplete version of capoeira.

Despite assurances of anonymity, it was rare for anyone I interviewed to outright condemn the apolitical capoeira groups or people who are just interested in the fitness aspects of capoeira. Like Riser, they often said something along the lines of, "that's fine, everything is cool, there's space for everything." But they also made clear that at least for them, this would eventually ring hollow, and that if capoeira were reduced to just a physical art, it would eventually lose its hold on them. They would become bored and move on to something else. Riser said, "many people approach me and either they admire the work that I do because they feel like capoeira has become so gentrified, like sexy dance fighting or something to keep them in shape. Or it's whatever cool movement is popping now." He doesn't have any hostility toward those who practice an apolitical capoeira, but he would not want to see the social field become overwhelmed by people who are only interested in its physical aspects.

Kesler, a published author whose writings on Black masculinity stem from both personal experience and his doctoral training, used to be frustrated with people who he thought didn't engage enough with the history and culture of capoeira. In fact, it is why he left one of the better-known international organizations, a franchise that is known for producing skilled players with a unique stylistic signature. He sought out a different mestre, someone he thought could help him in his quest to "create a group that really uplifted the culture, really understood the roots of capoeira and embraced it." Now, however, he is more relaxed in his attitude. He personally believes in the transformative power of capoeira, but when it comes to other people, he says, "I could care less why you train capoeira. I know why I train capoeira, that's all that matters to me."

Rene similarly argues that as a teacher, "you have to honor the reason that anybody comes to train, to learn capoeira." For his own part, he believes that when we look at the history of capoeira, "there's nothing else besides revolution and sticking up for people's rights, the common good, and for nature and the environment. That is the ethos of capoeira." If they just want to come for the workout, that's their business, but they're still being given the opportunity to learn about its deeper aspects just by being in the environment he creates. "Not everybody who does capoeira is ready for all of capoeira," he says, but teachers like Rene who are committed to passing on the legacy of enslaved Africans' resistance through capoeira will be there if and when those students do become ready.

APOLITICAL TEACHERS AND GROUPS

Riser, Kesler, and Rene are all teachers with a personal commitment to social justice who are accepting of students with many different motivations for training. In time, some of their formerly apolitical students may become "woke"; others will not. Then there are teachers who create apolitical capoeira groups, either intentionally, because they think politics has no place inside the roda, or unintentionally, because they themselves are not particularly invested in the idea of capoeira as an art of resistance.

Obviously, one doesn't have to promote capoeira as a tool of social justice in order to do good things with it. When we spoke on his podcast, *Capoeira Connection*, Cory explained, "we haven't ever really used capoeira or our group as a method of resistance or protest." And yet, when I pressed him to describe the free classes his group offers for kids in lower-income parts of his city, his description was not terribly different from what Riser does in his community or what I saw my own mestre do. By targeting these specific communities for outreach, teachers are at least implicitly recognizing and seeking to address inequities, yet nothing in his answer about why his group provides youth classes as part of an after-school program related back to the origin story about capoeira being an art of resistance. Rather, the focus is on following the example one's mestre has set and doing good for others because it feels good or is the right thing to do. His group is doing wonderful work but in a far less overtly politicized manner than are others.

The first time I visited Os Provocadores, I was told that a lot of groups will kick you out if you bring politics into capoeira. DaleChé, who started the local chapter of this group, assured me that this was true, but also said that if you're not talking about the political implications of what you're doing, then you're not really doing capoeira. I agree with him. This particular group is known for its strong Afrocentric orientation and is sometimes (I would say mistakenly) accused of being exclusionary, but I have found its members to be nothing but genuinely warm and welcoming, their pride in Black culture a proportionate response to living in a racist society.

Geoff, who is in a much more left-leaning city than is DaleChé (a city with a long history of political activism), did not mention anyone getting kicked out of his group for bringing in politics. Rather, what he sees is a tendency among others to construct the capoeira school as a refuge from activism. Perhaps these people engage in other forms of activism outside of capoeira, whether in their workplaces or with friends and family, and therefore want capoeira to be the place where they don't have to think about social justice. "Capoeira's not that for me. Capoeira is for me to just go and get away from things and express myself," he characterizes them as thinking. Granted, the luxury of escaping from talk about race, racism, power, and privilege is something not everyone enjoys, and Geoff was quick to point out that some people are resistant to the justice-oriented innovations like codes of conduct his group has introduced because they are invested in maintaining the power they hold over subordinate members of the capoeira community.

Running an apolitical capoeira group doesn't necessarily mean shutting down conversations about politics or social issues. In Barrett's academy, political conversations sometimes happen on the margins of class time. He maintains that "capoeira is a vehicle . . . to make people better people, and if that includes having political discussions, as long as everybody can be respectful, I have no problem with that." But he holds firm to the idea that class time is for training, and for him, that means movement and music, not ideology or activism. Barrett doesn't disavow political behavior or antiracist activism, but he disassociates that part of his life from his work as a capoeirista. While capoeira is a passion for him, it is also work, his job, a way to pay the bills. Some people have criticized him for this, particularly because he is a white man profiting from a Black art. His relative silence on certain social issues also creates a vacuum, leading capoeiristas from other groups to make assumptions about his political leanings that may or may not be correct. Yet he remains unapologetic. After all, he never set out to build a consciousness-raising organization; he sought to make a living for himself and his family.

COUNTEREXAMPLES AND IRONIES

In response to a query I posted on Facebook, one capoeirista—who incidentally is himself very politically aware and steeped in the literature on the African diaspora—expressed a recognition that capoeira may value resisting oppression, but stated that merely singing about slavery or inequality does not solve the contemporary manifestations of these problems. There is a good deal of truth to this; many groups perform the product of resistance (i.e., capoeira) without it being performative, meaning it fails to bring about a new state of being. Some students, teachers, and groups simply are not interested in engaging with capoeira as a form of resistance, which is their prerogative. In this section, however, I want to acknowledge that there are at least some capoeiristas who—despite singing about the *orixás* (gods and goddesses in the Candomblé religion) or parroting the foundational myths about enslaved Africans using capoeira as an art of resistance—fail to see how oppression operates in their own society and may inadvertently perpetuate it even within their own communities of practice.

No one in the capoeira community should have been caught off guard by what happened to George Floyd. Or Breonna Taylor. Or Philando Castile. Or Eric Garner. Or any of the other Black people who have been murdered by someone who either actively abused their power or let implicit assumptions cloud their judgment in a situation that ultimately only had life-or-death consequences for one party. No one should have been surprised. And yet they were.

Bram's frustration was palpable as he described how many capoeiristas in his network were shocked by what happened to George Floyd. For these students, all of whom are white, "this situation was so jarring, so mind-blowing" that they struggled to comprehend it. For him, sadly, it was not at all surprising. In the summer of 2020, most of the capoeira community probably could have been divided into two groups: those who were already "woke" and therefore not surprised by what happened to George Floyd, and those who were shaken because they didn't grasp the pervasiveness of structural racism and implicit bias in our society despite practicing an art form that traces its roots back to the actions of enslaved Africans. Some of those in the second group were in the right place at the right time to connect the dots and become activists. No doubt many people in both categories made blunders and explicitly or implicitly asked their Black camaradas to do the emotional labor of educating them about racism. Some Black capoeiristas accepted that burden, but the expectation that Black people will educate the white capoeiristas in their groups should still be recognized for the microaggression it is.

Beyond such microaggressions, there were some more blatant aggressions throughout the entire capoeira community that highlight the unevenness of the affective habitus I have been describing. When a semitruck on Interstate 35 failed to stop before reaching a crowd of protesters, Bram heard that one capoeira instructor made a disparaging reference to "all those monkeys on the bridge." Not only did this teacher thus signal her lack of support for the Black Lives Matter cause, but she also employed one of the longest-standing and most odious caricatures of Blackness. I was told that her mestre kicked her out of the group because of her statement, but it stands to reason that she is not the only one with these kinds of opinions.

After telling me about that incident, Bram recalled how other capoeiristas he knows laughed about an encampment for the unsheltered being forcibly closed by the authorities. Though he wasn't there for the conversation on the day the camp was finally cleared, he saw some of it on video:

> I see capoeiristas and they're just laughing. Some people, it's almost an absolute refusal to get it. It's like . . . how can you sing about quilombos and then not have empathy for people who are essentially living in a quilombo? . . . It really made me. . . . I try not to be judgmental. I try to be very fair, but it really made me see a lot of people very differently after that because not

only is that . . . that was something that I take very seriously. But capoeira's something I take very seriously. And I feel like it's not just a disconnect, but a blatant disrespect to see that type of oppression, to see that type of injustice, and mock it, and laugh at the people who are being victimized.

The inability of some capoeiristas to make this connection between modern-day situations and historical events within capoeira is not just ironic but painful for capoeiristas who consider it the absolute core of their practice.

There is a fine line between wanting capoeira to be an apolitical space and causing additional harm by refusing to see the oppressive practices happening in one's midst. When I was at Riser's evento where he screened a film on gender-based discrimination in capoeira, I happened to briefly chat with Darrias. He is a man training in a hyper–politically engaged part of the country among a lot of activists, and yet he still expressed discomfort with the politicization of capoeira. He did express interest in how capoeira could be used to support local communities—or at least he said he was interested in the Brazilian mestres' perspectives on that issue—but he had no interest in engaging with the identity politics of capoeira itself. Despite having just been presented with evidence of gender-based discrimination happening both in Brazil and in the United States, he clung to his own counternarrative that men experience just as much violence in the roda as do women, perhaps even more because people are more likely to be gentle with female players. He seemed to have completely missed the film's point about the barriers to advancement women face within capoeira, as well as the issue that the women in the audience raised during the Q and A session about the pervasiveness of sexual harassment within capoeira.

For teachers committed to social justice, there is a question of how to help students see the acts of injustice in front of them without ironically abusing their own power by imposing their beliefs on others. "Please come and explain the *emboscada* [ambush attack]," Rene says, calling Riser up to the front of the room. Riser is well versed in this tradition and eager to share the special knowledge he has acquired through Mestre Bimba's son Mestre Nenel. The emboscada is the stuff of legends. Before Mestre Bimba would award his students the silk scarf that could purportedly protect their throats from being sliced in a knife fight, the students would be sent out into the forest, where they would have to defend themselves from an ambush attack, not knowing when or from what direction the attack would come. Rene's students tend to enjoy the martial side of capoeira so they, and the others attending the evento, are excited. As Riser explains, they stand and wait, thinking, "Oh, this is great. We're going to throw each other around." The doors close; the locks click into place. Sit down, everybody. Rene has the floor again. This is the ambush: "We're going to talk about something none of you want to talk about." And thus begins a discussion unpacking the nuances of consensual sex and respectful dating within the context of capoeira.

Rene created a learning environment in which participants at the evento were forced to experience what might have been an uncomfortable conversation. The attendees had implicitly consented to participate in the activities that Rene organized for his evento just by being there, but had they consented to this particular conversation about consent? I have the utmost respect for both Rene and Riser, but I highlight the potential irony of this incident because it raises larger questions about how teachers should use their influence to create a more just community.

When I spoke to my own mestre, he said that he is "getting more strict with [his] capoeira." When I was actively training with his group, the principles of social justice were always in the background and would sometimes surface during the speeches he would make before performances, but social justice wasn't something that needed to be explicated often because we were all on the same page already, or at least I had the impression that we were. Today, however, he frequently finds himself lecturing his students about social issues. "That's my way actually to bring consciousness and social justice now to my white students," he says. "If you guys [disagree], this is not the right place for you . . . you should go [take] a jiu-jitsu class . . . because [this is] not the right place for you to learn capoeira."

My mestre didn't demand that anyone accompany him to the Black Lives Matter march after George Floyd's murder, but he tells them explicitly that if they don't support movements like Black Lives Matter, then his class is not the right place for them to be. And some of them do leave. He's also not afraid to kick people out if they express homophobic beliefs. He holds a hard line because he believes that a capoeirista must stand against injustice in all its forms, and that extends beyond race-based activism. In his words, "every struggle, every fight, gotta to be the same fight. You cannot push the LGBT people away and say Black lives matter. Everyone's got to be together." By taking a more active role in cultivating the affect of his group, he makes it a safe space for marginalized and underrepresented peoples. Yet at the same time, he is using his position of power to inhibit beliefs out of alignment with his own, which some might consider to be oppressive.

In some cases, a group can have great intentions of using capoeira to serve the community but execute the plan in such a way that it causes harm to people within the group. Take Jordan's group, whose Brazilian mestre focuses his outreach on youth. Jordan thinks this is "a beautiful mission." He explains: "I have no qualms with it. That's what they decided to pursue and use capoeira for. It's gorgeous. I have no issue. The only problem is that in order to do that, they feel that they have to push under the rug, or at least keep more quiet or more esoteric, the references to African culture." They still sing about the orixás, but it is presented as folkloric color more than as spiritual or social commitment.

Within the group, there is a subset of people whom Jordan characterizes as being strongly "pro-Black" and "pro–social justice," himself included. They feel alienated by the leadership's adoption of color-blind rhetoric and unwillingness to see that the most vulnerable youth in their community happen to be youth of color. So while the group is engaged in outreach work, its focus on a single issue (youth empowerment) without an accompanying acknowledgment that racism affects different groups of youth differently—or an interest in understanding why the African Americans in the group (and a small handful of sympathetic white allies) would want to focus their outreach on Black neighborhoods and Black youth—is a manifestation of white supremacy.

SEXUAL HARASSMENT AND OTHER ABUSES

In January 2019, I attended a performance that Grupo de São Miguel put on at a local community center. The audience mainly consisted of elementary schoolchildren as well as some senior citizens to whom the show had been marketed. The program was roughly an hour long and included several different scenes. Some presented movement for movement's sake (e.g., a samba demonstration), and others had a plot.[1] One scene in particular is worth examining closely both because it challenged some of the taken-for-granted norms about gender that have been dominant within capoeira since its inception and because it cleverly played on what Grupo de São Miguel knew about its audience's expectations in order to do so. I was a plant. Deacon asked me that morning to make sure I really played up my shock at the pivotal moment in the skit. But as it turned out, there was no need.

Approximately halfway through the show, the curtain rises on a roda made up entirely of men wearing jeans and formfitting white tank tops. Then a woman walks onstage, with nothing to suggest that she is a capoeirista. Two men are playing in the center of the ring. When they catch sight of her, the game in progress is abandoned and one player starts showing off his moves for her. Her body language suggests that she is impressed, but before he has a chance to capitalize on the impression he has made, the other man displaces him and starts showing off his moves. The woman is even more impressed by this guy, and pantomimes holding a phone to her ear, inviting him to call her. Then, a third capoeirista enters the ring and shows off his moves. The woman is so impressed that she walks offstage with him arm in arm. Not content to have yielded the competition for her affection to this interloper, however, the original two players come after the victor. He turns around and kicks one of the men, who falls to the ground. Rather than being concerned by this display of violence in her new beau, the woman demurely smiles and takes his arm and they exit stage left together.

The scene was cute, and well played by everyone involved. The audience loved it. And yet when I saw it the night before, during the dress rehearsal, I felt vaguely unsettled, though I could not put my finger on why. I had to interrogate my own discomfort at the scene. After all, it has all the markings of a classic hero tale. Men do manly things to demonstrate to one another and a female onlooker that they are worthy suitors. A woman is (indirectly) threatened when the defeated wannabe lovers come after the new couple. The hero further solidifies his worthiness by subduing the two others, who have breached the apparent norms of what is considered a fair fight for winning the lovely maiden's hand. So, what was it that bothered me?

Beyond the practical circumstances of the dress rehearsal—the main character's post-skit monologue was abbreviated in the interest of time, meaning that I lacked some of the framing the audience would receive in the show—I found the connection between love and violence to be potentially dangerous. I assume that I was more concerned with the heteronormative underpinnings of this skit than were most of the audience members, but what really stood out to me was the way in which it seemed to be reinforcing a common problem in capoeira today. Many women, and some men, I interviewed through this project have told me stories about male capoeiristas exploiting their power to coerce women into sexual relationships. This skit seemed to reinforce the stereotype of the sex-driven African/Latino male and the passive, receptive female. I was initially taken aback because I know this group to be keenly aware of gender dynamics within capoeira and supportive of female capoeiristas. The group has one of the largest, most diverse, and most skilled assemblage of women capoeiristas I have had the pleasure of meeting, and the group takes steps to actively protect female students from predatory capoeiristas at large eventos. What I grasped upon further reflection was that this skit *intentionally* brought up those themes so that they could be challenged in the next scene. When the skit is considered in its entirety, rather than as an isolated "meet-cute" scene, it becomes clear that the performance does indeed fit with the group's commitment to gender equity.

In the next scene, Deacon is playing the berimbau and another man is playing the *atabaque* (drum). The victor from the previous scene strolls in with the woman in much the same way two lovers in Brazil would take an evening *passeio* (stroll) through the plaza, focused on their own pleasure but also performing conspicuous coupling. When they reach the two capoeiristas, the beau motions to Deacon, silently asking to be given the berimbau. He plays, and while proficient, his performance is not virtuosic by any means. Then the woman reaches for the berimbau, indicating her desire for a chance to play. She is denied. Deacon even laughs at her and waves his hand dismissively. Again, she tries, using an even more exaggerated tap on her lover's shoulder, and again she is denied. She takes a few steps away and gathers her loose hair into a ponytail. She means business, and a few members of the audience seem to sense what is about to happen.

Unable to acquire the berimbau through polite (i.e., socially acceptable) means, the woman simply grabs it out of his hands. This is where I was told to react loudly, signaling a breach of etiquette. In truth, there was no need for me to do that because the audience did react strongly. But rather than sounding shocked or miffed by her obvious breach of norms, the audience members sounded satisfied and approving, even applauding her. She strikes the wire ever so hesitantly, shrinking back from the sound it makes, and the men laugh at her. But in her next attempt, she nails the basic rhythm, performs variations on it, and ends with a little flourish of a kick in the general direction of the men, who have by this point stepped back to look at her with wonder. She starts again, moving to the front of the stage, and this time smugly overpronounces the word "berimbau" in a mockery of the way Deacon had taught the audience the word just ten minutes or so earlier. One by one, all the women in the show come onto the stage, and the men retreat to the wings. Thus begins a skilled musical performance with a number of different songs, most notably "Gunga é meu" (Gunga is mine).

I had asked the star of this skit earlier that morning whether the choice of "Gunga é meu" was intentional. She said that it was more of a coincidence. I told her that in Brazil I had once seen a skilled African American man try to take the *gunga* (the largest and most authoritative of all three berimbaus) during a roda. He was denied, and then the person leading the roda began singing "Gunga é meu," which I took as a dismissal of the American's legitimacy and right to lead the roda. This prompted her to tell me that a similar thing used to happen to her all the time, and she knew it was because she was a woman.

As the curtain closed on the all-female orchestra, the woman from the skit stepped through to address the audience directly. During dress rehearsal the night before, she had skipped over the specifics of what she was planning to say, so I was extremely interested in hearing her speak. I was not surprised when she translated the title of the song and told the audience that there was a time in capoeira's history when women were prevented from playing but that through their perseverance and refusal to passively comply, capoeira was now open to anyone.

These scenes provided comic relief in the middle of the performance, but they also hinted at more troubling issues within capoeira. Most women I have interviewed mention their gender as a determining factor in how they experience capoeira. Almost all can relate to having to work harder than their male counterparts to receive the same recognition and respect, but several also discussed sexual harassment and predatory behavior. Instances of injustice within the capoeira community came up spontaneously in approximately 90 percent of the interviews I conducted for this project; most of those had to do with sex- or gender-based discrimination. Some comments I heard were irritating but not necessarily cause for serious alarm: Lucha, upon expressing frustration with the lack of female representation in the roda, was told by an extremely high-profile Brazilian mestre that women just needed to train harder and play better. Others were more nefarious: stories of mestres abusing their power by pursuing relationships with underage victims, who are legally unable to consent to a sexual relationship with an adult.

Any slight, no matter how seemingly small or insignificant, can hurt, and over time the combined weight of these microaggressions creates a climate that is oppressive. This book is focused on the diverse ways in which capoeiristas use their art as a tool for countering oppression, and I simply do not have space here to go into any real depth regarding the injustices that occur within capoeira itself. This is something that needs to be addressed further, and something that I focus on in other writings. Some capoeiristas are already tackling these issues within their own groups, often at great personal cost. When Lucha blew the whistle on some abuses, she was kicked out of her group and ostracized. And she is not the only one to have experienced this.

The hurt and anger that have resulted from these abuses cannot be overstated, and I am doing a disservice by mentioning them so briefly, but I would be doing even more harm by leaving them out entirely. Some groups have started requiring that students sign a code of conduct agreement. Others have pledged to only invite teachers "of character" to their eventos, or to intentionally bring more female teachers to their eventos so that they normalize female leadership. Some known abusers have been uninvited from eventos they were scheduled to attend. Of course, they sometimes show up anyway, and at one evento, I witnessed multiple people leave because of a certain individual's arrival. The organizer was in a bind. He holds the professor rank; the offender is a mestre. Many martial arts are characterized by extreme deference to those in higher ranks, but it is ironic that in capoeira—an art that claims to be rooted in the resistance of oppression—this structure would be used to protect abusers.

CONCLUSION

In the course of doing this research, I occasionally questioned my own premise. Is it true that capoeira as practiced in the United States includes a social justice component, or is this merely something I wanted to see in the data? Did I just happen to start my training with politically active groups and then keep running into like-minded people as I developed my research project? Perhaps it was just luck that the first group of capoeiristas I met happened to be communards living in a city that is known to be (and proud of being) "weird." Maybe it was a coincidence that the second group I joined was also politically engaged. At that time, our country was engaged in a war that many found unjust, and we were on the cusp of electing the United States' first Black president, so maybe everyone was political. Furthermore, both of these groups were located in university towns, and both universities were known to be the more liberal arts–oriented (and politically liberal) flagship institutions in their respective (conservative) states.

What erased my concerns was how quickly I identified individuals in roughly a dozen states who were doing this kind of work. Many of these states were traditionally "red" states with patterns of conservative politics, where I did not expect to find much left-leaning activism. Yet I also realize that not every capoeirista or capoeira group is committed to the principles of social justice, and injustice can be found in even the most woke group. This chapter has only scratched the surface of the gender-based discrimination and harassment that is unfortunately common in capoeira, and that needs to be further researched and theorized. There are also people who want to more aggressively pursue justice work through capoeira but feel constrained in some way.

The constraints may be fiscal, or the group may lack access to some other resource like a physical meeting/training space or a mestre who is willing to sponsor group members and their interests. Sometimes people have a special issue that they care deeply about, but they cannot get the rest of their group onboard. This is especially difficult in cases like Jordan's, where the issue he and his fellow students care deeply about (outreach in communities of color) is at odds with the color-blind worldview held by his Brazilian mestre, who holds far more power within the social field than does he. Sometimes a teacher may have a wonderful vision for the group, but the students are too busy with other responsibilities to put in the time it would take to bring this vision to fruition. In yet other instances, committed activists shy away from taking public actions because they fear repercussions like being arrested or physically harmed at a protest.

This is an especially poignant fear for capoeiristas of color, whose bodies are more at risk in such situations. Whereas Elijah, who allegedly defaced the Confederate monument, views his whiteness as a form of "active camouflage" that facilitates more radical activism, OC and other Black men I interviewed expressed concern that participating in a protest could turn deadly for them. When someone in OC's group proposed going to a protest for prison reform, he had to remind them that "this whole getting arrested thing is not viable for us," meaning the Black capoeiristas in the group. In that instance, the good-intentioned rush to do something had to be tempered with an understanding of the consequences of certain political actions. Overt participation in protests and social justice movements is also of higher risk for capoeiristas whose employment depends on having a clear background check, and these constraints shape the ways in which they express their social justice commitments.

To return to where Lua Negra was at that poetry reading so many years ago, some people just want to do backflips. Though the people I have worked with for several years choose to engage with the philosophical and ideological underpinnings of the art, this does not make it wrong for others to have a different relationship with capoeira. It is beautiful and fun; it is a great way to get in shape and to meet friends. Many people train for these reasons alone and are fully satisfied with their experiences. Yet even the most purportedly apolitical capoeiristas are still lending their bodies to the perpetuation of a Black art that the Brazilian government once tried to quell. As Tlaloc said, "the fact that it's still around, to me, is part of that resistance movement." Or as Lucha reminded me, just playing in a neoliberal society that demands constant productivity and hustle is a form of resistance. Even without meaning to endorse any particular vision of social justice, capoeiristas contribute to the African diaspora's ongoing struggles against both co-optation and erasure.

9

BOA VIAGEM

Activism will look different for everyone. Zenzele Isoke (2011, 117) defines "homeplaces" as "political spaces that black women create to express care for each other and their communities, and to re-member, revise, and revive scripts of black political resistance." What has been seen by many white feminists as the embodiment of patriarchal oppression—domestic labor and homemaking—is a liberatory tool in the hands of women who have been differently positioned vis-à-vis the society in which they live. The work of the Black female activists that Isoke interviewed does not end in the domestic realm; rather, homeplaces are important components of the overall landscape of Black activism. Similarly, scholars risk missing an important site of activist work if they only view leisure communities as ludic spaces where people "recharge" so that they can carry out the work demanded of them in their jobs and families. Leisure communities are a third space, neither work nor home, that can also serve as a political space. They are no less fruitful for not fitting traditional visions of activism.

Martial arts provide people with skills that are supposed to transfer into other arenas of their life, both literally and figuratively. That is one reason they are so successfully marketed to children (or their parents). This transference often draws on metaphors about dedication, discipline, and self-control. This happens in capoeira too, but the frequent references to Brazilian slavery and capoeira as an art of resistance alter practitioners' underlying emotional orientation to the world in a distinctive manner. In this vein, Paul H. Mason (2013, 4) writes, "the search for freedom of the African slaves in the history of Brazil is a potent metaphor for Capoeira performers who search for physical freedom in the confining space of the roda." However, I see much more than a metaphorical search for freedom in the groups that have opened their doors to me and the individuals who have reached out to share their stories about social justice.

Drawing from J. Lowell Lewis's (1992) excellent history of capoeira, Sophie Fuggle (2008, 207) argues that "capoeira is no longer about literal liberation from slavery yet the emancipation of the Afro-Brazilian slaves continues to operate as a metaphor for one's personal liberation from the constraints and limitations imposed not by slaveowner or plantation foreman but by one's social, financial and familial obligations." This is true, and yet going too far in the metaphorical direction risks equating all forms of personal struggle. Certainly, one can feel oppressed by the weight of a soul-crushing nine-to-five job in the corporate sector, but this is not the same as the fear a Black mother has for her son every time he leaves her home to navigate a sociopolitical system that disproportionately incarcerates Black men.

There is a fairly widespread assumption that capoeira angola is the more politicized version of capoeira. Most angola groups I have encountered are fairly politicized; however, it would be a mistake to assume that capoeiristas in the regional and contemporânea traditions are unconcerned with political issues and social justice. It may not be as closely linked in their institutional histories as it is in capoeira angola, thanks in large part to the personal ideological commitments of Mestre Moraes—who spearheaded the revitalization of capoeira angola in the 1980s against the backdrop of Brazil's growing Black pride movement—but it is still present in many groups I have come to know through this project. Bram, Deacon, Francis, Imani, Rene, and Riser are all examples of teachers in the regional and contemporânea traditions who take this work seriously.

Through a mixture of oral history and academic writing on the topic, the idea that regional is a whitened form of capoeira has crystalized into an apparent truth. Based on several conversations I have had with a teacher in Mestre Bimba's lineage, my understanding is that Mestre Bimba did take great pains to demonstrate to the government and the world at large that capoeira was a respectable art and had something beneficial to offer everyone. Some of these steps included the introduction of a streamlined pedagogy with assessments and markers of progress as well as an insistence on formal dress for public presentations and a requirement that students at his academy either be gainfully employed or attending school. These restrictions would have skewed the demographics of his academy, which is the justification typically given for calling regional whitened, but this does not mean Mestre Bimba had given up caring for the Black community. According to my interlocutor, Mestre Bimba wanted to show that capoeira was "something not just done by ruffians in the street," but at the same time he was not exclusionary and gave free classes in his neighborhood, which would have been predominately Afro-Brazilian. Improving access to capoeira and preserving African traditions within the practice of capoeira may not have been conceptualized by Mestre Bimba as a form of social justice (and it would be irresponsible to impose this modern-day concept on historical actors in early twentieth-century Brazil), but it is also a mistake to assume that angoleiros are the only ones who meld this political consciousness with their practice of capoeira.

A person who spends any time at all with Riser will come to appreciate his pride in being Black and the care with which he teaches his students about the importance of preserving African heritage. Sometimes he talks about these things explicitly, but just including Diaspora arts like the dance forms *maculêlê* and *puxada de rede* in his curriculum enculturates his students into a particular worldview. He says, "it's in the day-to-day things that [this worldview] becomes a part of you." The pride he has in capoeira and in African contributions to world culture more broadly affects his pedagogical

A group of evento participants practicing the puxada de rede dance. Photo by the author.

decisions, which in turn shape his students' affective habitus. And while novices need more explicit instruction about the history of capoeira and its connection to modern-day struggles, in more established groups with steady membership, this may already be a part of their shared understanding and orientation to the art, making explicit discussion of it unnecessary.

The teacher typically sets the tone and determines the ends to which capoeira is used by a particular group, but even in the absence of a teacher who uses capoeira for social justice, individual pursuit of knowledge about capoeira and its history may lead someone to make this connection independently. "Whatever lineage you come from, whatever group you train with," Doug said to me, "if you see capoeira as an expression of a culture of enslaved people you can't help but be focused on social justice. That, to me, is what ends up being the determiner." Opportunities to become involved in social justice causes—whether that means going to a protest or participating in a job training program—often come about because a member of the capoeira group just happens to be connected to that community, event, or program. During his speech after the Martin Luther King Jr. Day march in January 2019, Shaun King called on everyone there to tap into their networks and harness the power of people's connections in order to achieve the kinds of change we want to see. These capoeira groups are already doing this in an organic way, without it necessarily being part of an orchestrated campaign for social justice.

In an art so loaded with trickery, which was used to subvert the ruling class during and after slavery, it is almost inevitable that some lessons and attitudes will seep into one's teaching of capoeira. Focusing on the physical doesn't have to mean that one ignores the larger cultural dimensions of practicing capoeira, and even individuals who claim to avoid bringing social justice into their classes tend to implicitly teach about the power of capoeira to resist oppression. One African American man I interviewed was adamantly opposed to teaching these things to his students, especially the kids, and barely acknowledges the role played by Brazil/Brazilians in capoeira's history. Yet even if he makes every effort to avoid teaching culture to his students, there is—as he himself suggested—a hidden curriculum inside the physical art of capoeira, one that almost inevitably leads students to a more nuanced understanding of their own identities and place in the world. A brief encounter with a choreography or sequence of movements will not radically alter an individual's way of being in the world, but "the continuous practice (or rejection) of a particular set of embodied principles . . . eventually molds one's sense of selfhood." In turn, the repeated enactment of these "embodied knowledges" in various domains of social life becomes a structuring force in communal life (Rosa 2015, 12).

Even if capoeiristas never go to a protest or have a conversation about race, women's rights, or independence from industrial food systems, being part of the capoeira community is a challenge to the norms of contemporary society. Playing capoeira is sometimes called *vadiação* (loafing about); even though the physical training is hard work, it is a nonproductive sort of labor. This is a challenge to the neoliberal insistence on hyperproductivity (and the associated hustle, grind, and side gigs). Being part of this community also creates networks of caring and hospitality that are not part of the capitalist, consumerist mindset. And yet, despite the lofty ideals it embodies, the capoeira community is not (or not yet) utopic.

The first time I visited Grupo de São Miguel, I watched as a member who hadn't attended class that day stopped in after the official class ended and was pulled into the roda. She was wearing a T-shirt that read "Love Is Love, Black Lives Matter, Climate Change Is Real, Women's Rights Are Human Rights, Immigrants Make America Great, Kindness Is Everything." This list of phrases has been emblazoned on T-shirts, bumper stickers, and yard signs, becoming popular among the political left following the 2016 elections and the tide of conservative policymaking that followed. I wasn't surprised to see her wearing the shirt. These are the sentiments that most of my friends in capoeira promote. But of course, reality is always more complicated than a campaign slogan, and even within capoeira, homophobia continues to be a problem, white supremacy sometimes rears its ugly head, our practices are not always sustainable, women are routinely marginalized, immigrants struggle to find economic security, and people are not always kind.

Understandably, capoeira groups are at different points along their own path toward being more internally just. Some are ready to interrogate questions like why, in an organization that has many strong women in leadership roles, there are so few Black women in positions of power, and why they bear a disproportionate burden for service within the organization. These questions mirror conversations occurring at the national level and in many different types of organizations at the moment, but as Lucha points out, certain groups are not quite ready to interrogate their own practices this way. Many such groups *are* having conversations around race or gender but haven't reached the point at which they are ready to critically consider intersectionality. Even something that may seem relatively innocent, especially to outsiders, like calling capoeira a Brazilian art, may be a manifestation of latent white supremacy. It *is* an art that has come to the world via Brazil, but it never would have come into existence without the contributions of the enslaved Africans who nurtured its survival. Calling it Brazilian rather than Afro-Brazilian—or speaking of capoeira without acknowledging the contributions Africans have made—is a form of erasure and symbolic violence.

UNEXPLORED THEMES

I simply do not have enough space here to pursue all the themes that came up in my interviews, and there are several areas for future development that I wish to highlight before concluding. The first has to do with the idea of cultural appropriation and the way that non-Black capoeiristas' involvement in social justice work positions them differently than less socially engaged global consumers, who have a more straightforward transactional experience with the teachers of foreign cultural arts, particularly those that originated on the periphery of the world system. In fact, the original subtitle for this book was "appropriate appropriation," my attempt at explaining that when someone, regardless of their ascribed identities, adopts the affective habitus of a capoeirista and uses capoeira for purposes that are aligned with the underlying ethos of the art, then their usage of capoeira (or "appropriation" of it) is appropriate and likely to be legitimated by the community at large.

Most of the examples of social justice that I have explored here have to do with racial justice, which is perhaps the easiest cause to connect with capoeira because of how its history is entwined with Brazil's colonial legacy. There are at least two ways of thinking about capoeiristas' role vis-à-vis the African diaspora. On the one hand, capoeira is a practice that folds them into the diasporic traditions even if they are not Black. On the other hand, capoeira can be a bridge for people of the diaspora to find deeper connections with one another. For many Black capoeiristas I spoke with, this may feel like a homecoming, or become a source of strength and joy, a relief of sorts. For non-Black capoeiristas, being drawn into a diasporic art may carry with it a new sense of obligation. As they recognize their privilege and see how the absence of this privilege affects their camaradas in capoeira, they may feel obliged to take action on behalf of people of color.

In addition to race-based activism, capoeiristas use their art for the betterment of their communities in many other ways that also have a link to this history, even if that link is less obvious. Mestre Cobra Mansa is well known for his work promoting permaculture (Kugel 2018). Many capoeiristas from all over the world travel to Brazil both to train in capoeira and to volunteer on this project. I met several of them when I was conducting fieldwork in

Brazil in 2008, but at the time I did not see the underlying connection between the two practices. Yet when I described my interests in social justice to someone from Grupo de São Miguel, he pointed out that being able to grow one's own food enables individuals to decrease their dependency on industrial food systems. Being independent from large, industrial farms that are eerily reminiscent of colonial plantation systems is one way capoeiristas can avoid supporting the exploitation of migrant laborers. While I certainly don't mean to imply that migrant agricultural workers are enslaved, and in no way do I wish to diminish the gross disregard for enslaved Africans' humanity that fueled colonial empires, there are similarities in terms of modern-day laborers' exploitation at the hands of a more economically powerful class, their poor living conditions, and their restricted mobility. It is actually surprising that independence from industrial food systems isn't an explicit goal of more capoeiristas, and it would be worth asking why this is (see Aula 2020).

In chapter 8 I alluded to abuses that have taken place within the capoeira community, particularly sexual harassment perpetuated by teachers against their students. Nearly every woman I interviewed mentioned this to some extent. I could not do the topic justice within this book, and I will return to it in other writings. Some scholarship exists on this topic already, but more attention must paid to discrimination until capoeiristas can truly and unironically say that capoeira is for man, woman, and child, like Mestre Pastinha is credited with having said.

Scholars must also pay attention to capoeira outside of the United States. Scholarship on capoeira outside of Brazil has focused disproportionately on the United States, the United Kingdom, and a few other nations in the Global North (Contreras Islas 2021). Research on the Black Atlantic has been similarly narrow in scope, leaving us with an incomplete understanding of what it means to belong to the Black diaspora (see Joseph 2012). Because I am a US researcher and this is where most of my contacts live, I too have focused on the United States, but I want to briefly call attention to some initiatives being undertaken in other parts of the world, including the Global South, both as evidence for the pervasiveness of the social justice orientation within capoeira and as a call for sustained ethnographic explorations of capoeira in these regions.

Not long ago, a capoeira teacher in the Philippines was interviewed about his work with at-risk youth, who are given that label because it is anticipated that their environment may lead them to eventually run afoul of the law in some way (CNN Philippines 2019). Many of these children are living in an institutional setting, have behavioral issues, and may have suffered abuse or trauma in the past. In this interview, the teacher argued that children are drawn in by this dynamic, multifaceted art, which creates an opportunity to convey to them the values held within. After expressing quite possibly feigned skepticism that teaching a martial art to at-risk youth was a wise idea (see also Joseph 2015), the interviewer pressed the teacher on what exactly the children were learning beyond how to fight. The teacher focused on how capoeira instills respect and discipline in students. He also emphasized how music can be a form of therapy for the kids who have experienced trauma and abuse. The social worker who accompanied him on the show added that many of these children have become leaders among their peers. Having been raised in an environment where survival depends on looking out for oneself, the kids who were enrolled in capoeira were now helping others and seeing themselves as part of a community.

When Alejandro set out to establish the first capoeira angola group in the Southeast Asian nation where he lives, the regional teacher he had studied under previously warned him that he would have a rough road ahead. Because he connected more with the values of capoeira angola than with those of regional (which to him felt similar to just going to a gym for a workout), he was undeterred. Ultimately, however, he agrees that his former teacher was right. The angola mestre with whom he is affiliated has a "social" orientation to capoeira, "and that can be quite difficult for people at times to accept." An understanding of what parts of capoeira are embraced and which are rejected or downplayed in different locations will help us better understand not just capoeira, but ideoscapes (see Appadurai 1996) in general. We need to continue to focus on sites that represent or embody the tension between the global and the local, the insider and outsider, freedom and oppression, and other such dichotomies (see Conquergood 2013).

SOCIAL JUSTICE IN OTHER ARTS

From time to time I am asked whether capoeira is unique in terms of how (certain) practitioners merge its physical performance with seemingly unrelated social justice initiatives. And if it is unique, why might that be? When asked to articulate what it is that makes capoeira so special, particularly in terms of its readiness for use as a tool of social justice, Imani said that all traditional martial arts (though she excluded mixed martial arts from this) "talk about a journey, they talk about endurance, they talk about humbleness." She tells her students, "when you practice capoeira, you practice vulnerability." This too could be said of virtually any other art in which participants have to trust their training partners or coparticipants and risk public scrutiny. I have witnessed significant diversity, equity, and inclusion (DEI) efforts in the running community and know them to be present in other communities of practice as well. But what makes capoeira different, at least in Imani's estimation, is the "extra element of community" and the fact that it originated among marginalized peoples. There's a sort of camaraderie that comes from aligning oneself with the underdog.

This book has been premised on the idea that capoeira is a potentially useful tool for social justice because of the emphasis practitioners place on its origins as an art of resistance. Whether capoeira was successfully disguised as dance or helped quilombo residents like Zumbi resist capture is largely irrelevant for my present argument. Rather, what capoeiristas are motivated to do because of their belief in such stories is what matters. And in some cases—such as a man who told me he thinks we're "beyond" the point of talking about capoeira being disguised as dance—respect for this folklore matters more than actual belief in the tales.

Brazilian jiu-jitsu offers an interesting point of comparison because, from my admittedly limited vantage point, it does not seem to cultivate an activist orientation in the same way capoeira does, at least not in the United States. This may be at least partially explained by the way each has entered the global milieu. The entrepreneurs who have globalized capoeira and Brazilian jiu-jitsu differ in a number of key aspects (Rocha et al. 2015). Whereas capoeiristas have tended to come from the lower classes, Brazilian jiu-jitsu is represented by the middle class. Whereas capoeiristas tended to be Afro-Brazilian, teachers of Brazilian jiu-jitsu tended to be white, at least during the early days of its global diffusion, though now the field is much more diverse. Capoeira teachers working abroad also tended to be less educated than their Brazilian jiu-jitsu peers and less likely to be fluent in English prior to their migration. Furthermore, capoeiristas more often had to rely on their own meager earnings in their new countries than did Brazilian jiu-jitsu teachers, who often enjoyed at least some initial financial support from their families. Though the two arts/sports internationalized at roughly the same time, the drastic differences in the average teacher profile goes a long way toward explaining why these arts have taken such divergent paths in terms of the issues I am interested in (e.g., affective habitus). When a martial art becomes "sportified," which may happen for any number of reasons including globalization, it may become decoupled from its cultural roots. In some ways this makes it easier for people in other countries to learn the art, because one does not have to understand the cultural background of its originators in order to learn the movements and strategies associated with winning or performing well, but it also runs the risk of stripping away the core essence of the art.

COVID-19

Jill Dolan (2001) argues that liveness is essential to the transformative magic of performance. Post-2020, this claim needs to be revisited not only because of the advances that have been made in mediation technologies, but because of the pandemic, which has sometimes made live, embodied gatherings impossible. For many of us writing about society and culture in the present moment, there is a risk of our work being hijacked or derailed by the COVID-19 pandemic, which seems to be affecting every aspect of our lives. I do not want it to overshadow the social justice work all these capoeiristas were engaging in before they were forced to go into isolation; this work deserves to be elevated, celebrated, and studied, and I do believe that we will return to something close to normality soon. However, certain aspects of how capoeiristas dealt with the pandemic are relevant to the subject at hand.

I was listening to a podcast on capoeira, and someone I have gotten to know through this project was being interviewed. Finding a silver lining in the pandemic, he said one benefit of being forced to move online was the sense of community that developed and the way that people have been able to train together regardless of where they are in the world. "You can be in Brazil in five minutes" if someone sends you a link, he said. And while you won't be getting the full embodied experience of an apprenticeship pilgrimage—the smell of *acarajé* (a distinctive stuffed fritter) coming from a food stall in Bahia, the sway you develop from navigating the historic district's steep, cobblestone streets—it sure is a lot easier, less expensive, and, in a sense, more democratic.

His reflections also went beyond the physical aspects of training. He reminded listeners that capoeira teachers are more than just instructors: they are a key part of students' support systems. He acknowledged that people were suffering from isolation and said that being able to practice capoeira over the internet might be the one thing that really sustains them. He hoped that when life does go back to normal, capoeiristas will remember that they can lean on one another in times of need. "In moments when you find it difficult to train or just get through the day," he said, "remember . . . we're friends, we're like a family, and you can depend on family to be there."

All living bodies are, of course, subject to illness and death, but the social infrastructure in which we live determines—at least to some extent—which bodies are more likely to experience precarity and suffer more because of it (Butler 2015). The novel coronavirus may not discriminate, but a low-income supermarket worker whose labor is considered essential yet who has poor health insurance is both more likely to contract the virus and less likely to be able to seek appropriate and timely care than am I, a professor who has the luxury of teaching from home and whose university offers good health insurance.

Even in the best of times, it can be difficult to make a living from teaching capoeira or any other art form. The people I know who do this full time have put their hearts and souls into building their businesses, and they go above and beyond what is expected of most business owners because of how much they care for their students as individuals. They offer discounts to students in need, they sometimes pick students up or drive them home after class if they don't have transportation, and some of them have even opened their homes to students that needed a place to stay. Many of them have had to, at least periodically, pick up other work in the gig economy (e.g., driving for companies like Uber) or service industry. When the COVID-19 pandemic forced state and local governments to place restrictions on everyday activities, they suffered tremendously. Not only did many of them have to cease offering face-to-face classes, but they were also cut off from what used to be a secondary source of income. Some have benefited from crowd-sourcing campaigns; others have had to claim unemployment benefits. And through it all, many of them have still maintained that their suffering pales in comparison to the challenges faced by their counterparts in Brazil, where the virus circulated even more ferociously, and where people had less support from the state and less access to vaccines. As we recover from the damages brought about by COVID-19, I would like all martial artists and practitioners of globalized art forms to ask what responsibilities they have to the other members of their community both at home and in countries that occupy a more peripheral position in the world system.

BETTER CARING FOR ONE ANOTHER

Several people I talked to for this book marveled at the vast range of people who are drawn to capoeira. Lifelong friendships blossom between people who never would have hung out in any other context. It isn't that there would be animosity between them, just that it would be unlikely for them to meet. And even if they did, they wouldn't have had much in common, certainly not enough to be the basis of an authentic relationship characterized by vulnerability, generosity, and honesty. Capoeira brings these people together. It provides an opportunity to make a real difference in people's lives, provided that capoeiristas are ready to enact some of the principles I learned from this project. If you believe that friendships like these that transcend difference are important for a more tolerant, inclusive, and empathetic society, then you need to make sure that people from diverse backgrounds are able to participate in your group.

What does this mean in actual practice? Perhaps a young student is struggling to get to class. See if there is someone else in the group that can offer a ride. Francis did, and now the person that was once needing a ride is a mentor to other Black youth, showing them that their crowns have already been bought and paid for and just need to be put on. Perhaps you can offer scholarships to students who could not otherwise afford tuition. This has to be done with care, of course, since academies often operate with slim margins. Or perhaps you have the opposite problem. Perhaps, like Imani's group, there are not many affluent students in the group, which limits opportunities for students (and their parents in the case of youth classes) to network with those who may have resources from which they could benefit. You might be intentional about performing and recruiting in locations frequented by the upper middle class. Are women dropping out at disproportionate rates because they feel marginalized by sexual harassment? Maybe their domestic responsibilities (e.g., child-rearing) leave them with less time and flexibility to train than their male peers. Think about what strategies might be implemented to make them feel supported. Attendance policies might be relaxed, or children might be explicitly invited to come and play in the studio while their parent(s) train, even if that means asking the other students to take turns watching them during class. What I've learned through this project is that everyone has something to offer the capoeira community, and only by our making it as inclusive as possible can the benefits of diverse participation be fully actualized.

I have also learned that social justice takes many forms and that sometimes what seems on the surface to be supportive of DEI efforts actually undercuts the success of the very people who are meant to be supported. Using martial arts as a tool of encouraging a resistance mindset does not mean one wants to see actual fighting. The influence of Muhammad Ali proves that violence within certain contexts (the boxing ring) can coexist with peaceful and nonviolent activism in day-to-day affairs (Spencer et al. 2016). But there is a big difference between fighting for social justice and fighting because of social injustice.

As a white, female academic, I'm primarily interested in the former. I come at this topic from a privileged position, and I will rarely if ever have to physically defend myself. But the latter should not be discounted. The injustice of our society will continue to put certain bodies at more risk than others. As long as that is the case, people need to know how to defend themselves. When we approach the study of capoeira from this angle, instruction about how to use capoeira in real-world fights *is* a form of activism. If I do a *benção* (lit. blessing; kick to the stomach) with my weight thrown back because it gives my leg better extension and looks pretty, it is of little consequence. So what if I don't have as much force in the kick? In most rodas, it won't matter because my opponent is going to react to the image of my leg moving through space, not waiting around to test the strength of the kick itself. If we are making a beautiful game, he will dodge away and then issue a counterattack. If I were in a real fight, however, I would need that kick to have as much power as possible so that I could diffuse the threat or buy enough time to run away. Through this lens, teaching capoeira to people who are likely to encounter real-world violence without giving them the tools to implement it effectively may actually be doing them a disservice.

BOA VIAGEM (GOOD JOURNEY)

Is there a fundamental link between capoeira and social justice? How someone answers that question will have a great deal to do with which version of capoeira's history they endorse, and whether they put more emphasis on it as an African warrior art, an art of resistance born out of slavery, or an emergent cultural tradition that incidentally took place during Brazil's colonial period. Most people I worked with on this project fall into the second category. Even for those readers who do not buy into this idea that capoeira emerged as an art of resistance, I hope I have made it clear how many groups and individuals that practice capoeira today are making that connection. This in and of itself is a form of activist labor. It is not always fully realized, as is the case for much activist work, but the weight of this work readies capoeira to be used as a weapon of resistance when needed.

Barbara Browning (2001, 172) wrote that "it is important to reaffirm constantly the history of capoeira as an art of resistance." Whereas some will get caught up in their excitement and love of the movement itself, and others may get bogged down with an obsessive focus on authenticity and static traditionality, Browning called for greater focus on the "political potential of rootedness" in this long-standing tradition, a rootedness that is just as applicable today as it was in the colonial era. Although Browning focused on angoleiros who engaged with capoeira as a political art, I have seen it in all corners of the community, and it has not abated since she wrote these words two decades ago. If anything, it has intensified.

When I spoke with Bram, he said, "a lot of people in capoeira, I'm learning even more so, are having more conversation about liberation, and not just historical stuff in capoeira, but today." Using capoeira for justice is a way of finding hope. I conducted these interviews between 2016 and 2020, a period that was characterized by stress and anxiety for people of color, the LGBTQ+ community, and a host of others who have felt marginalized or oppressed. Even while feeling the stress of this, several interlocutors gave thanks for a political climate that encouraged people to bring their racist, homophobic views out into the open. Only by unmasking the hatred could it be engaged directly.

In the group that I trained with for many years, we ended our rodas by standing and walking around in a circle while the two capoeiristas inside the ring continued to play. Circling them, our mestre would sing *adeus, adeus* (goodbye, goodbye), and we would answer back *boa viagem* ([have a] good journey). That song was our last chance to build the *axé* (energy) that we needed to carry us through our week. In that same spirit, I cannot think of a better way to conclude than with what Rene told me. When you seek to do good in the world, "[your] circle of influence grows . . . that is the model of grassroots organizing and grassroots movements, period. So that is what capoeira is. Once you see it that way, then there are a million different things that you can do." There is no single right way to use capoeira for social justice, nor does capoeira have to be used in this way at all, but those who choose this path find a deep and meaningful resonance between the stories they have inherited about capoeira's past and its potential for positively changing the communities they inhabit today. Like capoeira, change is often hard and sometimes painful. It can also be achieved with style, a little bit of swagger, and grace.

GLOSSARY

angola—the style of capoeira formalized by Mestre Pastinha
angoleiro—practitioner of capoeira angola
atabaque—drum
axé—energy or "vibe"
bateria—the capoeira orchestra
batizado—baptism or graduation ceremony
benção—lit. blessing; also the name of a kick
berimbau—the most essential instrument in the capoeira orchestra; it
    "leads" the roda
boa viagem—lit. good journey; used as a farewell at the end of a
    capoeira roda
brincando—carefree and almost childlike play or "messing around"
camarada—lit. comrade; used to describe one's training partners within
    capoeira
cavalaria—in capoeira, a rhythm that warns of the police's impending
    arrival
communitas—intense experience of bonding with others whose status
    has been stripped away
conscientização—consciousness raising, associated with liberation the-
    ology and literacy projects
contemporânea—the globally predominant style of capoeira
contra-mestre—assistant master
emboscadas—lit. ambush; used by Mestre Bimba in the late stages of
    teaching his most advanced students

evento—a generic way of referring to a capoeira event, normally including lessons and lectures

ginga—the swaying, triangular step from which most attacks and defenses can be launched

habitus—the embodied dispositions one acquires as a result of membership in a social field

jogar/jogando—to play/playing; the most common way to talk about playing sports/games

jogue pra lá—an informal mandate to carry the lessons of capoeira beyond the roda/school

ladainha—the solo song or litany that opens a capoeira roda, often sung by a high-ranking player

maculêlê—a rhythmic stick-fighting dance

malandragem—a roguish quality

malícia—deceitful trickery or sneakiness

mestre—someone who has attained master rank

Othering—the exaggeration of differences, which results in dehumanizing other groups

performativity—doing something or causing some change through the act of performance

puxada de rede—a folkloric dance representing Afro-Brazilians' relationship to the sea/fishing

quilombo—community of freedom seekers (or quilombeiros); the most famous of these was Quilombo dos Palmares

regional—the style of capoeira formalized by Mestre Bimba

roda—the circle in which the capoeira game is played

treinel—teacher or coach

NOTES

Introduction

1. The names of individuals and groups used in this book are pseudonyms. While I wish I could give credit to some of the capoeiristas presented here for the work they are doing in their communities, there are both personal and legal reasons for some to remain anonymous. Given the intimacy of this community, revealing the true identity of any single individual could expose others.

2. Throughout the text, I use the Portuguese word *evento* to refer to capoeira-specific events; I use the English word *event* for more general gatherings, happenings, and historical moments.

3. Contemporânea refers to the style of capoeira, not a particular organization. Globally, it is the most popular style, deriving from Mestre Bimba's regional style but also incorporating some elements of the angola style.

4. In her work on capoeira in Canada, Janelle Beatrice Joseph (2012, 1090) noted that "Angoleiros' desire to practice traditional capoeira translates to maintaining a thread of social justice in their practice." In that cultural context, this desire manifests as a search for redress for the abuses suffered by Canada's First Nations population. Angoleiros in Toronto also reference themes of marginality and Blackness at their events and in their day-to-day practices; in contrast, Joseph found that *contemporâneos* were less focused on fighting for social justice and more interested in promoting a discourse of multicultural citizenship.

5. Kathleen A. Spanos (2019, 29) uses the term *dances of resistance* in reference to dances found across the globe that "are involved in strategic processes of liberation, activism, and/or marginalized racial, social, or ethnic identity formation for a specific group of people." While obviously a closely related concept, the term *globalized resistance arts* is broad enough to encompass arts other than dance yet narrower in the sense that it only refers to those arts that have circulated outside of their point of origin.

Chapter 1. The Making of a Politicized Art

1. Who "the ancestors" are is somewhat up for interpretation. In my experience, this phrase generally refers to the spirits of Africans who have long since died; however, it can also refer to any deceased individual whose legacy continues to inspire the living. For instance, within hours of her passing, Ruth Bader Ginsburg was being invoked as an ancestor by one of the capoeirista-activists I met through this project. An alternative interpretation of "the ancestors" refers to one's own personal genealogy. However, I have only encountered this interpretation once, from someone who claimed that invoking the ancestors in a roda comprised of multiracial participants created an antagonistic space in which old grievances were reanimated by the living.

2. See also Menara Lube Guizardi's (2011) work, which explores how Black bodies were co-opted by the Brazilian state in its creation of a mestizo national identity and how capoeira articulates with this ideological project.

3. In the film, a former Green Beret returns to Miami and finds that his old high school has been overrun with drug dealers. One of his former teachers recruits him to reform a bunch of at-risk youth using capoeira. While the theme of resisting oppression is not explicitly engaged, the film nonetheless articulates with the general idea of capoeira being a tool to resist negativity.

Chapter 2. Social Justice and Resistance as Analytical Frames

1. The term *decolonizing* will be familiar to most readers, but it might be more apt to say *recolonizing*, since these acts are not returning land to the Native peoples who originally occupied it but reconfiguring or at least troubling the nature of settler occupation.

2. Pastinha's 1966 trip to Senegal to perform in the First World Festival of Negro Arts was revolutionary given how the Brazilian state had repeatedly downplayed the significance of African cultural contributions through the discourse of racial democracy, muting its significance by absorbing it into a nationalist fantasy (see Rosenthal 2009).

Chapter 4. Capoeira's Pedagogies of Resistance

1. This is a pseudonym I affectionately assigned to the group based on the propensity of both the mestre and teachers in the organization to provoke critical thought and debate. Os Provocadores translates to the Provocateurs.

2. The additional classes offered at an evento like this are telling. Presenting samba, a musical form that retains its association with poor or working-class Afro-Brazilians (see Vianna 1999), rather than a middle-class martial art like Brazilian jiu-jitsu (see Rocha et al. 2015), can be interpreted as an intentional alignment with the poor or the African diaspora. Although samba is outside the scope of the current work, sambistas outside of Brazil, like capoeiristas, take pride in maintaining fidelity to

Brazilian sources, and instructors occupy a place of privilege within the global samba community (Kuijlaars 2019). Brazilian jiu-jitsu, as I explain in the final chapter, has taken a quite different path in its globalization.

3. Interestingly, among younger capoeiristas, I have found that many study Portuguese because they want to be able to communicate with Brazilian capoeiristas when these teachers visit from Brazil or when they themselves travel to Brazil. Now that information on capoeira is readily available in English and other languages, they are more concerned with learning Portuguese so that they may access the living, rather than the written, archive.

Chapter 8. Challenges to the Social Justice Perspective

1. Albeit on a more modest and less professional scale, capoeiristas like those in Grupo de São Miguel who produce shows featuring capoeira as well as other Brazilian arts are following a precedent set by Emília Biancardi and her company Viva Bahia, which toured domestically and internationally in the 1970s (see Höfling 2015). When folkloric traditions like capoeira, samba, and *maculêlê* (rhythmic stick-fighting dance) are presented in theaters more often associated with "high art," an aura of respectability is attached to the performers of folk traditions that have been marginalized because of their "low-class" associations. By integrating these arts into a larger production that may involve other arts, costuming choices, lighting decisions, and such, the artistic directors are (explicitly or implicitly) making commentary about the arts themselves.

BIBLIOGRAPHY

Acuña, Mauricio. 2016. "The Berimbau's Social *Ginga*: Notes towards a Comprehension of Agency in Capoeira." *Sociologia & Antropologia* 6 (2): 383–405.

Ahmad, Tania. 2016. "Intolerants: Politics of the Ordinary in Karachi, Pakistan." In Alexandrakis 2016, 135–60.

Ahmed, Sara. 2004. "Affective Economies." *Social Text* 22 (2): 117–39.

Alexander, Michelle. 2012. *The New Jim Crow: Mass Incarceration in the Age of Colorblindness*. New York: New Press.

Alexandrakis, Othon, ed. 2016. *Impulse to Act: A New Anthropology of Resistance and Social Justice*. Bloomington: Indiana University Press.

Almeida, Bira. 1986. *Capoeira, a Brazilian Art Form: History, Philosophy, and Practice*. Berkeley: North Atlantic Books.

Appadurai, Arjun. 1996. *Modernity at Large: Cultural Dimensions of Globalization*. Minneapolis: University of Minnesota Press.

Assunção, Matthias Rohrig. 2004. *Capoeira: The History of an Afro-Brazilian Martial Art*. London: Routledge.

———. 2007. "History and Memory in Capoeira: Lyrics from Bahia, Brazil." In *Cultures of the Lusophone Black Atlantic*, edited by Nancy Priscilla Naro, Roger Sansi-Roca, and David H. Treece, 199–218. New York: Palgrave Macmillan.

A Tarde. 1936. "A Inaguracao do Parque Oden." February 6, 1936.

———. 1948. "A Alegria Fez Praca no Largo da Conceicao." December 7, 1948.

Aula, Inkeri. 2017. "Translocality and Afro-Brazilian Imaginaries in Globalised Capoeira." *Suomen Antropologi* 42 (1): 67–90.

———. 2020. "Quilombist Utopias: An Ethnographic Reflection." In *The Revival of Political Imagination: Utopia as Methodology*, edited by Teppo Eskelinen, 57–77. London: Zed Books.

Boal, Augusto. 1993. *Theatre of the Oppressed*. Translated by Charles A. McBride. New York: Theatre Communications Group.

Bowman, Paul. 2016. "Making Martial Arts History Matter." *International Journal of the History of Sport* 33 (9): 915–33.

Brito, Celso de. 2012. "Berimbau's 'Use Value' and 'Exchange Value': Production and Consumption as Symbols of Freedom." *Virtual Brazilian Anthropology* 9 (2): 104–27.

Browning, Barbara. 1995. *Samba: Resistance in Motion.* Bloomington: Indiana University Press.

———. 2001. "Headspin: Capoeira's Ironic Inversions." In *Moving History/Dancing Cultures: A Dance History Reader,* edited by Ann Dils and Ann Cooper Albright, 165–73. Middletown, CT: Wesleyan University Press.

———. 2013. "Choreographing Postcoloniality: Reflections on the Passing of Edward Said." *Dance Research Journal* 35 (2): 164–69.

Butler, Judith. 2015. *Notes toward a Performative Theory of Assembly.* Cambridge, MA: Harvard University Press.

———. 2016. "Rethinking Vulnerability and Resistance." In *Vulnerability in Resistance,* edited by Judith Butler, Zeynep Gambetti, and Leticia Sabsay, 12–27. Durham, NC: Duke University Press.

Castro, Maurício Barros de. 2007. "Na roda do Mundo: Mestre João Grande entre a Bahia e Nova York." PhD diss., Universidade de São Paulo.

CNN Philippines. 2019. "Organization Uses 'Capoeira Angola' Art Form to Help Children, Youth at-Risk." YouTube video, 8:28. Uploaded November 7, 2019. https://www.youtube.com/watch?v=tsa6MwOwf_8.

Collier, John. 2006. "'But What If I Should Need to Defecate in Your Neighborhood, Madame?': Empire, Redemption, and the 'Tradition of the Oppressed' in a Brazilian World Heritage Site." *Cultural Anthropology* 23 (2): 279–328.

Conquergood, Dwight. 2013. *Cultural Struggles: Performance, Ethnography, Praxis.* Edited by E. Patrick Johnson. Ann Arbor: University of Michigan Press.

Contreras Islas, David Sebastian. 2021. "Mexican Capoeira Is Not Diasporic! On Glocalization, Migration and the North-South Divide." *Martial Arts Studies* 11:57–71.

Costa, Emília Viotti da. 1985. "The Portuguese-African Slave Trade: A Lesson in Colonialism." *Latin American Perspectives* 12 (1): 41–61.

D'Aquino, Iria. 1983. "Capoeira: Strategies for Status, Power, and Identity." PhD diss., University of Illinois.

Delamont, Sara, Neil Stephens, and Claudio Campos. 2017. *Embodying Brazil: An Ethnography of Diasporic Capoeira.* New York: Routledge.

Desch Obi, T. J. 2012. "The *Jogo de Capoeira* and the Fallacy of 'Creole' Cultural Forms." *African and Black Diaspora* 5 (2): 211–28.

Dettmann, Christine. 2013. "History in the Making: An Ethnography into the Roots of Capoeira Angola." *World of Music* 2 (2): 73–98.

Dolan, Jill. 2001. "Performance, Utopia, and 'Utopian Performative.'" *Theatre Journal* 53 (3): 455–79.

———. 2005. *Utopia in Performance: Finding Hope at the Theater.* Ann Arbor: University of Michigan Press.

Dossar, Kenneth. 1992. "Capoeira Angola: Dancing between Two Worlds." *Afro-Hispanic Review* 11 (1/3): 5–10.

Downey, Greg. 2002. "Domesticating an Urban Menace: Reforming Capoeira as a Brazilian National Sport." *International Journal of the History of Sport* 19 (4): 1–32.

———. 2005. *Learning Capoeira: Lessons in Cunning from an Afro-Brazilian Art.* Oxford: Oxford University Press.

Faubion, James D. 2016. "Cosmologicopolitics: Vitalistic Cosmology Meets Biopower." In Alexandrakis 2016, 89–111.

Fontoura, Adriana Raquel Ritter, and Adriana Coutinho de Azevedo Guimarães. 2002. "História da capoeira." *Maringa* 13 (2): 141–50.

Foster, Susan Leigh. 2007. "Choreographies of Protest." *Theatre Journal* 55 (3): 395–412.

Fuggle, Sophie. 2008. "Discourses of Subversion: The Ethics and Aesthetics of Capoeira and Parkour." *Dance Research* 26 (2): 204–22.

Gallant, Karen, Susan Arai, and Bryan Smale. 2013a. "Celebrating, Challenging and Re-Envisioning Serious Leisure." *Leisure/Loisir* 37 (2): 91–109.

———. 2013b. "Serious Leisure as an Avenue for Nurturing Community." *Leisure Sciences* 35 (4): 320–36.

Gates, Henry Louis, Jr. 2011. *Black in Latin America.* Episode 3, "Brazil, a Racial Paradise?" Directed by Ricardo Pollack. Aired May 3, 2011, on PBS.

Geertz, Clifford. 1972. "Deep Play: Notes on the Balinese Cockfight." *Daedalus* 101 (1): 1–37.

Gluckman, Max. 1954. *Rituals of Rebellion in South-East Africa.* Manchester: Manchester University Press.

Goffman, Erving. 1959. *The Presentation of Self in Everyday Life.* New York: Anchor Books.

Goldman, Danielle. 2007. "Bodies on the Line: Contact Improvisation and Techniques of Nonviolent Protest." *Dance Research Journal* 39 (1): 60–74.

González Varela, Sergio. 2013. "Mandinga: Power and Deception in Afro-Brazilian Capoeira." *Social Analysis* 57 (2): 1–20.

———. 2017. *Power in Practice: The Pragmatic Anthropology of Afro-Brazilian Capoeira.* New York: Berghahn Books.

Graeber, David. 2014. "Anthropology and the Rise of the Professional-Managerial Class." *HAU: Journal of Ethnographic Theory* 4 (3): 73–88.

Green, Thomas A. 2003. "Sense in Nonsense: The Role of Folk History in the Martial Arts." In *Martial Arts in the Modern World*, edited by Thomas A. Green and Joseph R. Svinth, 1–12. Westport, CT: Praeger.

Griffith, Lauren Miller. 2013. "Apprenticeship Pilgrims and the Acquisition of Legitimacy." *Journal of Sport and Tourism* 18 (1): 1–15.

———. 2016. *In Search of Legitimacy: How Outsiders Become Part of an Afro-Brazilian Tradition.* New York: Berghahn Books.

———. 2017. "Virtually Legitimate: Using Disembodied Media to Position Oneself in an Embodied Community." *Martial Arts Studies* 4:36–45.

Griffith, Lauren Miller, and Jonathan S. Marion. 2018. *Apprenticeship Pilgrimage: Developing Expertise through Travel and Training.* Lanham, MD: Lexington Books.

Guizardi, Menara Lube. 2011. "'Genuinamente Brasileña': La *nacionalización* y expansión de la capoeira como práctica social en Brasil." *Araucaria: Revista Iberoamericana de Filosofía, Política y Humanidades* 13 (26): 72–100.

Habjan, Urska. 2015. "Embodiment of Capoeira Skills." *Innovative Issues and Approaches in Social Sciences* 8 (3): 118–34.

Hamer, Lynne, Geneva J. Chapman, and Lucy Thelma Osbourne, eds. 1998. *Juneteenth: An American Holiday.* Curriculum guide. Toledo, OH: University of Toledo College of Education and Allied Professions.

Hanisch, Carol. 1969. "The Personal Is Political: The Women's Liberation Classic with a New Explanatory Introduction." *Writings by Carol Hanisch* (website). Last updated 2009. http://www.carolhanisch.org/index.html.

Hedegard, Danielle. 2013. "Blackness and Experience in Omnivorous Cultural Consumption: Evidence from the Tourism of Capoeira in Salvador, Brazil." *Poetics* 41 (1): 1–26.

Hejtmanek, Katie Rose. 2015. *Friendship, Love, and Hip Hop: An Ethnography of African American Men in Psychiatric Custody.* New York: Palgrave Macmillan.

———. 2016. "Care, Closeness, and Becoming 'Better': Transformation and Therapeutic Process in American Adolescent Psychiatric Custody." *Ethos* 44 (3): 313–32.

———. 2020. "Fitness Fanatics: Exercise as Answer to Pending Zombie Apocalypse in Contemporary America." *American Anthropologist* 122 (4): 864–75.

Höfling, Ana Paula. 2015. "Staging Capoeira, Samba, Maculelê, and Candomblé: Viva Bahia's Choreographies of Afro-Brazilian Folklore for the Global Stage." In *Performing Brazil: Essays on Culture, Identity, and the Performing Arts*, edited by Severino J. Albuquerque and Kathryn Bishop-Sanchez, 98–125. Madison: University of Wisconsin Press.

Howe, Cymene. 2016. "Negative Space: Unmovement and the Study of Activism When There Is No Action." In Alexandrakis 2016, 161–82.

Isoke, Zenzele. 2011. "The Politics of Homemaking: Black Feminist Transformations of a Cityscape." *Transforming Anthropology* 19 (2): 117–30.

Joseph, Janelle Beatrice. 2006. "Capoeira in Canada: Brazilian Martial Art, Cultural Transformation, and the Struggle for Authenticity." MS thesis, University of Toronto.

———. 2012. "The Practice of Capoeira: Diasporic Black Culture in Canada." *Ethnic and Racial Studies* 35 (6): 1078–95.

———. 2015. "Physical Culture and Alternative Rehabilitation: Qualitative Insights from a Martial Arts Intervention Program." In *Alternative Offender Rehabilitation and Social Justice: Arts and Physical Engagement in Criminal Justice and Community Settings*, edited by Wesley Crichlow and Janelle Beatrice Joseph, 55–77. London: Palgrave Macmillan.

Kim, Junhyoung, Jinmoo Heo, In Heok Lee, and Jun Kim. 2015. "Predicting Personal Growth and Happiness by Using Serious Leisure Model." *Social Indicators Research* 122 (1): 147–57.

King, Martin Luther, Jr. 1964. "Letter from Birmingham Jail." In *Why We Can't Wait*, by Martin Luther King Jr., 85–110. Boston: Beacon Press.

———. 1968. "I Have a Dream." *Negro History Bulletin* 31 (5): 16–17.

Kjølsrød, Lise. 2013. "Mediated Activism: Contingent Democracy in Leisure Worlds." *Sociology* 47 (6): 1207–23.

Kugel, Seth. 2018. "The Physical and Spiritual Art of Capoeira." *New York Times*, December 13, 2018.

Kuijlaars, Antoinette. 2019. "The Globalization of Samba Percussion: The Reconfiguration of the Legitimate Ways of Playing." In *Aesthetic Cosmopolitanism and Global Culture*, edited by Vincenzo Cicchelli, Sylvie Octubre, and Viviane Reigel, 222–45. Leiden: Brill.

Lave, Jean, and Etienne Wenger. 1991. *Situated Learning: Legitimate Peripheral Participation*. Cambridge: Cambridge University Press.

Lewis, J. Lowell. 1992. *Ring of Liberation: Deceptive Discourse in Brazilian Capoeira*. Chicago: University of Chicago Press.

Lilja, Mona. 2017. "Dangerous Bodies, Matter and Emotions: Public Assemblies and Embodied Resistance." *Journal of Political Power* 10 (3): 342–52.

MacAloon, John J. 1984. "Olympic Games and the Theory of Spectacle in Modern Societies." In *Rite, Drama, Festival, Spectacle: Rehearsals toward a Theory of Cultural Performance*, edited by John J. MacAloon, 241–80. Philadelphia: Institute for the Study of Human Issues.

Machado, Manoel Nascimento. 2018. *Bimba: One Century of Capoeira Regional*. Edited by Lia Sfoggia. Salvador, Brazil: Editora da Universidade Federal da Bahia.

MacLennan, Janet. 2011. "'To Build a Beautiful Dialogue': Capoeira as Contradiction." *Journal of International and Intercultural Communication* 4 (2): 146–62.

Madison, D. Soyini. 2006. "The Dialogic Performative in Critical Ethnography." *Text and Performance Quarterly* 26 (4): 320–24.

Marquese, Rafael de Bivar. 2006. "The Dynamics of Slavery in Brazil: Resistance, the Slave Trade and Manumission in the 17th to 19th Centuries." *Novos Estudos—CEBRAP* 74:107–23.

Marriage, Zoë. 2020. *Cultural Resistance and Security from Below: Power and Escape through Capoeira*. London: Routledge.

Mason, Paul H. 2013. "Intracultural and Intercultural Dynamics of Capoeira Training in Brazil." *Global Ethnographic* 1 (1). https://globalethnographic.com/index.php/intracultural-and-intercultural-dynamics-of-capoeria/.

McMillan, David W., and David M. Chavis. 1986. "Sense of Community: A Definition and Theory." *Journal of Community Psychology* 14 (1): 6–23.

Merrell, Floyd. 2005. *Capoeira and Candomblé: Conformity and Resistance through Afro-Brazilian Experience*. Princeton, NJ: Markus Wiener.

Mills, Dana. 2016. *Dance and Politics: Moving beyond Boundaries*. Manchester: Manchester University Press.

Mwewa, Muleka, Marcus Aurelio Taborda de Oliveira, and Alexandre Fernandez Vaz. 2010. "Capoeira: Cultura do corpo, esquemas, exportação identitaaria." *Agora para la educación física y el deporte* 12 (2): 151–62.

Owen, Craig, and Nicola De Martini Ugolotti. 2019. "'Pra homem, menino e mulher'? Problematizing the Gender Inclusivity Discourse in Capoeira." *International Review for the Sociology of Sport* 54 (6): 691–710.

Pickard, Sarah. 2017. "Politically Engaged Leisure: The Political Participation of Young People in Contemporary Britain beyond the Serious Leisure Model." *Angles: New Perspectives on the Anglophone World* 5. https://doi.org/10.4000/angles.1252.

Pires, Antônio Liberac Cardoso Simões. 2002. *Bimba, Pastinha e Besouro de Mamangá, três personagens da capoeira baiana*. Goiânia: Grafset.

Ratliff, Thomas N., and Lori L. Hall. 2014. "Practicing the Art of Dissent: Toward a Typology of Protest Activity in the United States." *Humanity and Society* 38 (3): 268–94.

Reis, Leticia Vidor de Sousa. 2004. "Mestre Bimba e Mestre Pastinha: A Capoeira em Dois Estilos." In *Artes do Corpo*, edited by Vagner Gonalves da Silva, 189–223. São Paulo: Selo Negro Edições.

Ribeiro, Nuno F. 2017. "Boxing Culture and Serious Leisure among North-American Youth: An Embodied Ethnography." *Qualitative Report* 22 (6): 1622–36.

Robitaille, Laurence. 2010. "Understanding Capoeira through Cultural Theories of the Body." 2009 graduate-level Baptista prizewinning essay. Centre for Research on Latin America and the Caribbean, York University, Toronto. https://www.yorku.ca/cerlac/lacs-at-york/prizes-and-grants/baptista-prizewinning-essays/.

Rocha, Angela da, Felipe Esteves, Renato Cotta de Mello, and Jorge Ferreira da Silva. 2015. "Diasporic and Transnational Internationalization: The Case of Brazilian Martial Arts." *Brazilian Administration Review* 12 (4): 403–20.

Rosa, Cristina. 2012. "Playing, Fighting, and Dancing." *TDR: The Drama Review* 56 (3): 141–66.

———. 2015. *Brazilian Bodies and Their Choreographies of Identification: Swing Nation*. London: Palgrave Macmillan.

Rosario, Claudio de Campos, Neil Stephens, and Sara Delamont. 2010. "'I'm Your Teacher, I'm Brazilian!': Authenticity and Authority in European Capoeira." *Sport, Education and Society* 15 (1): 103–20.

Rosenthal, Joshua M. 2007. "Recent Scholarly and Popular Works on Capoeira." *Latin American Research Review* 42 (2): 262–72.

———. 2009. "Capoeira and Globalization." In *Imagining Globalization: Language, Identities, and Boundaries*, edited by Ho Hon Leung, Matthew Hendley, Robert W. Compton, and Brian D. Haley, 145–63. New York: Palgrave Macmillan.

Rosner, Elizabeth, and Lee Brown. 2021. "Sign at George Floyd Square Gives List of Special Orders for White Visitors." *New York Post*, April 22, 2021.

Sansone, Livio. 1999. "From Africa to Afro: Use and Abuse of Africa in Brazil." Amsterdam: Sephis.

Schechner, Richard. 2002. *Performance Studies: An Introduction*. 2nd ed. New York: Routledge.

Schneider, Nicole. 2017. "Black Protest on the Streets: Visual Activism and the Aesthetic Politics of Black Lives Matter." *COPAS: Current Objectives of Postgraduate American Studies* 18 (1). http://dx.doi.org/10.5283/copas.276.

Schroter, Susanne. 2003. "Rituals of Rebellion—Rebellion as Ritual: A Theory Reconsidered." In *The Dynamics of Changing Rituals: The Transformation of Religious Rituals within Their Social and Cultural Context*, edited by Jens Kreinath, Constance Hartung, and Annette Deschner, 41–58. New York: Peter Lang.

Scott, James C. 1985. *Weapons of the Weak: Everyday Forms of Peasant Resistance*. New Haven, CT: Yale University Press.

Shrumm, Regan. 2016. "Who Takes the Cake? The History of the Cakewalk." *O Say Can You See? Stories from the Museum* (blog), National Museum of American History. May 18, 2016. https://americanhistory.si.edu/blog/who-takes-cake-history-cakewalk.

Spanos, Kathleen A. 2019. "A Dance of Resistance from Recife, Brazil: Carnivalesque Improvisation in Frevo." *Dance Research Journal* 51 (3): 28–46.

Spencer, Nancy E., Matt Adamson, Sasha Allgayer, Yvette Castaneda, Matt Haugen, Ryan King-White, Yannick Kluch, Robert E. Rinehart, and Theresa Walton-Fisette. 2016. "Teach-Ins as Performance Ethnography: Athletes' Social Activism in North American Sport." *International Review of Qualitative Research* 9 (4): 489–514.

Spry, Tami. 2006. "A 'Performative-I' Copresence: Embodying the Ethnographic Turn in Performance and the Performative Turn in Ethnography." *Text and Performance Quarterly* 26 (4): 339–46.

Stebbins, Robert A. 1982. "Serious Leisure: A Conceptual Statement." *Pacific Sociological Review* 25 (2): 251–72.

———. 1997. "Casual Leisure: A Conceptual Statement." *Leisure Studies* 16 (1): 17–25.

Stewart, Kathleen. 2017. "In the World That Affect Proposed." *Cultural Anthropology* 32 (2): 192–98.

Stuart, Elaine. 2013. "Capoeira: The Brazilian Tradition That's Sweeping through American Dance." *Dance Magazine*, July 2013, 46–48.

Talmon-Chvaicer, Maya. 2008. *The Hidden History of Capoeira: A Collision of Cultures in the Brazilian Battle Dance*. Austin: University of Texas Press.

Tamisari, Franca. 2006. "The Responsibility of Performance: The Interweaving of Politics and Aesthetics in Intercultural Contexts." *Visual Anthropology Review* 21 (1/2): 47–62.

Taylor, Gerard. 2005–7. *Capoeira: The Jogo de Angola from Luanda to Cyberspace*. 2 vols. Berkeley: North Atlantic Books.

"Tekken." n.d. Capoeira Mandinga Academy and Brazil Cultural Center. Accessed August 27, 2020. https://mandinga.org/media/tekken/ (site discontinued).

Theoharis, George. 2007. "Social Justice Educational Leaders and Resistance: Toward a Theory of Social Justice Leadership." *Educational Administration Quarterly* 43 (2): 221–58.

Thorp, Charles. n.d. "Meet the Martial Arts Expert Who Helped Chadwick Boseman Kick Ass in 'Black Panther.'" *Men's Journal.* Accessed September 21, 2020. https://www.mensjournal.com/health-fitness/inside-chadwick-bosemans-martial-arts-training-for-black-panther/.

Thrasher, Steven W. 2015. "In Baltimore We Need Protest in All Its Forms: Even Joyful Ones." *Guardian,* May 2, 2015.

Tuck, Eve, and K. Wang Yang. 2012. "Decolonization Is Not a Metaphor." *Decolonization: Indigeneity, Education and Society* 1 (1). https://jps.library.utoronto.ca/index.php/des/article/view/18630.

Turner, Victor. 1980. "Social Dramas and Stories about Them." *Critical Inquiry* 7 (1): 141–68.

Vianna, Hermano. 1999. *The Mystery of Samba: Popular Music and National Identity in Brazil.* Chapel Hill: University of North Carolina Press.

Wacquant, Loïc. 2004. *Body and Soul: Notebooks of an Apprentice Boxer.* Oxford: Oxford University Press.

Welsh, Kariamu, Esailama G. A. Diouf, and Yvonne Daniel. 2019. "Introduction: When, Where, and How We Enter." In *Hot Feet and Social Change: African Dance and Diaspora Communities,* edited by Kariamu Welsh, Esailama G. A. Diouf, and Yvonne Daniel, 1–17. Urbana: University of Illinois Press.

Wesolowski, Katya. 2012. "Professionalizing Capoeira." *Latin American Perspectives* 39 (2): 82–92.

White, Daniel. 2017. "Affect: An Introduction." *Cultural Anthropology* 32 (2): 175–80.

Willson, Margaret. 2001. "Designs of Deception: Concepts of Consciousness, Spirituality and Survival in Capoeira Angola in Salvador, Brazil." *Anthropology of Consciousness* 12 (1): 19–36.

Zonzon, Christine Nicole. 2014. "Algumas versões da malícia." *Revista de Humanidades e Letras* 1 (1): 45–81.

INDEX

Abadá-Capoeira, 38–39
abortion, 4–5
Acordeon, Mestre (Bira Almeida), 34, 39, 85
Acuña, Mauricio, 45
affective habitus, 67–72, 156; affect vs. emotion and, 68–69; anger sparked by injustice in, 116–17; in cultivating community, 90–91 (*see also* communities of practice); globalization and, 159–60; humility and, 70–72, 73; nature of, 19; nature of affect, 68; need to take action and, 117; power differentials and, 16, 69–70, 73, 102, 110–18; self-control and, 71, 72, 73, 151; unevenness concerning Black Lives Matter, 142–43
African Diaspora: activism relating to, 29, 52, 103, 107–8 (*see also* Black Lives Matter movement); African diasporic arts and, 60; call-and-response format of singing and, 15–16, 23–24, 25, 31; capoeira in respecting and supporting, 9, 29, 30, 51, 85–86, 110–11, 113, 114, 156; capoeira in valuing resistance to oppression, 30, 40, 60, 141; connection with the Black Lives Matter movement, 9, 110–11, 141–42; individual identification with, 1, 157; learning about, 85–86
agency: art as form of, 17–18, 47–48; feminism and, 17; in resistance (*see* resistance)
Ahmad, Tania, 48–49
Ahmed, Sara, 67–68

AIDS, 81
Alejandro (capoeirista), 87, 158
Alexander, Michelle, 79
Alexandrakis, Othon, 102–3
Ali, Muhammad, 162–63
Amado, Jorge, 35
Amen, Mestre, 40
Angelou, Maya, 24–25, 85
Angola, 31
angola/capoeira angola: as "African" form of capoeira, 9; Black consciousness and, 51–52; capoeira as therapy and, 130–32; decline in the 1970s, 51; Fundação Internacional de Capoeira Angola (FICA) and, 52–53; globalization and, 39–40, 52, 158; Grupo de Capoeira Angola Pelourinho (GCAP) and, 39–40, 42, 51, 52; nature of, 9, 28; political and social justice issues and, 51, 52, 152, 163–64; revitalization in the 1980s, 51–52, 152; *roda* vignette, 23–24, 28; *são bento grande* lineage, 36; workshops and multiday events, 78. See also *angoleiros*
angoleiros, 9, 28, 34, 36, 122, 137–38, 153, 164; Mestre João Grande, 39–40, 45–46, 52; Mestre Cobra Mansa, 52, 70–71, 156–57; Mestre Moraes, 39–40, 42, 51–53, 152; Mestre Pastinha (*see* Pastinha, Mestre)
Appadurai, Arjun, 158
apprenticeship pilgrimages, 41–42, 150, 160
Arai, Susan, 10, 13–14

LAUREN MILLER GRIFFITH is an associate professor of anthropology in the Department of Sociology, Anthropology & Social Work at Texas Tech University. She is the author of *In Search of Legitimacy: How Outsiders Become Part of the Afro-Brazilian Capoeira Tradition.*

INTERPRETATIONS OF CULTURE IN THE NEW MILLENNIUM

The University of Illinois Press
is a founding member of the
Association of University Presses.

University of Illinois Press
1325 South Oak Street
Champaign, IL 61820-6903
www.press.uillinois.edu